RAISING YOUR
SEXUAL
SELF-ESTEEM

RAISING YOUR SEXUAL SELF-ESTEEM

How to Feel Better About
Your Sexuality and Yourself

BEVERLY ENGEL, M.F.C.C.

Fawcett Columbine · New York

A Fawcett Columbine Book
Published by Ballantine Books

http://www.randomhouse.com

Grateful acknowledgment is made to Simon &
Schuster for permission to reprint an adapted version
of "A Spectrum of Sexually Abusive Behaviors" from Handbook of
Clinical Intervention in Child Sexual Abuse by Suzanne M. Sgroi, M.D.
Copyright © 1982 by Lexington Books. Adapted with the permission
of Lexington Books, an imprint of The Free Press,
a division of Simon & Schuster.

Library of Congress Catalog Card Number: 94-90597

ISBN: 0-449-90674-4

Text design by Holly Johnson

Manufactured in the United States of America

First Edition: April 1995

10 9 8 7 6 5 4 3

To S.L.K., my dear friend and constant supporter

Contents

Acknowledgments

I wish to thank my editor, Barbara Dicks, for her input and editorial guidance, and for her patience with what turned out to be a much bigger book than either one of us anticipated. I also want to thank Bob Tabian for getting the book sold.

I also wish to thank Patti McDermott for reading the first draft of the manuscript and giving me helpful feedback.

And last, but not least, I am deeply grateful to my dear friends, Sharon Kwast and Patti McDermott, for providing continual encouragement and support during the almost two years it took to write the book.

Beverly welcomes your feedback and ideas regarding *Raising Your Sexual Self-Esteem* but regrets that because of the volume of requests, she is unable to answer individual letters and phone calls. (Please refer to the organizations listed in the Sources Section at the end of the book for referrals.) To inquire about scheduling Beverly Engel for speaking engagements, you may write to her at the address below.

Beverly Engel
P.O. Box 552
Cambria, Calif. 93428

RAISING YOUR
SEXUAL
SELF-ESTEEM

Introduction

It would seem that in a time when many people are considering celibacy, or at least reconsidering their tendency to express their sexuality more freely, a book on raising your sexual self-esteem might not be too popular. But to the contrary, since more and more people are choosing to have sex only when they are in a relationship, and many are in fact staying in relationships longer because of their fear of AIDS and other sexually transmitted diseases, sex has become an even more important topic than ever. The fact is that because most of us are having fewer sex partners, the sex we do have is becoming more and more important to us. Quality has taken precedence over quantity. This is where sexual self-esteem comes in.

The pressure is indeed on for both men and women. When we do have sex we want it to be good and we certainly want to think that we do our share about making it a good experience for our partner. This makes us worry more about such things as whether we are physically appealing or not, whether we are sexually exciting enough, and whether we can satisfy our lover. Men worry more about the state of their erections and how long they can last, while women worry about whether they can have an orgasm and even whether they can have multiple orgasms.

Even though we have entered a time when sex can be dangerous, we are also in a time when there is a new freedom concerning our sexuality in an entirely different way—in terms of our sexual orientation and our sexual preferences. Ironically, although sex has once again become forbidden, sexual practices that have in the past been considered forbidden are now in vogue. Practices such as sadomasochism, exhibitionism, and voyeurism have all become popular. Questions concerning the issue of ambiguity in sexual gender and orientation such as in the cases of transsexualism, transvestitism, and bisexuality are not only out of the closet but in store windows and on television. And, at the same time, homosexuality has become the focus of debate as our country grapples with the complicated issues surrounding it in a way it never has before.

While the debates about these issues are much needed, they nevertheless complicate an already difficult situation. Not only do we need to worry about sexually transmitted diseases, we now worry more about whether we are gay or straight, whether our propensity for voyeurism is normal or abnormal, and whether we should act out our sexual fantasies. Sex has become more complicated than ever, and while we have more answers than ever before, we also have more conflicting answers.

Our sexuality is a wonderful gift, capable of bringing us great pleasures and relaxation, causing us to reach great heights of ecstasy, and providing us a way of connecting with another human being to create a sense of intimacy that is hard to reach any other way. Unfortunately, it can also cause us a great deal of distress, pain, frustration, and disappointment.

When our expectations of ourselves or our partner are too high, when our fears are too great, or when we begin to focus more on our performance than on pleasure, we find that our sexuality can begin to feel like a burden instead of a gift—a curse instead of a cure. Then we tend to either lose interest in sex, begin to view it as a chore, or compulsively focus on it as if it were the answer to all our problems.

Before I became a psychotherapist, I worked as a sex therapist for several years, mostly as a way of understanding my own sexuality. Because I have had many sexual issues throughout my life and because my clients often present sexual concerns, I have continued my interest in sexuality all during my career. Throughout the nineteen years I have been practicing I have noticed that those who suffer the most from sexual concerns seem to have several things in common—most significantly, the messages they received about sex while they were growing up, their personal histories, their body image, and the level of their self-esteem.

I have also discovered that as we worked to both uncover and change their negative messages concerning sex, as they talked about their first sexual experiences and released their pent-up emotions concerning them, and as we explored the true reasons for their poor body image, their self-esteem, and their sexual self-esteem in particular, increased considerably.

I would like to share with you the information and many of the processes that have served to help my clients feel better about their sexuality and that provided them a true sense of control over their sexuality.

The information in this book applies to all individuals, whether married or unmarried, heterosexual, homosexual, or bisexual. While there are obviously some differences between heterosexual and homosexual individuals and couples, these differences are far outweighed by the common problems all of us face concerning our sexual self-esteem.

Raising Your Sexual Self-Esteem is divided into three parts. In Part I we will discuss the common causes of low sexual self-esteem, helping you to come to an understanding, perhaps for the first time, as to why you feel inadequate about your sexuality. By discovering just where your low sexual self-esteem comes from, you can begin to raise it by letting go of the false beliefs, misinformation, shame, guilt, and other feelings that have kept it low, whether the cause is negative or inaccurate parental messages, a negative first sexual experience, sexual trauma as a child or adult, rejection, or a number of other possibilities.

Parts II and III of the book are devoted to helping you raise your sexual self-esteem. Part of this process will be helping you to make a distinction between what you can and cannot change about your body, your sexual identity, and your sexual personality.

For some, greater knowledge of their sexuality and more pleasurable sexual experience can enhance their sexual self-esteem. By expressing themselves more fully sexually they can begin to view themselves as warm, attractive, desirable individuals. By learning to give themselves and others sexual pleasure they may increase their feelings of connectedness and competence. But for many others, the key to improving their sexual self-esteem will be in gaining more self-acceptance.

Part II focuses on those things about yourself that you can readily change, while Part III focuses on helping you to accept those things about yourself that will be difficult if not impossible to change.

It is not the goal of the book to teach sexual techniques but to help you raise your sexual self-esteem by helping you get to the core of your insecurity, whatever it may be. Sexuality is a complex issue, not one that should be treated lightly and not one that can be separated from the rest of our lives. It is intricately tied in with our emotions, our mind, and even our spirituality. Thus, raising our sexual self-esteem is not just a matter of learning some techniques or "psyching ourselves up." It is a matter of carefully and scrupulously examining yourself—your history; your belief system; your body image; your deepest secrets; your dark side; your basic sexual nature; your emotions of anger, pain, and fear; your need for power; your creativity and spontaneity; and your need for and fear of emotional intimacy.

Raising Your Sexual Self-Esteem will encourage you to enjoy sex instead of performing it and to learn to appreciate your body for the pleasure it can bring you and your partner instead of focusing so much attention on how your body looks. In short, *Raising Your Sexual Self-Esteem* will help you to understand that you don't have to be beautiful or handsome, multiorgasmic or a sexual athlete in order to have a good sex life. What you do need is to learn to accept yourself and your body just the way they are.

PART I

UNDERSTANDING THE REASONS FOR LOW SEXUAL SELF-ESTEEM

Chapter One

DO YOU HAVE LOW SEXUAL SELF-ESTEEM?

No matter how financially secure or how successful we become, no matter how hard we work on having a "perfect" body, no matter how many books we read or how educated we are, many of us continue to feel insecure about a certain aspect of our lives—sexuality. Even though you may describe yourself as a competent, worthy, and loving person, when it comes to your concept of yourself as a sexual being, you may be far more negative and insecure. You are by no means alone with these feelings. We see evidence of sexual insecurity all around us—from the popularity of "sexperts" like Dr. Ruth to the fact that books on sexuality continually sell well, no matter what else is "in" or "out."

Melanie is a typical example. She is so obsessed with making sure that she is sexually attractive to men that she spends most of her money on cosmetic surgery. She has had a nose job, breast augmentation, two partial face-lifts, and liposuction on her thighs. This is how she explains her constant need for physical renovation: "Men want the perfect woman, one that is really gorgeous. That's who they fantasize about and that's who they go after. Beauty is sexy, ordinary is not. I know that if I hadn't had this work done no man would have wanted me."

Unfortunately, Melanie will probably never be satisfied with her physical appearance. There will always be some part of her body that isn't perfect, that needs improving. There will always be other women who are younger or more beautiful to compete with.

And while Melanie's beliefs about the value of beauty may reflect the beliefs of many people, they are nevertheless a sad indication of how she feels about herself. In reality, Melanie focuses on perfecting her body because she feels so insecure about her sexuality.

Why is it that even in these enlightened times, when sexual information is readily available, when nudity and overt sexuality are commonplace in the media, when we openly talk about this once forbidden subject, so many people remain so insecure about their own sexuality? One of the answers to this question is that so many people suffer from low sexual self-esteem.

What exactly is sexual self-esteem? Put simply, our sexual self-esteem is a measure of how we feel about ourselves sexually. The level of our sexual self-esteem determines just how sexually attractive we feel we are to others, how confident we feel about our sexuality, how responsive we are sexually, and how free we are to express our sexual feelings. It includes how we feel about our ability to satisfy our sexual partner(s), how we feel about our bodies, and how "normal" we feel we are regarding our sex drive, our sexual orientation, and our ability to perform sexually.

THE CONNECTION BETWEEN SELF-ESTEEM AND SEXUALITY

The words *sex* and *self-esteem* are rarely used together and yet it only stands to reason that they would be linked together. Even though human sexuality has been more frequently written about than almost any other subject, surprisingly little has been written about the links between sexuality and self-esteem.

Sexuality and self-esteem are indeed connected, but most people have it backward. Instead of the focus being on assuming that a good sex life will raise our self-esteem, I believe that many problems with our sexuality stem from low self-esteem. Our sexuality is immensely affected by how high or low our self-esteem is.

In order to define sexual self-esteem we must first understand what the connection is between our self-esteem in general and our sexuality. There are several ways in which our self-esteem affects our sexuality and vice versa. To understand this connection, we must define self-esteem.

Self-esteem is how you as a person feel about yourself, your overall judgment of yourself. Your self-esteem may be high or low, depending on how much you like and approve of yourself. If you have high self-esteem, you have an appreciation of the full extent of your personality. This means that you accept yourself for who you are, with both your good qualities and your so-called bad ones. If you have high self-esteem, it can be assumed that you have self-respect, self-love, and feelings of self-worth.

Many people use the words *self-esteem* and *self-concept* interchangeably, but these terms really have different meanings. Our self-concept, or self-image, is the set of beliefs and images we have about ourselves. Our self-esteem is the measure of how much we like and approve of our self-concept.

Our self-concept is made up of a wide variety of images and beliefs. Some of these are self-evident and easily verifiable (for example, "I am a woman," "I am a therapist"). But there are also other, less tangible aspects of the self (for example, "I am intelligent," "I am sexy," "I am competent").

Many of the ideas we have about ourselves were acquired in childhood from two sources: how others treated us, and what others told us about ourselves. How others defined us has thus become how we now perceive ourselves. Your self-concept—who you think you are—is a package that you have put together from how others have seen and treated you, and from the conclusions you drew in comparing yourself to others.

Nothing is as important to our psychological well-being as our self-esteem. The level of our self-esteem affects virtually every aspect of our lives. It affects how we perceive ourselves and others, and it affects how others perceive us and subsequently how they treat us. It affects all our choices in life, from what career we choose to whom we choose to get involved with. It affects our ability to take action when things need to be changed and our ability to be creative. It affects our stability, and it even affects whether we are followers or leaders. It only stands to reason that the level of our self-esteem, the way we feel about ourselves in general, would affect our sexuality and our ability to form intimate relationships.

How Our Self-Esteem Affects Our Sexuality

Low self-esteem can affect our sexuality in a number of ways. If you don't feel good about yourself, you may avoid sexual relationships because you are afraid of intimacy. You may be afraid of allowing another person to get too close to you and thus to find out who you "really" are. Or perhaps you have sexual relationships but tend to hold back from experiencing pleasure either because you don't think you deserve it or because it makes you feel guilty. You may avoid masturbation because it makes you feel guilty, you believe you are undeserving of pleasure, or you think physical pleasure is not worth the time or energy. Or you may become involved with one unhappy or abusive sexual affair after another, either because you are so uncertain of your worth that you feel driven to constantly prove your sexual attractiveness or prowess, or because you believe you do not deserve to be treated well.

When our self-esteem is low we tend to get involved with sexual partners and sexual practices that reflect and reinforce our poor image of ourselves, leaving us with less self-esteem than we had before. Promiscuity, prostitution, sadomasochism, and sexual addiction are all manifestations of low self-esteem and in turn perpetuate it by causing those involved to feel isolated and full of shame and humiliation.

No matter what your body looks like, if you don't feel good about yourself, if you don't basically like yourself, you will feel unattractive. The less we like ourselves, the harder a time we have understanding why someone else would like us or find us attractive. Low self-esteem thus causes us to focus too much attention on how our bodies look. We assume that it is our body that can turn the other person either on or off, not recognizing that it is our entire person—our mind, our personality, and our very spirit—that attracts another person.

When our self-esteem is high we feel more attractive, desirable, and confident about our sexuality. We neither shy away from nor focus too much attention on sex. It becomes a natural part of our need to express ourselves and our caring for others. We choose sexual partners who treat us with respect and tenderness and we get involved with sexual practices that are life-affirming and make us feel good about ourselves.

Our Sexuality Can Also Affect Our Self-Esteem

Not only does our self-esteem affect our sexuality, our sexuality can affect our self-esteem. This is especially true if we continually engage in sexual activities that cause us to feel shame and guilt or if we focus too much time and energy on our sexuality and not enough focus is put on other aspects of our lives.

In order to avoid the latter we must create a balance by gaining a proper perspective about sex. This is extremely difficult in a society that emphasizes sex so very much. We are constantly bombarded with advertisements that are couched in sexual terms. Sex is used to sell everything from cars to toothpaste. In addition, physical fitness has become intrinsically tied to sexual attractiveness, so much so that unless one fits the current image of physical beauty it is difficult to believe one is sexually attractive at all.

Raising your sexual self-esteem can indeed raise your overall self-esteem. When we feel good about our sexuality we are connected to a very powerful part of ourselves. Our sexuality is an aspect of ourselves that has the potential to provide us with a tremendous source of energy and pleasure as well as an outlet for pent-up tension and stress. Unfortunately, it also has the potential for causing problems in our relationships, for creating tremendous feelings of shame and guilt, and for making us feel tremendously inadequate.

If we could confine the damage to the bedroom, many with low sexual self-esteem might choose to be sexually inactive; but even that would not solve the problem. Low sexual self-esteem affects virtually every aspect of your life. For instance, if you have low sexual self-esteem, you may:

• Compete with other men or women for sexual attention at work. This will not only impede your performance, but chances are your relationships at work will be strained as well.

• Be hypercritical or judgmental of others because of your own insecurity.

• Not be able to maintain friendships with those who are sexually active.

• Withdraw socially for fear of sexual involvement.

• Put on weight.

• Deny yourself an intimate relationship.
• Avoid places like the beach or activities like boating because you are uncomfortable in a bathing suit.
• Be unable to form friendships with the opposite sex.

WHAT CAUSES LOW SEXUAL SELF-ESTEEM?

Although Stephanie constantly asks for and gets reassurance from her boyfriend, she is convinced she is a lousy lover and that her boyfriend will end up leaving her to find someone else who will be a better sexual partner for him. She has read every book she can get her hands on about improving her sexual technique and is constantly adding to her sexual repertoire, but nothing seems to change her feelings of sexual inadequacy. What could have caused this insecurity of Stephanie's?

While many things *affect* our sexual self-esteem (lack of sexual desire, inability to achieve orgasm or to perform certain sexual acts, a history of sexual promiscuity or sexual addiction, performance anxiety, or a lack of sexual experience), these things do not actually *cause* low sexual self-esteem. At the core of the problem lies one or more of these major causes:

• The amount of and type of physical affection and touch we received as infants and small children.
• The messages we received about sex during our childhood.
• Early childhood sexual experiences (including sexual abuse).
• Our first sexual experience as adolescents or young adults.
• The extent to which we accept our body.
• Our perception of our sexual attractiveness.
• The amount of acceptance/rejection we feel from others.
• How powerful we feel as individuals.
• The amount of shame we feel regarding our sexual feelings and preferences.
• The amount of shame/guilt we feel about past sexual experiences.
• Our overall sense of self-esteem.

As it turned out, Stephanie's low sexual self-esteem stemmed from early childhood messages she received from her father and mother regarding sex. From the time she was only about nine or ten years old she remembered hearing her parents fight late at night. Her mother would accuse her father of being with another woman and her father would yell back that if she was a better lover then he wouldn't have to get it elsewhere.

Stephanie grew up fearing that she, like her mother, would not be a good lover and that because of this her boyfriends would have affairs just like her father did. Even sadder, Stephanie has a deep-seated belief that *all* men are unfaithful and that no matter how hard a woman tries, she is never going to be able to keep a man home. Having received these messages from her parents at a time when her ideas about sexuality were just beginning to form, they became an integral part of her own belief system.

DO YOU HAVE LOW SEXUAL SELF-ESTEEM?

Generally speaking, if you are unable to participate in sexual activities without a great deal of fear or anxiety, if you spend an inordinate amount of time worrying about whether or not you are able to perform adequately, or if you are convinced that you are not sexually attractive—you probably suffer from low sexual self-esteem. Some other indicators of low sexual self-esteem include:

- Being so afraid of rejection that you don't even try.
- Being afraid to have sex.
- Believing that others do not find you sexually attractive.
- Being embarrassed to be seen naked by your sexual partner(s).
- Being afraid that if you were to become sexual with someone he or she would be disappointed.
- Always being attracted to those who reject you or find you unattractive.
- Being very sexually inhibited.
- Being sexually promiscuous.
- Thinking there is something wrong with you sexually.
- Needing constant reassurance that you are sexually attractive and sexually satisfying.
- Endlessly comparing yourself with others.
- Feeling guilty, insecure, or anxious after you have had sex.
- Being overly concerned about pleasing your partner.

In addition, if you answer yes to at least ten of the following questions, you most certainly suffer from low sexual self-esteem:

1. Are you afraid to have sex because you fear that you will disappoint your partner?

2. Are you afraid to have sex because you fear your partner will not like your body?

3. Are you self-conscious about the size of your breasts or penis?

4. Are you so self-conscious about stretch marks or a scar that you imagine your sexual partner would be repulsed by you?

5. Do you have difficulty having an orgasm?

6. Do you have an orgasm so quickly that you are embarrassed to have sex?

7. Does engaging in sex make you feel extremely vulnerable, self-conscious, and exposed?

8. Does engaging in sex make you feel extremely ashamed or guilty?

9. Do you avoid sex because it reminds you of being sexually abused as a child?

10. Do you avoid sex because you have been raped as an adult?

11. Do you feel out of control when it comes to sex—unable to stop yourself from having it even when it is with the wrong person or at the wrong time?

12. Do you feel compelled to have sex several times a day, even to the point of endangering your job or your marriage?

13. Do you feel compelled to masturbate many times a day, even to the point of causing yourself physical pain?

14. Do you risk contracting AIDS or other venereal diseases because you engage in sex with multiple partners but refuse to practice safe sex?

15. Do you frequent prostitutes even though you feel terribly ashamed about it?

16. Do you know you are homosexual but refuse to act on it because you feel so much shame about it?

17. Do you have homosexual experiences but hide the fact from those closest to you for fear of their criticism?

18. Are you engaged in any kind of sexual act in which you allow another person to control you, inflict physical pain onto you, or humiliate you?

19. Do you engage in sexual activities in which you control, humiliate, or inflict physical pain onto another person?

20. Do you allow your partner or partners to coerce, manipulate, or force you into having sex against your will?

21. Do you coerce, manipulate, or force your partner or partners to have sex against their will?

22. Do you engage in sexual activities that are against the law and which cause you a great deal of shame?

23. Do you engage in sexual activities that go against your own set of moral values and which cause you a great deal of shame and guilt?

24. Do you have sex with a partner or partners whom you do not like, respect, or care about?

25. Do you use people sexually, having sex with them even though you do not really like them, pretending that you care, or making false promises?

26. Do you use sex as a way of bolstering your ego?

27. Do you have sex even when you don't feel like it in order to feel loved by someone?

28. Do you use sex as a way of reducing stress instead of as a way of connecting with another human being?

29. Do you feel addicted to sex? Do you feel that you need it in order to get through the day?

30. Are you ashamed of your sexual fantasies?

31. Are you insecure about your masculinity/femininity?

WHO IS MORE LIKELY TO SUFFER FROM LOW SEXUAL SELF-ESTEEM?

While anyone can suffer from low sexual self-esteem, and in fact most of us do at some time in our lives, those who tend to suffer the most and for the longest duration are either those who had something occur in their lives that prevented them from developing high self-esteem in general, and high sexual self-esteem in particular, or those who have had their sexual self-esteem shaken in some way—by a traumatic or stressful event, for example, or by engaging in sexual activities that caused shame or guilt.

Those who are most likely to suffer from low sexual self-esteem are:

1. Those who were deprived of adequate touch and nurturing as children.

Children who were not given adequate nurturing and touching grow into adults who are emotionally handicapped. They will either be too rigid and cut off from their emotions or they will be extremely needy emotionally and sexually. Either way, they will have a continual (although often unconscious) yearning for the touch and nurturing they were deprived of.

2. Those who were sexually abused as children.

Probably more than any other experience, childhood sexual abuse damages our ability to express our sexual feelings in a genuine, uncorrupted way. Those who experienced childhood sexual abuse suffer from a great deal of shame, guilt, and self-hatred, as well as from a poor body image. In addition, since many survivors of sexual abuse also suffer from sexual dysfunction, lack of sexual desire, and flashbacks during sex, they feel insecure about attempting to be sexual again with a partner.

Many of you reading this book have been sexually abused as children or adolescents. Some of you already know this, while others of you may discover this fact as you read the book and work on raising your sexual self-esteem. The most recent statistics show that at least one in three women and one in five men were sexually abused when they were children. If you are one of these people or suspect that you are, you can be certain that the sexual abuse is responsible for most of your sexual problems and insecurities.

3. Those who have been raped as adults.

Women and men who have been raped not only have to suffer from the physical and emotional damage of the rape itself but from the shame and humiliation so often connected with the crime. Many end up feeling tainted and spoiled and fear that no one will ever want them sexually again. Others are so traumatized that they fear they will never again enjoy a sexual relationship.

My client Caroline told me: "Ever since the rape I have felt like damaged goods. Every time I think of that guy being inside of me I feel like my genitals are dirty. I don't want my husband to touch me, I feel so dirty.

"Of course, my husband's reaction hasn't helped. He made me feel like somehow I asked for it—like I encouraged the guy in some way. He acts as if I have been unfaithful to him instead of treating me like a victim of a violent crime. I blame myself enough anyway. I keep thinking that if I hadn't been so stupid to walk into a poorly lit parking lot at such a late hour it would have never happened."

4. Those who have been criticized by a lover or lovers about their physical attractiveness, their ability to satisfy sexually, their sexual drive, or any other aspect of their sexuality.

This is both a cause and a symptom of low sexual self-esteem. It is a cause because constant criticism is a form of emotional abuse, and the longer a person stays in an abusive relationship, the lower his or her self-esteem in general and sexual self-esteem in particular will become. It is a symptom because people don't tend to get into abusive relationships and certainly don't stay in them unless they already had low self-esteem and/or low sexual self-esteem.

5. Those who have a poor body image.

Those who are overweight or underweight or who think they are, those who have a physical disability or a scar that makes them feel they are no longer desirable, and those who feel unattractive because they are aging, are but a few of the people who suffer from a poor body image. Because they feel so unattractive they are self-conscious about becoming nude and making love. This self-consciousness will be expressed in a variety of ways, including avoidance of sexuality, problems with intimacy, and sexual dysfunction.

Ronetta's feelings about her body definitely influence her sexual self-esteem: "I can't imagine any man wanting to be with me sexually. I am so fat that I must be disgusting to them. All those rolls of fat disgust me, much less anybody else."

6. Those who suffer from a sexual dysfunction.

Those who have a sexual dysfunction have a tremendous burden to carry around since they go into each sexual experience with the fear that they are not going to perform the way they would like to. This of course has a tremendous effect on their sexual self-esteem, causing them to avoid sexuality altogether or to become so preoccupied with potential failure that they cannot really enjoy sexual encounters.

Roger has a problem with premature ejaculation. He is seldom able to last more than a few minutes before he climaxes, leaving him feeling so embarrassed that he never sees the woman again. He is becoming more and more reluctant to have sex because each time he tries he suffers from overwhelming embarrassment. The more he experiences prematurity, the more pressure he puts on himself to perform, which in turn almost guarantees he will fail again. This is a typical scenario for many men.

7. Those who are unable to perform certain sexual acts.

Sometimes, as hard as we try, we just can't perform a particular sexual act. Even if we understand the reason for our fear or repulsion it doesn't mean we will be able to get past our reluctance. To make matters worse, sometimes our partners continue to pressure us to perform the act, even when we have tried to make them understand why we can't.

Jenny's boyfriend is constantly pressuring her for oral sex but the thought of either giving it or receiving it repulses her. She is afraid that if she doesn't get over her hang-up she will lose her boyfriend, and yet she just can't get past her feelings of repulsion and nausea at the very thought of it.

8. Those who are inexperienced.

Virgins and those with little experience sexually sometimes feel inadequate sexually. They imagine that everyone else has much more experience than they have and they tend to fear that they will never catch up. Many also have fears that they will never be able to accomplish full sexual expression at all.

Jack has never had intercourse with a woman. At twenty-five, he is afraid to make advances to a woman for fear of rejection. "I am so afraid at this point that each date is excruciating. All I think about the whole time is how and when I can make my move, but by the end of the date I am so nervous and shaky all I can manage to do is feebly shake her hand or give her a peck on the cheek. I've built up so much fear and I feel like such a failure that I don't know if I will ever get over it."

Each failed attempt on Jack's part has left him more and more afraid of rejection. He is so ashamed of being a twenty-five-year-old virgin, and so fearful that he will remain one indefinitely, that he is now reluctant to even try.

9. Those who are having sexual thoughts or fantasies that are causing them a great deal of shame.

While we all have sexual fantasies, some people are plagued with sexual thoughts or fantasies that they are terribly ashamed of but cannot seem to stop. These fantasies and thoughts often involve violence or forbidden acts—things that the person would not actually consider doing. Nevertheless, night after night, day after day, they feel compelled to have these thoughts and fantasies, even though they know the guilt and shame will follow.

For instance, Sara told me: "Lately I have been having fantasies about letting a man beat me. I get so turned on I can't believe it. In fact, it's getting so that this is the only way I can have an orgasm when I masturbate. I must be really sick."

10. Those who are acting out sexually in ways that are causing them to feel a tremendous amount of shame.

Being involved with sexual activities that go against your value system will undoubtedly make you experience shame. Unfortunately, many people feel out of control when it comes to their sexuality and continually feel compelled to act out sexually in ways that make them feel very bad about themselves. This obviously affects their sexual self-esteem.

Dan is addicted to phone sex. He calls the 900 numbers advertised on television at least five to ten times a day, sometimes even more. Not only has this practice put him in debt, more importantly, it has damaged his already low self-esteem. "I can't tell you how very ashamed I am. I don't know what is wrong with me. I know I am a good-looking guy and I've had good sex in the past but this phone thing just got out of hand without my knowing it. Now I feel so bad about myself for getting caught up in this stuff that I feel like a giant scumball—like no decent woman would want me now."

11. Those who are sex addicts.

Anita is a sex addict. Even though she is aware of the risk she is taking by being promiscuous in this age of AIDS, she cannot control herself. She is obsessed with sex, sometimes having it three or four times a day, each time with a different partner and often with strangers. "I just can't control myself. Each day I vow that I will not let my impulses take control of me and each day I let myself down. I feel terrible about myself. I know all this is damaging my self-esteem, much less the risk I am taking with my life."

12. Those who are insecure about their femininity or masculinity.

Our sense of masculinity or femininity can be an important aspect of our sexual self-esteem. If we feel insecure or confused about this part of ourselves it can affect all areas of our sexuality, causing us to avoid sex or to overcompensate by becoming sexually promiscuous in an effort to prove our masculinity or femininity.

Justin feels deeply inadequate as a male. As an attempt to prove his virility to himself and to others he spends a great deal of time seducing women in order to verify his sexual prowess. Even though he is tired of the single life, he is incapable of making a commitment to a woman because he continually has to gather fresh evidence indicating he is thoroughly masculine.

13. Those who do not accept their sexual orientation.

There is still a lot of shame associated with being homosexual or bisexual, even in these so-called enlightened times. Many homosexuals and bisexuals still feel they must hide their sexuality from even their closest friends and relatives for fear of being criticized or, worse yet, ostracized. This is especially true of those who were raised in strict religious or conservative families.

Tony has been married for eight years and he has two children, ages seven and five. Five years ago he started having fantasies of being with other men. He tried to push away these fantasies but they kept coming back. Then he started looking at men in a way he never allowed himself to before. About three years ago he started an affair with a man at work. "I know that I would be happy with Matt. I love him very much and he makes me feel like I have never felt with my wife. But I hate the idea of being gay and living a gay lifestyle."

14. Those who have been rejected or betrayed by a lover.

We are so vulnerable in our love relationships. Our lovers have the power to hurt us deeply because we lower our inhibitions and let down our walls with them and let them really see us for who we are. When a lover rejects us, no matter what the reason, it hurts us to the very core, causing us to feel as if no one will ever want us again. When a lover betrays us, the hurt goes even deeper, causing us to feel as if we never want to love again, as was the case with Tina:

"Ever since Carl left me for another woman two years ago I have felt extremely unattractive. I just can't imagine any man finding me sexy because I feel so unsexy. I feel that if I had been sexy enough Carl wouldn't have left me for someone else and that the same thing is just going to happen if I were to get involved with another man."

15. Those who are recovering from alcohol or drug addiction.

Very often, when a person becomes sober his or her sexuality goes through a number of changes. First of all, many alcoholics and addicts have never had sex sober. They used alcohol or drugs to either lower their inhibitions, give them courage, or anesthetize themselves. They found it was easier for them to have sex when they were stoned or drunk since they could then ignore their sexual self-esteem problems. Once they are sober many alcoholics and addicts find that they are unable to become sexual. They are faced with their conflicts regarding sex, whatever they may be. Many alcoholics and addicts have a tremendous fear of intimacy and many were physically, emotionally, or sexually abused as children. These issues must be cleared up before they are able to enjoy sober sex.

16. Those going through a midlife crisis.

A midlife crisis can cause us to go into a tailspin—questioning our beliefs and values, our life choices, and our sexuality. Things we took for granted are all of a sudden in question, things we thought we wanted we no longer find appealing. Time seems to be racing by and we feel older by the minute. Some people want to grab every moment of happiness they can get while others feel their time is already up. Zachary felt this way:

"I've always felt so sure of myself with women. I always knew how to please them sexually and they always came back for more. But lately I have begun to doubt myself. I think it has to do with the fact that I'm pushing fifty and, well, frankly, I'm slowing down a bit, if you know what I mean. I used to be able to go all night and now I'm lucky if I can get it up sometimes. Suddenly I just don't feel all that attractive or all that sexy."

17. Those who have genital herpes, venereal warts, or other sexually transmitted diseases.

Having either genital herpes or venereal warts can be devastating. Many people are so ashamed that they avoid new sexual relationships completely, while others do so with much trepidation, fearing rejection as soon as they tell a potential partner. Even those in relationships feel ashamed and disfigured with each new outbreak.

Like thousands of other Americans, Rebecca has genital herpes. "When I found out I had herpes I was devastated. I feel like my sex life is over. No one is going to want to have sex with me when they find out I have herpes and I cannot in all good conscience have sex with someone unless they know the risk they are taking. I feel like I have the plague or something—like no one would ever want to touch me again."

18. Those who have recently had a mastectomy, hysterectomy, prostate surgery, a vasectomy, or other surgery or procedures involving their sexual organs or a part of the body that is strongly associated with sexuality.

Any kind of surgery can be traumatic, but when the surgery involves our sexual organs we are particularly vulnerable. Even if the surgery should not cause any permanent change in our sexual functioning we feel threatened and often feel less sexually attractive. If the surgery causes us to be disfigured in any way we are particularly fearful of losing our sexual appeal as Martha did:

"Ever since my mastectomy I have felt totally repulsive sexually. I can't imagine having another relationship in my lifetime because there is absolutely no way that I am going to allow anyone to see my scarred chest."

While I have tried to list as many examples of those who suffer from low sexual self-esteem as possible, I undoubtedly have missed some. In general we can assume that included in this list is anything else that has occurred to make you doubt or question your sexual desirability, sexual identity, or ability to perform sexually.

Chapter Two

PARENTAL AND SOCIETAL MESSAGES ABOUT SEX

The verbal and nonverbal messages we receive as children from our parents and society in general concerning the importance of touch, the role of sexuality in our lives, our bodies, intimacy, and the stereotypes about males and females lay the foundation of our sexual self-esteem. From these early messages we begin to form our beliefs about whether sexuality is good or bad, our ideas about the sexes, and our feelings about our own bodies and our own sexuality. These beliefs in turn determine how good or bad we feel about expressing our sexuality, how we feel about our bodies, and how we feel about our gender.

TOUCH AS SEX EDUCATION

The importance of touching in human life can hardly be overemphasized. Touching is essential for healthy development—in fact, the tactile sense is the first to develop. Babies who have not received sufficient tactile stimulation—hugging, cuddling, kissing—do not develop normally and many do not grow at all. In the months following birth, touching can literally mean the difference between life and death; the mortality rate for babies deprived of touching is extremely high.

Most mothers seem to understand this instinctively, and these mothers provide their infants with a lot of physical contact, but some mothers provide their babies with only the barest of necessities, giving them bottles, changing their diapers, and bathing them without any real time spent cuddling, admiring, or talking to their infants.

The relationship between infant and mother is the single most important factor contributing to the health, well-being, and eventual sexuality of the child. It is through the mother's loving touch that children are given the ability to love themselves, to love others, and, most importantly, to love life. One of the most important aspects of the relationship between mother and infant is bonding—the amount of physical and emotional connectedness between mother and child. This physical and emotional connectedness begins with eye contact, caressing, and holding.

The intimacy of loving interactions between mother and baby—soothing skin-to-skin experiences, peaceful feeding pleasures, and playful facial games—is actually the child's introduction to bodily pleasure, which is a basic characteristic of sexuality.

Research shows that the amount and the kind of touching we received as infants and young children strongly affects the strength of the adult sex drive and the urge to nurture. For the human being to learn to give love he or she must first receive love. Each time a parent cuddles, hugs, rocks, or pats a baby or toddler he or she gives the experience of taking in love. The manner in which the child is touched and treated affects whether he or she finds physical contact pleasurable or not and it influences future capacity to enjoy touching and intimacy.

When the child is provided with enough nurturing and safety he is taught that intimacy and personal involvement are not to be feared and that opening oneself up psychologically to a significant other is nurturing instead of dangerous. On the other hand, a child who is pushed away, neglected, or smothered by his parents' love learns that intimate contact is too risky and may grow up preferring alienation or physical sex to the vulnerability of genuine intimacy.

Touching is the simplest, most direct, and most powerful means of expressing affection, and it is a fundamental part of intimacy, our means of connecting with one another. Perhaps the most important gift parents can give their child is the ability to give and receive touch. Certainly, touching is an essential part of a fulfilled sexual life.

In addition to learning about touch from his physical interaction with his parents, a child learns about touching from his parents' behavior with each other. Aside from occasional hugs and pecks on the cheek, many children rarely see their parents being physically affectionate.

While it is difficult to determine whether or not you received adequate touching and nurturing as an infant and small child, most of us have an internal sense as to how much touching we received. In addition to this internal sense we can begin to put the pieces of the puzzle together by noticing the following:

• How much do you remember being touched and held by your parents throughout your childhood?
• Are your parents affectionate with you now?
• How free do you feel to be affectionate with those you are close to?
• Were you able to bond with your own children when they were infants?
• Were you or are you able to be affectionate with your own children?

PARENTAL MESSAGES

A child's training about sex begins fairly early. The earliest and most deeply influential messages we got about sex were from our parents, since they reached us when we were the most impressionable. Unfortunately, most parents do not discuss sex with their children in an open, calm way. Instead, parents communicate their fears, discomfort, embarrassment, and attitudes about sexuality to their children.

For example, Carlotta's mother passed on her own negative attitudes about men to her daughter, which in turn ended up influencing Carlotta's attitudes about men and sex: "My mother warned me from the time I was very young that all men wanted was sex. I never thought of sex as pleasurable for the woman—it was just a thing you put up with if you wanted to have a man, or something you used to bargain with to get things you wanted."

Consequently, because Carlotta went into each sexual experience with no expectations of pleasure but with the attitude of "When is this going to be over?" she had no chance to experience enjoyable sex. This further reinforced her mother's message. By the time Carlotta came into therapy, she had become so cut off from her body that she suffered discomfort whenever she had intercourse.

In the typical family, parents teach only the mechanics of sex and spend very little time discussing either the responsibilities that go along with sex or the issues of intimacy and caring. Most parents give their children incomplete and confusing information about their sexual development, inadequate sex education, and little or no information about what they can expect during sexual experiences. Many parents feel a great deal of shame and embarrassment about sex, and this is communicated to their children, who in turn internalize their parental feelings of shame. If your parents seemed ashamed, embarrassed, or confused when discussing sex, your chances of developing a healthy sexual identity were probably limited. Most people in our society have no consistent model for, or firsthand experience of, healthy sexuality.

On the other hand, some parents react against their own puritanical upbringing by providing their children with too much information about sex and too much permission to explore their sexuality. Some mothers who consider themselves enlightened provide their daughters with the Pill and then retreat into the background, and some parents go so far in the opposite direction of how they were raised that they end up encouraging their children to be promiscuous.

Parental messages about sex are not just those that are verbalized, but those that are conveyed to us nonverbally, such as the way our parents interact with one another. For example, were your parents openly affectionate with one another or did they confine any evidence of intimacy behind closed doors? Or was the reverse true: Were your parents inappropriate in the ways they showed affection toward one another, becoming too overly sexual in front of you? Did you see your father try to be affectionate with your mother only to be rebuffed with "Not in front of the children?" Or did you see your father grab at your mother's breasts or butt without showing regard for her feelings, forcing her to slap him away or retreat in embarrassment?

Parental Messages Regarding Genitals

Parents' handling of their child's early body explorations has a marked affect on the child's attitudes toward his body. For example, when a baby delights in the discovery of his feet his mother is warmed by his enthusiasm, and yet when the same baby discovers his penis and tries to examine it the same mother grows tense and pushes his hand away. In this way she is teaching her child that certain parts of the body are taboo.

Every child forms attitudes toward his genitals and these attitudes color his view of sex. If a child's parents believe the organs for elimination and reproduction are shameful or nasty these beliefs will be communicated to the child and he or she will likely develop similar reactions.

Typically toddlers are taught the correct names for all body parts except the genitals. This inability to apply straightforward names to sexual organs contributes to a sense of mystery about sex—simultaneously bestowing it with importance and shame. Mave told me about how her family handled this issue: "In our family we had silly names for our genitals. We called them our 'pee-pees' and the boys' penises were called 'wienies.' This continued up until we were teenagers. Although at school we were learning words like *vagina* and *penis*, our parents continued to use these cute names. Mother would always say 'I have to use the little girl's room' when she had to go to the bathroom and 'I have my visitor' when she started her period. All this tended to give me the message that my genitals and our natural bodily functions are shameful and I tend to still feel this today."

Parents don't have to say a word in order to communicate their attitude about genitals. It can all happen nonverbally—a mother's facial expression when she changes a diaper, her obvious distaste when her child wants to show her his "number two," her anger when her two-year-old wants to examine his penis. These and other reactions tell children that their genitals are unacceptable, that elimination is dirty. Each time parents toilet train, bathe, or dress a child their attitudes toward his body, and his genitals specifically, are being communicated to the child.

Parental Messages About Masturbation

There are three stages of normal development during which masturbation occurs almost universally. During infancy, the healthy, alert child investigates the genital area with the same curiosity that he shows when he pokes at his ears. Since the nerve endings around the genital area are quite sensitive, the infant naturally experiences a generalized pleasant sensation. This feeling is not the intensely exciting feeling of the mature adult.

Between the ages of three and five, when children are emotionally attached to the opposite-sexed parent, another period of genital play can occur. Children handle some of their sexual feelings at this stage by self-manipulation. Because boys have a noticeable organ for elimination that is pleasurable to touch, they are more apt to play with themselves than girls.

The third period of self-manipulation occurs in adolescence, when the specific activity of the sex glands makes itself felt. Because direct outlets for sexual expression are restricted until they are older, adolescents turn to masturbation to handle the new intensity of their feelings.

Some genital play, then, is a part of normal development. In addition, the ability to continue to give ourselves sexual pleasure is an important part of developing positive feelings about ourselves sexually. If handled unwisely by the parent, though, a youngster will conclude that the genitals and the feelings coming from them are bad and wrong.

Because their penises are so much more accessible, masturbation generally begins earlier with boys than with girls. Boys normally begin to masturbate at anywhere from six or seven years old to twelve or thirteen years old. Girls, on the other hand, vary more in terms of when they begin to masturbate. Some girls tend to explore their bodies more than others and, consequently, may experience pleasurable feelings in their genitals when they touch or rub themselves against something. Other girls don't explore their genitals or don't feel pleasure when they do and so do not begin masturbation unless they are taught by other children, introduced to it inappropriately by an adult, or accidently experience pleasure when they are horseback riding, bicycling, running, or playing on the monkey bars.

If our experience with masturbation was positive, it sets the stage for a lifetime of pleasurable masturbation experiences, as Donald experienced:

"I remember the first time I masturbated. I was eight years old and I was taking a shower. As I was washing my penis I suddenly got a different kind of sensation than I had ever had before. I got an erection and it felt wonderful to touch myself and so I continued lathering up the soap and rubbing myself. I had what I now know was an orgasm. At first I felt a little scared because I didn't know what had happened. But my fear subsided and by the time I took my next shower I was back at it. To this day the shower is one of my favorite places to masturbate or to make love. The whole experience—the water, the lathering of the soap, is all very erotic to me."

If, on the other hand, our experience with masturbation was a negative one, filled with guilt and shame, it can set the tone for how we feel about it for the rest of our life. This was Melissa's experience:

"I was raised Catholic and so I grew up thinking that masturbation was a sin. I did it anyway, of course, but I always hid it from my parents and I always felt guilty about it. One night when I was twelve I was masturbating before going to sleep and my mother walked in on me. I had never seen her so angry. She told me that I should be ashamed of myself because I was sinning against God. Then she stormed out of the room.

"I was so humiliated to have my mother catch me like that! I felt terrible. The next day she wouldn't even look at me or speak to me. That went on for several days until I finally couldn't stand it any longer. I went to my mother and told her I was sorry and asked her to forgive me. She made me promise I would never do it again.

"I tried to keep my promise but I just couldn't. I'd become aroused and before I knew it I had done it again. Each time I masturbated I promised myself it was the last time but I just couldn't stand by my promise. That made me feel even worse about myself."

The message Melissa had received from her religion and her mother in particular was that masturbation was unnatural and that her natural tendency to want to masturbate was wrong. Even though she continued to masturbate, the experience was always followed by intense guilt and shame and this in turn affected Melissa's feelings about herself and her sexuality. To Melissa, sex is always cloaked in shame and feelings of sexual arousal are looked upon as a betrayal by her own body. Because of this she has not been able to have a successful sexual relationship with a man.

Those raised in deeply religious households, like Melissa, often experience tremendous guilt and shame about masturbation. As I stated earlier, as children and adolescents we lack knowledge about sex, our bodies, and our sexual organs in particular. The most basic form of learning about our bodies is to touch and explore them. But touching ourselves and exploring "down there" have been especially discouraged by religious teachings. Masturbation, while practiced by almost everyone, is considered depraved and sinful by many religious organizations.

Parental Messages About Personal Privacy

Parents can also give negative messages about sex and intimacy by not respecting their children's personal boundaries. Our boundaries are those physical and emotional barriers that separate us from others and from the world. We need firm boundaries to define us ("This is where you end and I begin") and to prevent us from merging with others.

In dysfunctional, unhealthy families, physical boundaries are either overly rigid or enmeshed. Rigid boundaries are like walls between parents and children, giving the child the message that touching is not permissible within the family. When a child receives these messages from his or her parents' behavior ("No one ever touched in my family," "When my parents did hug or kiss us it felt like a duty"), he or she will undoubtedly grow up to have difficulties learning how to be intimate.

Enmeshed boundaries, on the other hand, give children the message that they do not have a right to their own privacy and separateness or a right to have control over their own bodies. Boundary violations by parents include: exposing children to their parents' sexual behavior or naked bodies; denying privacy to a child by walking in on the child in the bathroom or in his or her bedroom; making inappropriate remarks to children about their bodies and their sexual development; asking teenagers and even young adults about their sexual experiences; talking inappropriately about sex in front of their children; or being overtly sexual in their children's presence.

Parents with a blurred, unclear sense of their own and others' boundaries behave in overly intrusive ways that serve to engender an unhealthy form of closeness and intensity of feeling. Children raised in such families don't know how to define their limits and are unable to protect their rights. They lack a healthy sense of separateness and individuality that might enable them to know and to say what feels okay and what doesn't. Such children grow into adults who unconsciously violate others' boundaries and allow others to violate theirs.

If your boundaries were continually violated by other family members you will probably have problems with setting limits yourself. This can mean that you get too close to someone too fast, that you become invasive or intrusive sexually, that you become overly possessive of your lovers, or even that you have crossed the line and acted out inappropriately sexually, either by forcing others to have sex, by continually getting involved with illicit affairs, or by acting out sexually with children.

Others have the opposite reaction and build walls around themselves to protect themselves from being hurt or intruded upon again. Intimacy and even friendship is a problem for them. Wary of close love relationships and commitment, they have compensated for being intruded upon by becoming overly protective of their emotions.

In healthy families sex education is provided but sex is not talked about in a derogatory or teasing way. There is open affection between the mother and father but no explicit sexuality is exhibited in front of the children. Individual privacy is respected—especially the child's right to privacy concerning his or her own body and sexual experiences—and nudity is confined to the bathroom and bedroom, and these doors are locked to ensure further privacy.

Parental Messages About Sex and Role Identification

For many years, it was assumed that gender identity—the sense of oneself as male and masculine or female and feminine—was determined biologically. But now it is believed that while biology is influential, it alone does not dictate gender identity. How parents react to the sex of their infant is also a vital cause of the toddler's early gender sense.

For example, recent research has shown that beginning as early as infancy, girl babies are treated differently than boy babies. Girls are spoken to in a soft, melodic, or high voice while boys are spoken to in a deeper, rougher voice. Girls are treated as if they are more fragile than boys, while boys are treated in a rougher manner and are expected to not only accept the roughness but like it. These behaviors are subtle but nevertheless extremely influential.

Most parents encourage their children to accept that they are male or female and learn the differences between male and female behavior. For instance, when children discover that they cannot be both girl and boy, they are often confused and disappointed. Two-year-old boys may play "mommy," put on her clothing, or declare that they will grow up to be a mother. These behaviors and the feelings underlying them are temporary, however, as the boy's misconceptions are quickly and routinely corrected. Repeated positive interactions with both parents regarding one's particular sex minimize any unhappiness. It also becomes clear to him that his emerging male gender-role behaviors please both his mother and father, as is evidenced by comments such as: "That's my boy!" and "What a big boy you are!"

In order to accept the label "boy," the child has to accept being different from his mother and accept the fact that his future is tied to maleness. A mother can promote male gender-role behavior in her son by subtly encouraging him to be different from her. But when the mother has a need to prolong the infantile closeness with her son, she may cause the toddler to be afraid of trying new things, of taking part in rough-and-tumble play, and of being a boy. Fathers usually play a subtle, supportive role in this process if they are loving models for sons to identify with, and if they take an active role in their sons' upbringing.

Andy's mother, Dorothy, inadvertently caused him to be effeminate because of her deep hostility toward males. Andy told me during our first several sessions that his mother's own father had abandoned his family and left his grandmother to raise five children all alone. Dorothy grew up hearing her mother constantly complain about "good-for-nothing men." To make matters worse, Andy's father had left Dorothy as soon as he discovered she was pregnant. All during Andy's childhood his mother had given him the message that to be male was to be selfish and unreliable, traits that Andy remembers feeling strongly that he did not want to have. This caused Andy to reject any innate "male" behaviors that he might naturally exhibit and to take on more effeminate mannerisms in order to please his mother.

These effeminate mannerisms were the motivating factors for Andy's seeking help. As he explained it: "My life has become simply unbearable. I am either being made fun of by straight people or being hit on by gays. Even though I'm not gay most people think I am. I'm very attracted to women but none of them take me seriously. I've even had a few women friends try to fix me up with one of their gay friends or relatives. I'm twenty-six years old and I'm still a virgin. I'm tired of being hit on by gays and ignored by women."

Uncaring parents and frightening events can discourage a child from accepting the biologically appropriate label. A father's drunken rages, which terrify both a mother and her two-year-old son, may cause them to cling to each other and may frighten the boy about growing up to be a man. Another mother's harshness and disinterest may also leave her son frightened about maleness and uncertain as to how to elicit affection.

Many children are given the parental message that they are of the wrong sex. Because a child is helpless to alter this message, feeling its particular sex to be second-best tears at the child's self-respect in a devastating way, making him feel unacceptable at a very basic level. Part of any child's high self-esteem is feeling "I'm glad I'm a girl" or "I'm glad I'm a boy." If parents are not happy with a child's sex, the child certainly cannot be. A small percentage of children who develop conspicuous disturbances in gender identity were once treated by their families as though they were members of the opposite sex, as was the case with Frankie.

Frankie's parents had already had three female children by the time she was born. Each time her mother became pregnant her father would be certain that this time he was going to get the boy he so longed for, and each time he had been terribly disappointed. When Frankie was born it seemed that her father just couldn't cope with one more disappointment and so, beginning with her name, he began treating her like a boy. Frankie's mother just didn't have the heart to tell her husband he was out of line.

By the time Frankie was five years old, she had become her father's sidekick. He took her with him fishing, camping, and hiking. He taught her how to play softball and fought to have her included in boys' Little League, where he was the coach. Frankie watched her dad while he worked on the family car and by the time she was a teenager, thanks to his teaching, she was a first-rate mechanic.

When other girls began to take an interest in dressing up for boys, Frankie thought they were all crazy. She had better things to do, like working on projects with her father in the garage, or taking off on hiking trips. All during high school she was a star athlete on the track team. She hated the home economics classes she was required to take and fought unsuccessfully to take shop instead. She was popular with both the boys and the girls but no one ever asked her out on a date and she was secretly glad.

In college, however, things started to get a little more confusing for Frankie. Away from her parents and the group of friends who had become accustomed to her differentness, Frankie became more uncomfortable with the fact that she was expected to date men but really didn't want to. And while her tomboy ways had been tolerated and even considered "cute" among her family and friends, in college she began to be ridiculed. Many of her classmates thought she was a lesbian and one lesbian friend made a sexual pass at her.

This last event is what brought Frankie into therapy. She was extremely upset by the woman's approach and what it meant in terms of her sexual orientation. Before the first session was over, however, Frankie confessed to me that she didn't think she was a lesbian at all but that she felt like a male. She was, in fact, what we call "male identified," meaning that in all respects, she identified with men far more than women. As it turned out, Frankie was so confused about her gender identity that she had no sexual desire for men *or* women, and this bothered her immensely because she wanted to have a family later on in life.

The formation of core gender identity does not suddenly happen; it gradually emerges from a seeming gender neutrality in early life. While a fifteen-month-old boy has more in common with all toddlers than with boys in particular, he has already begun learning about and identifying with males. His sense of himself as a boy will progressively appear during the next year or so. The sex of the child begins as a powerful factor in the parents' minds but by the first birthday it is becoming a powerful factor in the child's mind.

Another key factor, therefore, of core gender identity is the quality of the child's relationships early in life. In order for a child to develop a healthy core gender identity parents must:

• Consistently behave as though the child belongs to his or her biological sex.
• Understand the child's nonverbal expressions and be willing to meet his or her needs.
• Protect the child from overwhelming separations from trusted people.
• Protect the child from physical and psychological abuse.

Parental Messages About Sexual Orientation

The second landmark of sexual identity development is the establishment of sexual orientation. Our culture continually steers children toward heterosexuality through messages from the family, the schools, the media, and peer relationships. Children's erotic preoccupations are directed toward heterosexuality by their need to obtain and retain the approval of others. Children learn to hide any homoerotic impulses or feelings when they see the negative, anxious responses they produce in parents, teachers, and friends. This most certainly was the case with Quintin:

"From the time I was seven or eight years old I knew I was different from other kids. While my brothers wanted to play baseball and war, I preferred to spend time with my sisters and their friends, playing house and dressing up. My father really didn't like it and he gave me a really hard time about it. So when he was around I'd play with my brothers just to please him.

"Then, when I was older, I really got into art. I could sit for hours drawing and painting and be as happy as could be. But my father told me it was for 'sissies' and tried to get me to stop. He made me feel bad about myself because I wasn't on the baseball teams or the basketball teams the way my brothers were. I think my father knew I was gay long before I did. And I know that even today he doesn't accept it.

"It's taken me years to finally learn to accept my homosexuality, in spite of the fact that my father does not. But with the help of a gay support group and lots of loving friends I have finally learned to not just accept my gayness but to be genuinely proud of it. I've stopped acting straight just to pacify my father and that feels especially good."

WHAT IF I DON'T REMEMBER ANY MESSAGES ABOUT SEX?

Some people are unable to remember much of anything about the way their families dealt with sex or about sexuality in the family in general. This inability to remember any childhood family sexual experiences may be an indication that you have blocked out memories that were too painful to remember—more specifically, a sexual trauma. Those who were abused as children, for example, often have little recall of their childhoods. Forgetting painful experiences is the way children protect themselves from emotional traumas they are too vulnerable to handle.

Talking to your brothers or sisters about what they remember concerning the sexual climate in your parents' home may be helpful, but don't be surprised if you get little cooperation or help from them. They also may have blocked out passages of time, they may be defensive or embarrassed about talking about this issue, or they may have entirely different memories and perceptions about what happened.

Talking to your parents about the messages they gave you regarding sex may prove to be even less helpful. You and they may feel extremely embarrassed talking to one another about sex. On the other hand, now that you are an adult, your parents may find it easier to talk about their uneasiness and embarrassment about sex when you were a child. They may have become more knowledgeable, enlightened, and flexible regarding sex and may welcome the chance to apologize to you about the negative or inaccurate messages they passed on to you. In addition, they may be able to share with you information about the messages they themselves received from their parents. This information will not only put things in perspective but can provide you with valuable information regarding some of the beliefs you have about sex that you don't actually remember hearing from your parents directly but have acted on nevertheless.

Exercise—Parental Messages

List all the messages, both verbal and nonverbal, that you remember receiving from your parents regarding sex. Try to recall not only specific verbal messages but also behaviors, attitudes, and specific incidents that also reflected your parents' attitudes regarding sex.

If you have some difficulty, the following questions may help spark your memory:

1. How did your parents express their affection toward one another?

2. Were your parents ever overtly sexual with one another in front of you?

3. Did your father ever make jokes about how difficult it was to get your mother to have sex, or complain about how he "never got enough"?

4. Did your mother act as if sex was a burden she had to endure or complain about how your father never got enough?

5. How did your parents handle sex education?

6. How did your parents respond to you as you developed sexually? (Was it considered a joyous time or a negative time?)

7. Did your parents caution you against premarital sex?

8. Was there a double standard for the boys and the girls in the family? (Was it okay for boys to have premarital sex, not okay for girls?)

9. What was your parents' attitude about unmarried couples living together?

Negative messages about sex, our genitals, masturbation, gender identity, and sexual orientation can affect our sexual self-esteem immensely because we end up believing things that are not only untrue but that hamper our sexual spontaneity, make us feel bad about our normal sexual urges, and make us feel shame about our bodies.

MESSAGES YOU RECEIVED ABOUT SEXUALITY FROM SOCIETY IN GENERAL

Attitudes About the Sexes

Another message we received, both from our families and from society in general, is how women and men are to be perceived. Our attitudes about the sexes directly affect our feelings about ourselves and can severely interfere with our relationships with the opposite sex. Spend some time thinking about your mother's attitude about men and your father's attitude about women. Also think about the attitudes about the sexes that permeated your environment. This is what Amber shared with me:

"My mother's attitude about men was extremely confusing to me. On the one hand, she seemed to take on what was then the typical passive role of women while in the presence of men and to give them a tremendous amount of power. On the other hand, she often voiced such things as 'Why would I want a man around? All they do is demand that you feed them and then sit with their feet up on the coffee table and get in your way.'

"I also grew up in the fifties, when fathers typically had very little involvement with their children. Although I did not have a father in my home, I noticed that my friends' fathers just seemed to go to work and then come home and sit in an easy chair watching TV or reading the paper all night, spending little or no time interacting with either their children or their wife.

"These images remained firmly in my mind until I was well into my twenties, when I began to meet some fathers who were different. It was no coincidence that at seventeen I escaped from my hometown and what I assumed would be my destiny—to marry a man like the kind of men I grew up around.

"It is also no coincidence that I have never married. The picture my mother painted of domestic 'bliss,' coupled with the images of my friends' fathers, has been a significant factor in my remaining single."

Sometimes both parents, and in fact the entire family, will teach their children to have a particular attitude about the sexes. This was the case in Sophie's family:

"My entire family preferred males. When a male was born it

was time for celebration; when a female was born condolences were in order. I grew up wishing I was a male and feeling less than any male I had contact with."

A good way of discovering what your attitude is about the opposite sex is to look at the words you use to identify them. If you grew up hearing your parents or your peers talk about the opposite sex in derogatory terms, it is likely that you adopted these same terms and, consequently, the same attitudes. Many women, themselves raised among men who used derogatory words to describe females, seem to take these terms for granted. This was the case with Hope:

"My father used very derogatory words when referring to sex and female genitalia in particular. He used words like *bang, pork, poke,* for intercourse and *cunt, hole,* and *slit* to describe the vagina. I was keenly aware from the time I was very small that he did not respect women—that he only saw them as objects to be used. Naturally this made me feel ashamed to be a female, ashamed of my body, especially my genitals."

We are also trained by family and society about how our own sex is expected to act and how our sex is perceived by others. Females are often trained to be seductive and sexy and to derive their good feelings from winning male approval and turning men on, while at the same time remaining virginal and innocent.

Males, on the other hand, are supposed to be aggressive and experienced. While girls are guaranteed a bad reputation for being sexually curious or sexually active, boys are guaranteed admiration for the exact same behavior. This puts some boys in the precarious position of having to find a girl to have sex with even if they aren't ready for the experience.

Contraceptive pills, antibiotics, and the sexual revolution have caused some parents to become more permissive with their female children, but even today our culture is still steeped in the belief that young men need to sow their wild oats—while it teaches girls that boys do not want "used property." Many a father is secretly proud of his son's sexual escapades, believing that they underscore his son's virility. Promiscuity in boys is more likely to be sanctioned by society—"Boys will be boys!" we say. But male promiscuity has nothing to do with masculinity: in fact, it can signify precisely the reverse.

RELIGIOUS MESSAGES ABOUT SEX

Although we live in the twentieth century, the archaic belief that sex is evil and dirty still lurks in our minds. We may not consciously admit to this outmoded view, but we certainly act as if we do.

In the fifteenth and sixteenth centuries earthly pleasure was regarded as sinful. Sex was seen as necessary for the continuation of the race, but enjoyment of it was publicly viewed as the work of the devil. Sex symbolized man's fall. Even between married couples, sex was meant for procreation only. It pointed out the beast in man, and for a woman to enjoy sex meant she was immoral and depraved.

Religion today, based on Judeo-Christian ideas of morality, teaches us that sex is primarily intended for procreation. The traditional Christian view of the body is that it is the source of all temptation and sin. Rather than being considered a sacred vessel of the divine, the body is seen as a vehicle for the profane, with a relentless potential for sin.

Marci grew up in a very religious household. Most of the family's activities were centered around going to church. Very early on Marci learned that sex was the work of the devil. The women in her congregation were not allowed to wear makeup and they were required to wear their dresses below their knees and to never wear short sleeves. Dancing was also forbidden because it was seen as the devil's way of tempting them. They were also forbidden to go to the movies or to listen to rock-and-roll music for the same reason.

Needless to say, Marci grew up being very afraid of her sexual feelings. But she also grew up thinking that women were the ones who were responsible for tempting men. The message she received was that if a woman conducted herself properly, did not wear makeup, and covered her body properly, then men would not be tempted to have sex with her. This message ended up nearly destroying Marci when she was eighteen.

Marci was on her way to her car after leaving the library late one night when a man attacked her. He grabbed her, pulled her into his car, and sped away with her. On a deserted road outside of town he brutally raped her and then threw her out of the car.

Marci had no choice, given her upbringing, but to blame herself for the rape. She felt that she must have tempted this man in some way—perhaps by something in her manner. She also blamed herself for being out after dark, since her parents had warned her about doing this. After this incident, Marci, who still lived at home, became even more isolated and dependent on her parents, seldom venturing out on her own at all.

It wasn't until after her parents' death in a car accident when Marci was thirty years old and considered an "old maid" within her religious community that Marci began to doubt her religion's teachings about sex. Deeply depressed by both her parents' death and the prospect of spending her entire life alone, Marci went against her religious tradition and sought help from the therapeutic community. This in itself was a major step for Marci, but it still took quite some time to free herself from the negative messages she had been raised with regarding sex and to overcome the damage caused by both the rape and the self-blame she felt for the rape.

Eventually, though, Marci worked through her conflicts regarding what she believed to be appropriate behavior and what wasn't. While she is still a religious person, she is no longer a member of the more rigid congregation she was raised in. She chose to include dancing, movies, and music in her life, and this enabled her to break out of her isolation. Today Marci is engaged to a wonderfully kind and considerate man who understands her need to wait until marriage to have sex.

SEXUAL MESSAGES CHECKLIST

Which of the following messages about sex did you receive from your parents, from other family members, from society in general, or from your church?

___ Touching the genitals is bad.
___ Sexual pleasure is bad.
___ Sexuality is animalistic.
___ The genitals are dirty and are organs to be ashamed of.
___ Sex is something to be endured.
___ Sex is something "nice" people don't enjoy.

___ Don't look, dress, act, or feel sexy.
___ Sexual secretions are dirty.
___ Using sex to hurt others is okay.
___ Withholding sex is a good way to get even.
___ Something is wrong with you if you don't experience an orgasm with every sexual act.
___ You should not enjoy sex—it is for procreation only.
___ You should not enjoy foreplay.
___ Masturbation is evil.
___ Masturbating your partner is evil.
___ Only men should be sexually aggressive.
___ It is only important for a man to have an orgasm, not a woman.

Your sexuality, which includes your most basic ideas of what sex is, what it means, and how and when it is appropriate, was formed early in your life, most notably by your family experiences, where you began to absorb the messages about sex that would stay with you all of your life. It is vital, therefore, that you work on remembering just what those messages were, how they affected you, and most importantly, which of them you still believe and which ones you need to discard in order to make room for healthier, more sexually liberating ones. Remembering and gathering information about the messages you received from your family, from religion, and from society in general regarding sex will help you to understand more about your own sexual attitudes and where they come from.

Chapter Three

SEXUAL SELF-ESTEEM AND
YOUR BODY IMAGE

How we feel about our bodies is crucial to our sense of self-esteem, and as we have learned so far, self-esteem is closely related to our sexual adjustment. If we think of ourselves as unattractive, our self-esteem as a whole is lower. This in turn can prevent us from fully enjoying sex.

A person's view of his or her own physical appearance is called *body image*. Body image is the picture a person has of his or her body—what it looks like to the person and what the person thinks it looks like to others. Body image is subject to change and usually does change with aging, pregnancy, illness, surgery, and other major physical events.

For many people, low self-esteem is caused by a negative body image, while for others it is the low self-esteem that comes first and the negative body image that follows from it. These people know what is wrong with them—if only they had a better body, they would have a better life.

People who have strong negative body images, such as those who are embarrassed about some physical flaw (real or imagined), can become so strongly convinced of the abnormality or repulsiveness of some physical feature that it prevents them from feeling confident and sexy in a relationship, as was the case with Odetta:

"I know that if I felt better about my body it would probably help me a lot in my relationships. There have been many times

45

when I didn't think I looked good and so I turned down a date or avoided physical intimacy even though I felt turned on to the guy. If I finally do get in bed with a guy I worry so much about how my body looks to him that I can't even enjoy myself sexually."

Some are so embarrassed by their body that it prevents them from entering a relationship at all, as it did with Jacob:

Jacob was certain that his penis was so small that any woman he would become involved with would laugh at him when she saw it. He was so convinced of this, in fact, that he avoided getting involved with women sexually. When it came time for the relationship to proceed toward physical intimacy he would stall for so long that the woman either stopped seeing him or they just became friends.

A positive body image is an important part of self-esteem, and having high self-esteem is vital to establishing intimacy with others. Having high self-esteem is having the belief that one is valuable and deserving of loving relationships and being secure enough to risk having a lover find out that you are not completely perfect.

Not surprisingly, the way we feel about our body directly affects how we feel about our sexuality. If we like the way our body looks, if we feel attractive physically, we will have a lot more confidence in our sexuality and our sexual attractiveness than if we don't like our body and don't feel physically attractive. This all seems rather logical, but what isn't logical is how each of us determines whether he or she is physically attractive. Why is it that someone who by most people's standards would be considered extremely attractive can be as insecure about how he or she looks as someone who is far less attractive? And why is it that some people who actually have less to work with in terms of physical attributes can end up coming off as extremely sexy and extremely attractive? And even more important, who really determines what is attractive and what is not?

For many people, their *view* of themselves has as much impact on their ability to form intimate, loving relationships as does their actual physical condition—in some cases more. We've all known people we consider to be especially blessed in the looks department—the gorgeous woman at work, the handsome guy who lives down the street. We usually think that these people know they are attractive and we even assume they are probably conceited about their looks.

No matter how many times it happens, we always seem shocked to discover that often these good-looking people are insecure or shy or that they even feel unattractive. And time after time in television interviews we hear beautiful movie stars tell us that they don't really feel attractive at all, and we are always surprised to hear it.

I had this kind of experience with Jennifer, an actress and model who came to me for counseling. She told me, "Even though everyone tells me now how beautiful I am and a lot of men are interested in me, I just don't *feel* attractive. I still feel like the awkward teenager who had braces and acne, who sat home alone on the weekends while my friends went out on dates. People think I'm kidding or I'm pretending to be modest or something when I tell them I don't think I'm pretty, but I really mean it."

The sad truth is that some of us are simply not able to appreciate our beauty no matter how much others recognize it in us. Often this is because as children and adolescents we felt we were ugly. In fact, research shows that the self-image we had as adolescents tends to stay with us throughout our lifetime. That means that if you were an awkward, pimply-faced teenager who was made fun of, you probably are carrying around that picture of yourself in your mind no matter how you look today. And the reverse can be true. If you were an attractive, popular teenager, you probably tend to feel pretty good about yourself today, no matter what shape you are in. While you may be critical of the fact that you have gained weight, or of some other aspect of your body, you probably still feel better about yourself than the person who was less popular and attractive as a teenager.

Those who experienced constant criticism or teasing about how they looked as children or teenagers are usually self-conscious about their appearances as adults and often suffer from both low self-esteem and low sexual self-esteem. This was the situation with Alexis:

"I was a fat kid and you know what that means. I felt like an outcast and in most respects I was. Even though I lost weight in college and guys started asking me out, I still felt inadequate somehow, as if I was not as good as the other girls. This caused me to give in to guys too quickly as a way of making sure they'd like me. While I don't do this anymore, mostly because of my fear of AIDS, I still feel like that fat teenager who isn't going to get a date for the prom. When a good-looking guy asks me out I am always surprised and I find myself wondering, 'What's wrong with him?'"

Most people have negative body images not because they have unattractive bodies, but because they see themselves inaccurately. Their images of their physical selves are distorted, either because they see their overall size and shape inaccurately (seeing themselves as much fatter, thinner, taller, or shorter than they actually are), or because they see specific body parts in a distorted way. When the latter occurs not only do they perceive their long nose, acne, wide hips, sagging breasts, or large behinds as more grotesque than they are, but they see their imagined or real flaws dominating their entire physical selves, as Clarissa did:

"Everyone tells me that I am so pretty but I know I'm really not. They don't know that I have these huge hips and thighs. That's because I do such a good job of hiding them. All I see when I look in the mirror are my hips and thighs. They disgust me so much that I know they would disgust other people if they saw them."

Unfortunately, Clarissa has been blinded to her other physical attributes—her beautiful skin and hair, her lovely shoulders and breasts, her striking facial features. All these beautiful parts of her are overshadowed by her dislike for her hips and thighs.

Many people are very poor judges of themselves and have a distorted view of how they impress others. Most people, especially women, are not as unattractive as they think. About one third of people, particularly women, report being strongly dissatisfied with their bodies. And women are more likely to have a negative self-image than men. In fact, studies have shown that relatively few women look in a mirror without focusing on all the things they'd like to change, whereas men tend to be more accepting of what they see. Women tend to distort their perceptions of their bodies negatively, while men—just as unrealistically—distort their perceptions in a positive, self-aggrandizing way.

Almost all women say there is something they don't like about their bodies. Women put an overemphasis on the way their bodies look and assume that men are attracted to them solely or primarily because of their bodies. They don't take into account their personality, their wit, their mind, their sensitivity, their ability to relate to others, and most important, their ability to love.

HOW WE LEARNED TO DISLIKE OUR BODIES
Parental Messages

To a great extent, our body image comes from the physical and emotional input we received as children. Experiences from significant others have a dramatic impact on how we feel physically and emotionally about our bodies as adults. Our parents, of course, have the most profound effect on our body image. If they like how we look and tell us so, we face the world with a head start. If, on the other hand, our parents dislike our appearance, our body image will be tremendously influenced in a negative way.

Kevin began to dislike his body very early on due to the fact that he knew his father disliked it. "My dad was a jock and he wanted me to be one too. But I was more frail like my mother. He was constantly on me to gain weight and to 'toughen up,' as he put it, but no matter how much I ate or exercised I remained thin with very little musculature. By the time I was in high school I was convinced that no girl would want to date me with all the jocks around, so I just never asked anyone out. It wasn't until I was in my early twenties that some girls seemed to find me attractive. Today, even though I have girlfriends, I'm always self-conscious about them seeing me without my shirt on because my chest is so underdeveloped."

Some parents place a great deal of importance on physical appearance, while others do not. Unfortunately, those that do instill in their children a tendency to overemphasize looks.

This was the case with Amanda: "My mother was very pretty and she spent a great deal of time on her appearance. She taught me to do the same, starting when I was quite young. My father loved my mother very much and he talked about how beautiful she was and how I looked just like her. I grew up thinking that beauty seemed to be the most important thing a woman had to offer a man and that in order to keep a man you had to work on looking good all the time."

In addition to whether or not our parents like the way we look and how much importance they place on physical appearance, another factor that influences our body image is whether our parents are satisfied with the way *they* look. Parents with a poor body image can pass on their negative attitudes and feelings to us, causing us to dislike our bodies. This is especially true if we resemble a parent who dislikes his or her body.

Roberta's mother had a great deal of body hair. She had dark hair on her arms, thighs, and calves. "When I was little I remember my mother was always using a product call Nair to remove hair from different parts of her body. She was always worried about the hair growing back and was always complaining about having to use this product.

"When I was about eleven and starting to develop, she began worrying about my body hair. She taught me how to use the depilatory and nagged at me to use it as soon as the hair started coming back at all. I didn't like to use it—it smelled bad and sometimes it gave me a rash, but she insisted. I began to feel really self-conscious about being so hairy and became as obsessed as my mother about always making sure it was removed. I didn't know anybody else who used a depilatory and somehow it became a source of shame for me. I began to hate my body for being so hairy."

Toni's family handled a similar situation in a completely different way. An extremely attractive woman who carries herself regally, Toni told me her story: "In my family we all have big noses, but my parents and grandparents always taught us to have pride in them because they were a mark of our ancestry. My grandparents came from Italy and in the particular region where they were born a big nose was a sign of the aristocracy. So I grew up liking my nose even though it is very large. I have always felt very fortunate to have been raised to have pride in the way I look because I see so many others who are always trying to change their features with plastic surgery."

Unfortunately, most parents are not like Toni's. Since many are critical of their own bodies they are equally critical of their children's bodies, as was the case with Selina: "From the earliest I can remember my mother was always battling with her weight. She went on diets of all kinds, sometimes starving herself for days. When I reached ten years old she started to focus on my weight as well. The doctors told her I was of normal weight and that I would grow out of my baby fat but she didn't believe it. She started putting me on diets and paying a lot of attention to what I ate.

"This continued throughout junior high school. By the time I entered high school I had a serious problem with my self-image. I imagined I was fat even though I was not and even saw myself as overweight when I looked in the mirror, although I was getting thinner and thinner. By the time I reached sixteen I was throwing up any food I ate and had become anorexic. I have spent the past seven years overcoming my problem and working on seeing myself accurately instead of so critically."

OUR CHILDHOOD ENVIRONMENT

Most people's low self-esteem and poor body image reflect the fact that there must have been something in their childhood that eroded their confidence.

We are all taught from an early age that those who are attractive are also more worthy. And we are all taught just what *is* considered attractive in our particular social circle. This training begins very early on when the cutest babies and toddlers are given the most attention by outsiders. Slowly, as the child grows up he or she will be treated well or not, depending upon how cute he or she is, what kind of clothes he or she wears, and what color skin she or he has.

Studies have shown that attractive children tend to develop more self-confidence and have higher self-esteem than those children who are perceived as less attractive. If adults smiled approvingly and told you how cute or how pretty or how handsome you were as you were growing up, you probably felt very good about your body and the way you looked. On the other hand, if insensitive adults said things such as, "My, she is a fat one, isn't she?" or "He must look like his father" (implying that he doesn't look like his *attractive* mother), you probably ended up not feeling very good about your appearance at all.

HOW EMOTIONAL, PHYSICAL, AND SEXUAL ABUSE AFFECTS OUR BODY IMAGE

Nothing erodes a child's confidence more than experiencing emotional, physical, or sexual abuse, particularly when that abuse comes from his or her parents. When a parent abuses a child that child will tend to blame himself or herself instead of being willing to experience the alienation that feeling anger toward the abusive parent would create. A great deal of this self-blame turns into self-loathing, in particular a hatred of the child's own body.

Many emotionally abusive parents will include attacks concerning the child's physical appearance, as was the case with Bianca: "My father would periodically go on a rampage—shouting and throwing things at my mother and then bursting into each of our bedrooms and yelling at me and my siblings. He seemed to know each of our weaknesses and vulnerabilities and would go after them with a vengeance. My particular vulnerability was my physical appearance. I was a homely-looking kid with glasses and big ears. My father would yell at me that I was ugly and that no man would ever want me. I can't tell you how many times those words have come back to haunt me."

Fathers have a tremendous effect on their daughters' body image for several reasons. If a girl knows that her father loves her and thinks she is attractive she is more likely to feel attractive to other males. If, on the other hand, she feels rejected by her father or thinks he sees her as unattractive she will generalize this to all males.

Many fathers have a difficult time when their daughters reach puberty. They may feel proud that their little girl is growing up and at the same time want to hold onto her. Because of this internal conflict some fathers give double messages to their daughters, such as "You look so pretty" one time and "You look like a tramp" another time. Still other fathers, who had always been very affectionate with their daughters, suddenly push them away when they reach puberty and no longer show them any physical affection. This kind of behavior may cause a girl to hate the changes going on with her body.

If a child is physically or sexually abused she or he is especially likely to have a problematic body image. Those who were physically or sexually abused as children often ignore, neglect, and even abuse their bodies, since they see them as objects of shame. Survivors of abuse tend to cover up their bodies, hiding them from themselves and the rest of the world.

PEER ACCEPTANCE OR REJECTION

It is very important to children and adolescents to be accepted by their peers. Those who have this acceptance tend to have high self-esteem while those who experience rejection, teasing, or indifference tend to have lower self-esteem. Rejection or indifference from the opposite sex can be particularly devastating and can be the start of a child's believing that he or she is not attractive or desirable, as it did with Sue Ellen:

"Boys just never paid any attention to me in school. I was taller than most of them and my parents couldn't afford to dress me very well. I was so envious of the girls who wore frilly dresses and matching socks. By the time I was in junior high I just gave up trying to get their attention. I didn't feel like I had a chance of getting a boyfriend so I tried to convince myself that I really didn't want one."

Name-calling is particularly hurtful to children and can affect their body image negatively. Names such as "Beanpole," "Fatso," and "Four eyes" can stay with someone a lifetime and take a prominent place in someone's self-concept, as happened to Hank:

"It's pretty difficult to think of yourself as sexually attractive to women when you were called a 'nerd' or a 'fag' most of your childhood. Those words still ring in my ears every time I even think of asking a girl out."

THE DEMAND FOR THE PERFECT BODY

One of the main reasons so many women perceive their bodies as problems is that we live in a culture that dictates that women must be beautiful to be worthwhile, and then sets up standards of female beauty that are not only impossible for most women to live up to, but are unhealthy as well. For example, many diets and all surgery to control weight are physically dangerous.

Getting and staying thin have become major pastimes for women, consuming a significant amount of their time, energy, and money. According to Judith Stein of the Fat Liberation Movement, the emphasis on thinness in our culture not only oppresses overweight women, it also serves as a form of social control for all women.

Until very recently, men have not had to suffer quite as much pressure regarding the way their bodies should look, but all that is rapidly changing. Today men are constantly being pressured to work out, pump up their muscles, and stay physically fit. The message that men get today is that all women prefer a man who is athletic and muscular, even though that is not actually true. Many women prefer men who are slender, and some even prefer men who are overweight—kind of the "bear" look. Some others find muscular men threatening because they feel either physically or emotionally overwhelmed by them.

The entertainment and advertising media not only promote certain ideals in terms of how the body should look but often, in the absence of other sources of information, teach us what a normal and healthy body should look like. By trying to conform to our culture's ridiculous ideals we place ourselves in a no-win situation where we will never be satisfied with our bodies.

For example, women tend to compare themselves with the kind of physical perfection they see on TV or in magazines, and as a result, even very attractive women are certain that they're too fat or too thin or that something is wrong with their thighs or their breasts.

Although there are some exceptions, such as Lena Horne and the late Audrey Hepburn and a few older "super" models, rarely do we consider older women to still be sexy and beautiful. Older men fare a little better; Sean Connery was *People* magazine's "sexiest man alive" at sixty. It is still generally agreed that while older men look distinguished, older women just look old.

Men are also bombarded with advertisements for gyms and home exercise equipment and the constant message that women only like men who are physically fit. When all a man sees on television or in magazines is a suntanned Adonis with a huge chest and arms and all the women going crazy over him, he cannot help but feel bad about himself.

Messages from Lovers

With just a comment or two, a lover has the ability to either raise our sexual self-esteem or lower it. Because we are generally so vulnerable with our lovers their opinions about our bodies affect us tremendously.

Whether a lover tells you that he or she wishes you would lose or gain weight, exercise more, or buy some new clothes, the message can shake your confidence. If he or she begins to nag at you continually, the damage to your body image can become more severe. And, in the heat of an argument, a lover's calling you "ugly," "repulsive," "a fat slob," or "a thimble dick" can cut you to the very core. Not only will the insult devastate you in the moment, and make it impossible for you to ever feel safe with that lover again, but chances are you will replay that insult over and over in your head hundreds of times, the result being that your self-esteem will be continually whittled away.

What Are the Messages You Have Received?

1. Make a list of all the messages you remember receiving concerning your body from the time you were a child until the present. Include verbal and nonverbal messages from your parents, nicknames and insults from your siblings and peers, and things that have been told you by friends and lovers.

2. Put a star beside each message that still has an affect on you (those you still believe, those that are still replayed in your head).

As we have seen in this chapter, the way you feel about your body has a lot to do with how high or low your sexual self-esteem is. Improving your body image will be a major part of raising your sexual self-esteem. In Part III I will address the issue of learning to accept your body the way it is and methods of improving your body image.

Chapter Four

YOUR "FIRSTS"

Our "firsts" with sex—the first sexual contact we have with another person, the first time we decide to have sex with a partner
of our choice, and our first serious love affair—all have a profound
effect on our sexual self-esteem. Like the first time for anything,
there is the initial excitement, the heart-thumping anticipation,
the fears, and then the relief when it is all over. Sometimes a first
is a surprise to us, sometimes it is planned, but always it is significant. Our firsts with sex are always incredibly intense, leaving
memories that can last a lifetime.

YOUR FIRST SEXUAL CONTACT WITH ANOTHER PERSON

Aside from the messages you received from your family, your peers,
and society in general about sex, there were other experiences that
you had as a child that strongly affected your sexual self-esteem.
Most notably, your first sexual contact with another person is one
of the most significant events influencing your sexuality. It is to be
hoped that your first sexual experience was either a positive or a
neutral one, not one that elicited tremendous shame or fear. If the
person who introduced you to sex was another child, the chances
are that the experience might have been one of innocent explora-

tion and curiosity and that it left you with positive feelings, as Lucy's first sexual experience did:

"My friend Brian and I started playing 'doctor' together when we were around six. He showed me his 'pee-pee' and I showed him mine. It was fun and a way of satisfying our curiosity about what the opposite sex looked like. I remember one time I asked him if I could touch his penis and he said I could only if I let him touch me. I realized that I was too embarrassed to have him touch me so I understood why he didn't want me touching him. I look back on this as a beginning lesson about respecting other people's boundaries."

How do you feel when you think of your first sexual experience with someone else? No matter how innocent, no matter how young you were, you probably remember the moment quite vividly and probably have strong feelings about it, as these people did:

"My first memory of sex was playing strip poker with my girlfriend and her brothers when I was eight. Their parents were never at home so we were alone a lot. Her brothers were a few years older than us and it was their idea. I felt really embarrassed but also curious. I liked having older boys pay attention to me because I wasn't a very attractive kid and the boys in my class didn't pay any attention to me. I didn't really know what we were doing and it all seemed to be a lot of fun and I was curious to see the boys' penises. But then I started losing and had to take off my clothes and suddenly it wasn't much fun anymore. The boys ended up stealing my clothes and those of my girlfriend's and hiding them from us. We had to sit with our clothes off until the boys finally agreed to return them. That part of the experience was really embarrassing and I remember feeling tricked by the boys. I thought they were mean and we refused to play the next time they asked because we didn't trust them anymore."

Another woman tells us:

"I was twelve years old and I had just started to develop. Jason T., the boy I was 'going steady' with, asked me if he could feel my breasts to see what they felt like. I remember getting so angry with him that I threw his ring in his face and ran away crying. I felt so humiliated and so hurt that I missed two days of school. I was afraid to face Jason again. Somehow, it made me feel cheap that he even asked me. I didn't 'go steady' with anyone else for a long,

long time because I was afraid that was what all boys would want to do."

Sometimes our first experience with sexuality is a pivotal point in our life, as it was with Luke:

"I was thirteen years old and I was playing with some of the kids in the neighborhood. One boy, a new kid in the neighborhood, suggested we see who could pee the farthest. All the other boys unzipped their pants and pulled out their penises so I did too. I didn't want to be different from the others in the group. Everyone was giggling and starting to pee. I got an erection but I couldn't pee. Instead, I ended up ejaculating. I was so embarrassed that I ran home. I felt so humiliated. I was afraid they were all going to think I was homosexual, and in fact it turned out to be true. I had become aroused by looking at the other boys' penises instead of getting into the macho thing about seeing who could pee farthest. This was the first time I became aware that I was different from the other boys."

Childhood is full of embarrassing experiences, but the ones involving our genitals and our sexuality can be especially humiliating. As you can imagine, in each of these examples the person being introduced to sex was greatly affected by the experience. You will notice that in two of the above examples my clients ended up feeling humiliated or embarrassed by the situation. This is very common. Children are extremely preoccupied with "fitting in," so they will often go along with other children, even when they don't really want to. Sex is a very private matter, even for children, and being introduced to it, even by another child, is fraught with potential embarrassment. If the feeling of shame or humiliation was significant enough, it may follow the child into adulthood, coloring adult sexual relationships.

WHEN YOUR FIRST SEXUAL EXPERIENCE WAS SEXUAL ABUSE

While many people do not recognize it as such, our first sexual experience was often sexual abuse. Thousands upon thousands of children are sexually abused every year by relatives, other caretakers, and other children. The majority of perpetrators are relatives, most notably stepfathers, fathers, uncles, grandfathers, and older siblings, as well as mothers, grandmothers, and aunts. In addition, having a stepfather constitutes one of the strongest risk factors, more than doubling a female's chance of being sexually molested, since a stepfather is five times more likely to sexually victimize a daughter than is a natural father. It has been estimated that ninety percent of child sexual abuse occurs in the home or at the hands of people known to the family. Many children are sexually abused as well by coaches, camp counselors, baby-sitters, doctors, dentists—people the child trusted and cared about.

One of the reasons so many victims of child sexual abuse do not recognize they were indeed abused is that many people believe that they were willing participants when, in fact, they were being coerced or manipulated by an older, more experienced person, whether it was a child or an adult.

Sexual curiosity is normal in children. All children explore their own bodies, and to some extent and at some time they may engage in visual or even manual exploration of another child's body. This is one way in which children discover sexual differences or verify what they have been told by their parents or others about the differences between boys and girls. But often children may appear to consent even though they actually do not. In many instances what appears to be consent may actually be only passive consent or the inability to make a rational decision because of limited cognitive skills and life experiences.

Many of my clients, when answering my question "What was your first sexual experience?" will tell me that an older sibling or older neighborhood child introduced them to sex, not realizing that, in fact, they had been sexually abused. Sometimes this introduction to sex was made by someone several years older than themselves and there was a great deal of coercion, and yet seldom do my clients consider the experience abusive. The following example is representative of this type of experience:

"My older brother and I would play with each other sexually, starting when I was three years old. He'd touch my vagina and I'd touch his penis. We did this for several years until my brother started taking girls out on dates. Then I felt terribly abandoned by him. I thought I had done something wrong and I would go into his room at night and touch his penis and try to get him to touch me again but he would just get angry and push me away, saying, 'We're too old for that now—go back to bed.' I grew up being terribly afraid that a boy would reject me just like my brother had."

It wasn't until several months into therapy that Marsha came to realize that the "playing" she and her brother had engaged in starting when she was three years old was, in fact, sexual abuse. First of all, her brother was seven years older than she was. That means that when the touching started, she was three years old and he was ten. Obviously, because of the differences in their ages and experience, her brother was the instigator. While she might have been curious about her brother's penis when she was three and might even have wanted to touch it out of curiosity, she was not old enough to understand the implications of allowing him to touch her. What had, in fact, happened was that by introducing her to sex at such an early age she became sexualized far too early. Children are not equipped to handle the intensity of strong sexual feelings and it is likely that she was overwhelmed by her feelings of arousal.

Second, her brother had a tremendous amount of power over her since he was so much older and she wanted to please him, very much like a child wants to please its parents. She couldn't have said no to him if she had wanted to.

Third, even though Marsha says she felt no shame or guilt about their touching when she was little, she was made to feel horribly ashamed when she wanted to continue the touching after her brother had lost interest. She felt that she must have instigated it all along and that she was a tramp for continuing to be sexually attracted to her brother long after he had rejected her. Most victims of child sexual abuse feel tremendously guilty and ashamed about the sexual incidents and most blame themselves. This is one of the most damaging effects of sexual abuse of children, since it lowers self-esteem—and sexual self-esteem in particular.

Sexual contact between children is often misunderstood as being just normal sex play. But normal sex play and exploration occurs *only* between those of the same age, sexual experience, and power. For example, "playing doctor" by consenting age peers is likely to represent normal sexual experimentation, while sexual activity between an adolescent and a young child most likely represents sexual abuse.

Only under certain special circumstances is sex between children *not* sexual abuse:

1. The children are young and of approximately the same age.

2. They each have equal power, both with each other and in the family if they are related. This rules out any situation where one child is in charge of another or has any authority over the other. It also generally rules out any sexuality between an older male child and a female child even one year younger since males generally have more power in our society than females.

3. There is no betrayal of trust between them. This would be possible only if they were of the same age and each had equal power. For example, a younger child has a certain amount of trust in an older child, especially if it is an older sibling, a baby-sitter, a scout leader, and so forth. If the child in authority misuses this trust the abused child feels betrayed in an extremely profound way—sometimes causing her or him to mistrust all authority figures in the future.

4. There is no coercion or physical force.

5. The sexual play is the result of natural curiosity, exploration, and mutual sexual naïveté. This is not the case when an older or more experienced child "teaches" the younger one what he or she has learned. In fact, what is generally going on here is that the more experienced child may have, in fact, been sexually abused himself and is reenacting the sexual abuse he suffered by repeating it.

6. The children are not traumatized by disapproving parents who may "catch them in the act."

How Old Do You Have to Be for It to Be Considered Sexual Abuse?

Many people have a memory of sexual interaction with an adult or an older child when they were a child or a teenager and yet they believe they were either too young or too old for the experience to be classified as sexual abuse. Several studies have determined that there are two age periods when children seem most vulnerable to sexual abuse. These are the period between ages six and seven, and the period between ages ten and twelve. But children are vulnerable to sexual abuse at all ages, from as early as infancy to as late as age eighteen.

More and more I have clients coming to me who suspect that perhaps they were molested even as infants, although they have a very difficult time believing their own feelings. Some clients describe it as a feeling, an inner "knowing," while others feel it in their bodies, as body memories. Some see and feel themselves as infants and then feel a tingling in their genitals or a sharp pain in their vagina or anus, as Tabatha did:

"Whenever I think of myself as an infant I feel a sharp pain in my vaginal area. This tells me that something really did happen to me as a baby, even though I don't have a clear memory of it."

Many people do not think they were sexually abused because they feel they were old enough to consent. Unfortunately, even a teenager is not old enough to understand the ramifications of having sex with an adult, especially if that adult is a relative. The adult always has more personal power, and usually more physical power, and is always the one responsible for the act, no matter how much the child or adolescent feels he or she wanted to do it.

Some victims report being abused throughout their teen years and even into adulthood. This is particularly true of girls who are abused by their brothers, as Dee was:

"I was so relieved when my brother went away to college. He had been sexually abusing me ever since I was five years old but now it was finally going to stop. But one weekend I visited him at school and he attacked me in his dormitory. Even though I was seventeen years old I was still no match for him."

What Is Child Sexual Abuse?

In addition to the fact that many people have blocked out the memory of sexual abuse, blame themselves for the abuse, or think they were too young or too old to be sexually abused, there are other reasons people are confused as to whether or not their particular experiences was that of child sexual abuse—most notably that unless intercourse took place they do not believe they were sexually abused.

Many forms of sexual abuse do not involve intercourse or any kind of penetration. Below is an abbreviated version of a list that originally appeared in the *Handbook of Clinical Intervention in Child Sexual Abuse* by Suzanne M. Sgroi. The list contains many of the types of sexual abuse toward children of either sex:

1. *Nudity.* The adult parades around the house in front of all or some of the family members.

2. *Disrobing.* The adult disrobes in front of the child, generally when the child and the adult are alone.

3. *Genital exposure.* The adult exposes his or her genitals to the child.

4. *Observation of the child.* The adult surreptitiously or overtly watches the child undress, bathe, excrete, or urinate.

5. *Kissing.* The adult kisses the child in a lingering or intimate way.

6. *Fondling.* The adult fondles the child's breasts, abdomen, genital area, inner thighs, or buttocks. The child may similarly fondle the adult at his or her request.

7. *Masturbation.* The adult masturbates while the child observes; the adult observes the child masturbating; the adult and child masturbate each other (mutual masturbation).

8. *Fellatio.* The adult male has the child fellate him, or the adult of either gender fellates the male child.

9. *Cunnilingus.* This type of oral-genital contact requires either the child to place his or her mouth and tongue on the vulva or in the vaginal area of an adult female or the adult to place his or her mouth on the vulva or in the vaginal area of the female child.

10. *Digital (finger) penetration of the anus or rectal opening.* Perpetrators may also use inanimate objects such as crayons or pencils.

11. *Penile penetration of the anus or rectal opening.*

12. *Digital (finger) penetration of the vagina.* Inanimate objects may also be inserted.

13. *"Dry intercourse."* This is a slang term describing an interaction in which the adult rubs his penis against the child's genital-rectal area or inner thighs or buttocks.

14. *Penile penetration of the vagina.*

If any of the above-listed acts took place in your infancy, childhood, or adolescence with someone older and you felt uncomfortable or strange about them, then you were sexually abused. Of equal importance is any indirect or direct sexual suggestion made by an adult toward a child. This is called *approach behavior.* It can include sexual looks, innuendos, or suggestive gestures. Even if the adult never engaged in touching or took any overt sexual action, the child picks up these projected sexual feelings.

Keep in mind that the *intention* of the adult or older child while engaging in some of the acts (nudity, disrobing, observation of the child) will determine whether the act is actually sexually abusive. If an adult watches a child bathe, for example, but does so in a *nonsexual* way that does not upset the child, it may not be sexually abusive. But if the adult becomes sexually aroused while watching, it is then sexual abuse.

Pornography often plays a part in child sexual abuse, with the perpetrator using it to introduce the child to the idea of sex.

"I was nine years old when my uncle, who was watching me for the evening, started showing me pictures from magazines of naked women and men. He put me on his lap and started stroking my back while we looked at the pictures. He told me that when a woman loves a man that is what they do and then he asked me if I loved him. I told him that yes, I did, and then he took me into the bedroom, where he showed me his penis. That was the beginning of several months of sexual activity between us until he moved away. I don't know what he did to me exactly because I disassociated while it was all going on. All I know is that I can't stomach pornography of any kind and the smell of a man's ejaculate makes me sick."

Another common misconception is that sexual contact with a child doesn't really cause any damage to the child as long as there is no violence or pain. While the list of types of sexual abuse seems to indicate that the severity of the abuse increases as the list goes on, all types of sexual abuse, even nudity and kissing, can be emotionally and psychologically damaging to a child for a lifetime, even if the abuse is not violent, overly physical, or repeated. There is always damage and pain, even if it is emotional rather than physical, and much of this damage is caused by the betrayal of the child by someone previously trusted and cared about. Children need time to be children before they are capable of handling any sexual relationship. Sexuality foisted upon them too early amounts to abuse, and it is still abuse even in the complete absence of physical pain.

"I was five years old and my female baby-sitter showed me her breasts one day. She asked me if I'd like to touch them. I didn't really but she seemed to get mad that I didn't want to so I did. They felt soft but I was very uncomfortable. I knew we weren't supposed to be doing this. Then she told me to pull out my penis so she could touch it. I really didn't want to do this but again, I was afraid she'd get mad at me so I did it. She started rubbing it and it felt really good but I was really scared.

"After that, I didn't really want to have her baby-sit for me again. I tried to talk my parents out of going places but I couldn't really tell them why I didn't want her to baby-sit. I think she baby-sat for me for several years but I'm not sure. She continued to touch me and have me touch her but I think I have blocked out other things she did. I don't have any memory of those years with her so I can only assume she must have abused me further. God knows what she did to me. All I know is that I have both a tremendous fear and a sick attraction to being around domineering women and being controlled sexually by them."

The Long-Term Effects of Child Sexual Abuse

There are many other long-term effects of childhood sexual abuse. Not every person who is sexually abused as a child suffers from each specific problem listed under the following broad categories, but most suffer from all the broad categories themselves.

1. *Damage to self-esteem and self-image:* feeling ugly inside; feelings of worthlessness; a tendency to overapologize; feelings of being stupid, a failure, a loser, tremendous guilt feelings and feelings of shame; a tendency to blame oneself for whatever goes wrong; a tendency to sabotage success; a tendency to be victimized by others; feelings of helplessness.

2. *Relationship problems:* difficulty trusting others; a tendency to be distant and aloof; a tendency to get involved with destructive people who abuse one physically, emotionally, or sexually; a lack of empathy or concern for others; a deep sense of isolation; difficulty with physical affection; secrecy, evasiveness, and a tendency to withhold information from others—or the opposite, a tendency to "tell all"; a tendency to "give oneself away," helping others to the point of not taking care of oneself; difficulties with authority figures; difficulties communicating desires, thoughts, and feelings to others; difficulty receiving from others.

3. *Emotional problems:* intense anger and rage that sometimes bursts out unexpectedly; mood swings, ranging from deep depression to extreme anxiety; chronic depression; dissociation or a

"splitting off" from oneself, including time blockages and feelings of numbness in various parts of the body; extreme fears or phobias; sleep disturbances; addiction to food, alcohol, or drugs; obsessive/compulsive behavior such as compulsive shopping, shoplifting, gambling, or cleaning; eating disorders; flashbacks that are triggered by certain sights, sounds, smells, or touches; abusive behavior; self-destructive behavior such as suicide attempts and self-mutilation.

4. *Physical problems:* frequent sore throats; difficulty swallowing; migraine headaches; unexplained vaginal or anal pain; frequent bladder and vaginal infections; skin disorders; numbness or tingling in legs or arms.

5. *Sexual problems:* some of the many long-term symptoms that victims of child sexual abuse suffer as adults are specifically focused around their ability to function sexually:

- Lack of sexual desire or inhibition of sexual feelings. Inability to have an orgasm.
- Sexual dysfunctions such as vaginismus (an involuntary contraction of the vaginal muscles, making penetration difficult or impossible) and painful intercourse.
- Inability to enjoy certain types of sexuality (can't be penetrated but can engage in oral sex; can't be fondled but can be penetrated; can't be touched on certain parts of the body).
- Problems with sexual identity.
- Promiscuity, continuing to be a sexual object.
- Attraction to "illicit" sexual activities such as pornography and prostitution.
- Anger and disgust at any public (or media) display of affection, sexuality, nudity, or partial nudity.
- Sexual manipulation. This includes using seductiveness or other forms of sexual manipulation to get what you want in your marital, social, or business relationships. Sexualizing all relationships (which can cause victims to become sexual victimizers of their own or other people's children).
- Sexual addiction, wherein victims, sexualized early on, often become addicted to daily sex or masturbation as a way of alleviating anxiety and comforting themselves.

As you can see, the experience of being sexually abused as a child can have a tremendous effect on your ability to have healthy sexual relationships as an adult. If your first experience with sex was indeed sexual abuse, or if you suspect that you may have been sexually abused, please refer to chapter five, where I will discuss more long-term effects of childhood sexual abuse and offer further information about the more hidden types of sexual abuse.

"GOING ALL THE WAY" FOR THE FIRST TIME

Whatever your experiences of sex were when you were a child, the first time you voluntarily decide to have sexual intercourse (or its equivalent if you are gay) with someone of your choosing will be a tremendously significant event in your life. This occurs for most of us when we are adolescents.

The clumsy initial intimacies of adolescence may have an excitement that will never again be matched. On the other hand, this very clumsiness can be devastating. Lack of accurate information about sex shaped our first sexual experiences with another person, and those experiences—good or bad—often colored our general feelings about sex:

"I'll never forget my first time. I was out with this really popular girl and she was really fast. She let me go further than any girl ever had and pretty soon it was obvious that she was willing to go all the way. I was scared to death because I didn't really know what to do. I tried to get my penis inside of her but I missed and started entering her anus by mistake. She pushed me away and yelled: 'What an idiot—you can't even find the right hole!' I was absolutely mortified.

"I took her home right away and never called her again. I was sure she had told her friends about me so I felt like an outcast at school. And believe me, it was a long time before I ever tried to have intercourse again—in fact, it wasn't until I was in college and then I was drunk at the time. I still feel insecure with women and afraid I'm going to make a wrong move."

Our first sexual experience with another person can set the tone for our sexuality. If it was basically positive—with tenderness, mutual respect, and caring—then we are not so devastated by later negative sexual experiences. But if our first sexual experience with another person was painful or humiliating, we are far more likely to believe that sex is a negative experience.

Claudia's low sexual self-esteem came directly from her first sexual experience. The boy, unable to achieve an erection, blamed her for his own inadequacy: "He told me that this had never happened to him before and that I wasn't sexy enough to turn him on. I was so humiliated that I wasn't willing to try it again with another partner for a long, long time. I was convinced that the same thing would happen again because I just wasn't desirable. To this day I still blame myself if a man has trouble maintaining an erection."

While our first sexual encounters have a tremendous effect on our self-esteem in general, and our sexual self-esteem in particular, the reverse is also true. Our first sexual encounters will almost always reflect whatever fears, confusion, and self-esteem problems already existed within us. For instance, a young girl who feels inadequate and unattractive may hope to find approval through sexual acting out, but finds only disappointment and shame. A young man who is insecure and afraid concerning his own abilities may seek out sexual experiences, but his fear will permeate these experiences, coloring them in such a way as to make him feel even more insecure.

In addition, sometimes our first sexual experiences are aimed more at "getting back" at our parents or at resisting the control of our parents than they have to do with our being ready for sex. In these cases, the first experiences are not filled with love, connection, or nurturing, but rather with anger, hurt, and confusion.

WHEN YOUR FIRST TIME WAS DATE RAPE

Carrie's first experience with sexual intercourse was when she was date-raped at seventeen. "I was on my second date with a really popular guy at school, a football star. He was really nice to me the first part of our date but later in the evening when we parked up on the hill where all the kids go to make out, he became really persistent. I tried to push his hands away gently but he wouldn't take no for an answer. I started to become frightened and insisted that he take me home but he just became more and more aggressive with me. Before I knew it he had me pinned down on the front seat of the car and was forcing himself into me. I tried to scream for help but he had parked so far away from the other cars that no one heard me.

"Although it seemed like it took forever because the pain was so excruciating, it was all over within minutes and he was starting up the car. We drove home in silence and he unceremoniously dropped me off in front of my house.

"I know now that I should have told my parents and the authorities because God knows how many other girls he raped, but I was too ashamed. I felt responsible somehow, probably because he had called me a 'prick-tease' while he was raping me. I was a virgin when he raped me and I was more concerned about having lost my virginity and possibly being pregnant than I was about him being punished or even being stopped."

Needless to say, this experience was tremendously traumatic for Carrie. And as is true in many date rapes, Carrie didn't define what had happened to her as rape. Instead she blamed herself for parking with the boy in the first place and believed that she had indeed "led him on."

"After this experience occurred," Carrie says, "I felt like a 'fallen woman.' I was no longer a virgin and back in those days that was a big deal. I imagined that everyone at school knew that he'd 'gone all the way' with me and that they all thought I was cheap. I became extremely withdrawn and dropped out of most of the extracurricular activities I had been involved in. Since I had gotten in trouble for being a 'prick-tease' I started dressing much more conservatively and hardly looked at boys at all."

The trauma caused by Carrie's experience is typical for most women who are date-raped. Most experience a tremendous amount of shame and blame themselves for the rape. Because they knew the rapist most victims do not report the crime and, in fact, many do not even consider it a crime. Although they try to minimize it, the effects of date or acquaintance rape are often extremely severe, especially in cases like Carrie's, when the rape was the victim's first sexual experience.

In addition to feelings of shame, date-rape victims suffer from a myriad of symptoms, many of which are similar to those suffered by victims of child sexual abuse—difficulty trusting others, sleep disturbances, anxiety and panic attacks, fear of the dark, fear of being alone with a man, inability to have sex, feeling like used property, intense anger toward men, and self-hatred.

YOUR FIRST LOVE AFFAIR

While our "first time" strongly influenced our sexual self-esteem, it continued to be shaped by our later experiences. Most significantly, our first consummated "love" relationship, our first real love affair, affects how much confidence we have in ourselves sexually and how willing we are to open ourselves up once again to future relationships.

Many, many people have had their sexual self-esteem damaged by a first love affair. Rejection by a lover, no matter what the reason, is devastating, even if we don't really know the reason, as was the case with Dena:

"I was twenty when I fell in love with Tom. I'd had sex with a couple of guys I dated in high school but I hadn't really been serious about either one of them. As soon as I started dating Tom I knew this was going to be different. I really loved him and this made our sexual experiences all that much better. I felt so secure with him that I was able to express myself very freely. I thought we had a great sex life. Then one night he got up after we had made love and said he was going out for a while. He seemed really agitated but wouldn't tell me what was wrong.

"When he came back about an hour later he told me he had to have a serious talk with me. He said he wasn't happy with our sexual relationship, that I just wasn't meeting his needs. I asked him what he needed that I wasn't giving him but he wouldn't be specific. I told him I would do anything necessary to make our relationship work and this seemed to satisfy him for the time being.

"The next day I went out and got several sex manuals and pored through them on my lunch hour and after work. That night I surprised Tom with some of my new techniques. He seemed pleasantly surprised and I breathed a sigh of relief, thinking that I had solved our problem.

"But several weeks later I noticed that Tom didn't seem as interested in having sex and when we finally did have it he seemed restless afterward. When I asked him if he was satisfied with our new sex life he was so evasive that I once again began to worry. I started talking to my friends about it and getting suggestions from them that I would enthusiastically try out with Tom when I saw him. But the same pattern continued—he seemed pleased when I brought something new into our lovemaking but soon afterward seemed to get bored once again.

"I began to become more and more self-conscious about my abilities to please my man. Pretty soon I was just performing for him and not enjoying it myself. I began to feel like I was on trial—like I had to perform or Tom was going to leave me. I became more and more desperate to please him and more and more insecure about how to go about it. Finally, Tom broke up with me, but not before he had completely demoralized me about my ability to please a man.

"To this day I don't know what was wrong with my sexual relationship with Tom. My friends tell me that it was clearly his problem, not mine, and that he was probably just looking for an excuse to get out of the relationship. Some have even speculated that maybe he was gay. But no matter how I try to reason it out, I still blame myself and I have been extremely reluctant to start a new relationship. When I do begin to sleep with a man I am like a sexual acrobat, performing all my tricks for him to ensure his interest. But I'm not really able to relax and enjoy my own sexual feelings and I am constantly needing reassurance even though I know that this turns guys off."

When a lover says or does something that makes us doubt our desirability or our ability to please him or her it can seriously damage our self-confidence sexually, as it did with Ann:

"When I met Jerry I was very inexperienced. I'd had sex with my boyfriend in high school but that was in the backseat of his car and it lasted all of three minutes. Jerry was quite a bit older than me and he seemed to like the role of being the teacher. I was an eager student and soon we were having great sex. He loved my body and I was completely comfortable with him—walking around nude, trying all kinds of positions—really having fun.

"Then he seemed to change and become more and more critical of me. He told me I should firm up and began to teach me about nutrition and exercise. Once again I was an eager student and we started an exercise regimen together. I toned up and felt and looked better than I had in my entire life.

"But Jerry once again became critical of me. This time it was because I wasn't educated enough. I wasn't as well-read as he was and I didn't use proper English. I once again became his student but this time not so eagerly. Nevertheless, I went along with him because I loved him so much and wanted so desperately to please him.

"It wasn't long after this that Jerry left me for another woman—someone who was younger, less experienced, less attractive, and even less educated than myself. I was devastated. By the time he left me I was desperately insecure about my sexuality, my body, and even my intellect. If he had left me for someone who was prettier, sexier, and more intelligent it would have still hurt but it wouldn't have messed me up so much. The message I got from the experience with Jerry was that you can't please men no matter what you do and that they get threatened by anyone who is pretty, sexy, or intelligent."

Like Ann, many people formed a set of beliefs about the opposite sex and the role of sex in a relationship from that all-important first serious relationship.

Betrayal by a lover is demoralizing no matter when it occurs—whether you are twenty or fifty—but when it happens with your first love it is all the more painful. Our first love symbolizes so many things to us—opening up and trusting another person in a very special way, being vulnerable emotionally and sexually, sharing secrets about ourselves we may have never shared. When this same person that we loved and trusted so much betrays us it can make us want to protect our heart from ever being broken again. And it can make us doubt ourselves, our attractiveness, and our sexuality, as it did with Cal:

"I'd had flings with several other women before I had my first serious relationship with Karen, when I was twenty-three. We had been living together for two years and I thought we were really happy. Then I came home from work one day for lunch and found her in bed with my best friend. I felt horribly betrayed by both of them. To this day I have a difficult time trusting women, especially around my friends. The whole situation has made me doubt my masculinity. I keep thinking that there is something wrong with me, with the way I make love. No matter how much reassurance I get from women I keep thinking that I am probably not satisfying them and that they are probably looking around for some other guy who will."

WHEN THERE HASN'T BEEN A FIRST TIME YET—VIRGINITY

While some people choose to remain virgins, even into their thirties, most men and even most women become concerned if they are still virgins past the age of twenty-one. Things have changed even for females. Where remaining a virgin until the wedding night was once a virtue, today it has become a burden for many young women, as it is with Francesca:

"I'm a twenty-five-year-old virgin and I've reached a point where I'd just like to get it over with. I wish I would have had sex a long time ago because now I've waited so long that it's become too big a deal. Now when a guy finds out I'm a virgin he gets afraid. No one wants to be the first one. I've had guys tell me to come back after I've lost my virginity. But I don't want to just lose my virginity to just anyone either. I really feel trapped."

Some people choose to be virgins for religious reasons, believing that it is a sin to have sex before marriage. Others want to save themselves for that special person, as is the case with Michael, a twenty-eight-year-old virgin:

"I just haven't met the right woman. It is really important to me that I be in love with the woman I have sex with, especially the first time. It's such a special experience, why waste it on someone you don't even care about?"

But even those with deep convictions about remaining virgins go through a tremendous amount of embarrassment about their state of virginity. Michael continues:

"I don't know why people have such a difficult time with my being a virgin. I know I'm a lot older than most virgins, especially men, but it really is my own business. People always want to make such a big thing out of it—accusing me of being gay or thinking that I must be afraid of sex. Their accusations made me really insecure for a long time. I started to believe that maybe there was something wrong with me."

Your first sexual experience can either be a wonderful experience, opening you up to your passions and the pleasure of intimacy, or it can sour you on the idea of sex. It can be fulfilling or embarrassing, something to "get over" or something to savor, something that whets your appetite for more or something that turns you off.

In addition, your first sexual experience is highly charged. The sights, sounds, smells, and sensations of that first experience often remain indelibly imprinted in your mind and in your body. Whether the experience was a good one or a bad one, whether it was by choice or by coercion, the fact remains that the experience was extremely powerful and stimulating. Because of this we will often replay that first experience over and over in our lifetime, whether it is reflected by our choice of partner or our preference in terms of location, position, or type of sexual act. This reenactment can have tremendous ramifications on our sexual self-esteem, as we will discuss throughout the book.

Chapter Five

THE IMPACT OF CHILD SEXUAL ABUSE ON YOUR SEXUAL SELF-ESTEEM

If you were sexually abused as a child or think you might have been, this chapter is vitally important to you. As was mentioned earlier, sexual abuse has, beyond a doubt, more of an impact on your sexual self-esteem than any other experience. In order to raise your sexual self-esteem it is important that you learn to identify the many ways in which sexual abuse has affected your sexual identity, attitudes, and behaviors, and that you make connections between past abuse and your current sexual issues.

When your first sexual experience is one of manipulation, exploitation, or pain, the effects on your self-esteem and your sexuality can be devastating. One or more experiences with sexual abuse, no matter how seemingly minor, cause a child to feel tremendous shame, which in turn lowers self-esteem. Since most children blame themselves for the abuse, and since most are too afraid to tell anyone, their shame stays with them, spilling over into all their future relationships. This pervasive shame affects self-confidence, body image, sexual desire, sexual functioning, and our ability to form intimate relationships, as it did with Kiko:

"After I was molested by my uncle I felt so terrible about myself. I felt so ugly and dirty that I knew no one would ever like me again. And when someone did seem to like me I would just tell myself that they wouldn't like me if they really knew who I was.

It was like I had some horrible secret disease that was silently eating away at me from the inside."

Instead of being an experience of exploration and tenderness, sexual abuse is an initiation to sex characterized by exploitation and sometimes violence. It is extremely difficult to overcome this violation and make sexuality a positive experience. Instead, sexuality brings with it fear, pain, and anger, as each encounter may be accompanied by memories and flashbacks of the abuse and the abuser. In addition, because of the early age of sexualization and the negative circumstances surrounding it, there has been little opportunity to differentiate between love and sex, intimacy and sex, and sex and violence.

Child sexual abuse is not something that happened to you in the past and is now over. Sexual abuse influences every aspect of your current sexuality—your sexual identity, your body image, your attitudes toward sex, the types of sexual behaviors you will become involved in, your choice of sexual partners, and even your sexual fantasies. Many of the sexual concerns discussed in this book—poor body image, sexual dysfunctions, and concern over the types of sexual practices one is involved in, are all directly related to the issue of sexual abuse.

Many of the effects of sexual abuse are hidden in your sexual attitudes and lifestyle and may only become apparent many years after the abusive experience. For example, your current behavior may not feel like a consequence of your sexual abuse experience at all. Even though you may avoid sex you may rationalize that you just have a low sex drive. Although this may be true, if you were sexually abused the chances are high that your current feelings about sex were shaped by the abuse experience.

Conversely, if you are constantly seeking sex you may tell yourself it is because you have an abnormally high sex drive, when in actuality your high desire for sex may come directly from your experience of sexual abuse.

YOUR SEXUAL ATTITUDES AND BELIEFS

Those who were sexually abused tend to develop negative, false, or distorted attitudes and beliefs about sex. Some survivors are aware of these attitudes, but since many are unconscious, most are unaware. One of the primary attitudinal problems with survivors is that they have a difficult time separating abusive sex from healthy sex. This is due to the fact that sexual abuse and its perpetrators teach victims an abusive way of thinking about sex. Sexual abuse teaches its victims the following attitudes and beliefs:

- In sex, there is always a victim and a victimizer.
- Sex is dirty, bad.
- Sex is something to be endured.
- Sex is something you do in exchange for something else.
- Sex is secretive.
- Sexual desires must always be acted out.
- Sexual energy is uncontrollable.
- Sex is power.
- Sex is used as a way to control others.
- Males have a right to demand sex of women.
- Sex is humiliating.
- Sex is dangerous.
- Sex is a game.
- Sex is addictive.
- Sex is a way to escape painful emotions.

HOW SEXUAL ABUSE HAS AFFECTED YOUR SEXUAL SELF-CONCEPT

As was mentioned in Chapter One, our self-concept is who we think we are based on a set of beliefs and images we have about ourselves. These beliefs and images are in turn based partly on how others have treated us. The same is true of our sexual self-concept. We have certain ideas about ourselves sexually based in part on how we have been treated sexually. Sexual abuse and its effects have influenced your sexual self-concept more than any other influence or event. Your sexual self-concept is measured by how you feel about your sexuality, your body in general, and your genitals in particular, and even your sexual identity. For example, after being sexually abused you may have seen yourself as being sexually damaged, as being used property, or as being dirty and contaminated. Or you may have developed a self-concept that is inflated, meaning you believed you were more powerful as a result of sex. Some of the common beliefs caused by sexual abuse that reflect problems with your sexual self-esteem and self-concept are:

- I hate my body.
- My body/sexuality is disgusting.
- Certain parts of my body are especially disgusting.
- There is something wrong with me sexually.
- If someone wants to have sex with me I can't say no.
- I feel like a victim in sex.
- I can easily be sexually dominated.
- I am a sexual object.
- I fear I will lose control if I let myself go sexually.
- I am oversexed.
- The only thing I am good at is sex.
- The only way to keep partners is to please them sexually.
- I wish I were of the opposite sex.
- I am confused as to whether I am gay or straight.
- I am inferior to other people because of my sexual past.
- There are some things I have done sexually that I can never forgive myself for.
- I'd be happier in a world where sex didn't exist.
- I am undersexed.
- I hate sex.
- I just put up with sex.
- I use sex to get what I want.
- I am a sexual pervert.

HOW SEXUAL ABUSE AFFECTS YOUR REACTIONS TO TOUCH AND SEX

Sexual abuse causes its victims to have strong, long-lasting reactions to physical touch and to sexual experiences. The abusive experience(s) actually conditions or "programs" victims to react in ways that they neither have control of nor are aware of. Survivors experience spontaneous reactions to sex that cause them to numb their bodies or their sexual feelings, to dissociate (separate their mind from what is happening physically), or to become sexually aroused at inappropriate times. Certain sights, smells, touches, or sounds can elicit feelings of terror or repulsion and take them back to the abuse experience. Flashbacks can occur during sex that cause them to confuse their current partner with the perpetrator. And certain settings or contact can bring back negative feelings associated with abuse.

Sexual abuse causes its victims to react to sex in extreme ways. For example, some survivors want to run the other way when sexually approached and try to avoid sex altogether, while others are preoccupied with sex and continually seek out sexual partners and experiences. Some survivors freeze when they are sexually approached and are unable to ward off unwanted sexual advances, while others become sexual predators, stalking those who are helpless or less powerful than themselves. Some survivors are repulsed and turned off to any form of sexual expression that is in anyway "kinky" or unconventional, while others are drawn to illicit, "kinky" sex and seek out dangerous sexual encounters. Below is a summary of some of the reactions to touch and sex from which survivors typically suffer:

- Little interest in sex.
- Feelings such as fear, panic, anger, shame, guilt, or nausea when touched sexually.
- A fear of certain parts of your partner's body.
- A feeling of repulsion when asked to touch certain parts of your partner's body.
- A fear of being touched on certain parts of your body.
- A feeling of repulsion when asked to perform certain sexual acts.
- Being unable to protect yourself when sexually approached.
- Feeling emotionally distant when having sex.
- Feeling like another person during sex.
- Feeling smothered during sex.
- Having flashbacks to past sexual abuse during sex.
- Being sensitive to certain smells, sounds, sights, or sensations during sex.
- Unwanted sexual fantasies intruding upon your sexual experiences.
- Being sexually aroused by thoughts of forceful, hurtful, or violent sex.
- Feelings of shame, guilt, emotional pain, or anger after sex.
- A preoccupation with sex.

- Continually looking for sexual opportunities.
- Having sexual thoughts you cannot control.
- Becoming extremely anxious when you become aroused.
- Feeling extremely powerful when you are having sex.
- Becoming sexually aroused when it is inappropriate.
- Believing that when a person touches you he or she wants to have sex.
- Having unhealthy sexual interests and desires.

HOW SEXUAL ABUSE AFFECTS YOUR INTIMATE RELATIONSHIPS

Sexual abuse almost always affects a survivor's ability to establish and maintain healthy sexual and intimate relationships, often severely. The sexual abuse you experienced may have interfered with your ability to choose partners who are sensitive, caring, and sexually healthy. Or, even though you may have chosen emotionally supportive and healthy partners, you may be unable to trust and feel safe with them. You, like many survivors, may actually fear intimacy or have a limited capacity for experiencing closeness. Some of the signs that you may be having difficulties either in choosing an appropriate partner or in being able to be intimate are:

- Being attracted to partners who are sexually or emotionally smothering.
- Being attracted to partners who are sexually or emotionally rejecting.
- Being attracted to partners who are sexually demanding.
- Being attracted to partners who are never happy with your sex life together.
- Being attracted to partners who are addicted to sex.
- Staying in an emotionally abusive relationship.
- Staying with a partner who continually pressures you into performing sexual acts that repulse you.
- Staying with a partner who forces you to have sex.
- Being afraid to become emotionally vulnerable in relationships.
- Being unable to show your real feelings in a relationship.

* Being unable to communicate your sexual needs and desires.
* Needing to get away from your partner immediately after sex.
* Believing that all men (women) want is sex.
* Believing that all men (women) are unfaithful.
* Difficulties initiating sexual contact in a relationship.
* Being unable to remain faithful to one partner.
* Having a tendency to pressure your partners for sex.
* Receiving complaints from sexual partners that you are sexually abusive.

HOW SEXUAL ABUSE HAS AFFECTED YOUR SEXUAL FUNCTIONING AND BEHAVIOR

As has been stated earlier, sexual abuse can cause specific difficulties with sexual functioning. Sometimes this means that survivors suffer from sexual dysfunctions such as impotence or an inability to achieve orgasm, while at other times it means that certain types of sexual acts or positions are so repulsive that they are off-limits. In addition, survivors often experience a tremendous amount of stress and anxiety around the issue of sexuality, making a relaxed, satisfying sexual experience almost impossible. Some of the types of sexual difficulties suffered by survivors are:

* Difficulties becoming sexually aroused.
* Becoming sexually aroused too quickly and easily.
* Difficulties experiencing sexual sensations, a tendency to become physically numb when touched.
* Feeling uncomfortable about touching your own genitals.
* Difficulties achieving orgasm when you masturbate.
* Lacking sexual desire.
* Difficulties achieving orgasm with a partner.
* An inability to experience much sexual pleasure with orgasm.
* Being very limited as to the positions or types of sexual acts you can comfortably engage in.
* Only wanting certain parts of your body to be touched.
* Feeling frightened or repulsed when someone attempts to touch you in certain places or in certain ways.

Not only do victims of this kind of abuse suffer from many long-term effects that tend to lower both self-esteem and sexual self-esteem, but the abuse causes victims to act out in ways that reinforce and deepen their negative feelings about themselves. Sexual abuse not only introduces children to adult sexuality long before they are emotionally or physically equipped to handle it, it can also introduce victims to many unusual and harmful practices. The types of sexual activities survivors are attracted to and tend to get involved with can be extremely unhealthy. Sexual abuse teaches abusive patterns of sexual behavior and introduces the child to abnormal, compulsive, and unhealthy sexual activities such as: sadomasochism, pornography, prostitution, group sex, violent sex, child-adult sex, homosexuality, and compulsive masturbation. In addition, survivors of sexual abuse may associate sexual expression with shame and secrecy.

This behavior can cause tremendous feelings of pain, loneliness, and self-loathing. It can prevent you from experiencing sex as a normal, healthy, positive experience and as something that increases self-esteem and intimacy. Instead, this behavior tends to reinforce the feelings you experienced during the sexual abuse— shame, guilt, fear, and anger—leading you to continually feel damaged, intrinsically bad, or to see yourself as a sex object. In addition, it reinforces the idea that sex is something that is hurtful, secretive, outside of normal moral boundaries, and something that cannot be controlled.

If you are currently engaging in behaviors such as those listed above you may be unconsciously replaying your own sexual abuse experience. Sometimes referred to as the *repetition compulsion*, replaying the sexual abuse can be a survivor's unconscious attempt to understand what happened and to resolve internal conflicts by acting out the abuse again and again, either by continuing to be victimized or by becoming a victimizer.

Many survivors, especially women, reenact or replay their earlier abuse by continually getting involved with people who either sexually, physically, or emotionally abuse them. Another common way in which some survivors reenact the abuse of their childhood is by getting involved with partners who are either sexually compulsive, sex addicts, or sex offenders. A common pattern for many female survivors is to repeat the cycle of abuse by getting involved with or marrying a child molester who sexually abuses her children.

Other survivors take the opposite route and reenact the abuse by victimizing other people, either physically, emotionally, or sexually. This most often occurs with men, especially in terms of sexual abuse, since male survivors are more likely to identify with the perpetrator as a way of avoiding feeling like a victim. Females have also been known to victimize others, of course, but are more likely to reenact by emotionally or physically abusing their children than by sexually abusing them. And, since females are less physically strong than males, females do not tend to physically abuse their male partners (although they can emotionally abuse them) or to physically overpower them sexually.

It can be enormously upsetting to realize just how profoundly you have been affected by sexual abuse and to see, perhaps for the first time, that something is definitely wrong with how you approach sex. But before you can recover from the effects of sexual abuse you must first identify just how sexual abuse has affected you. While this process can be painful, not understanding the effects can be even worse. If you remain unaware of the many ways in which the sexual abuse has harmed you sexually, you may suffer years of confusion and pain unnecessarily, denying yourself the pleasure and enjoyment of healthy sexuality.

EMOTIONAL INCEST

Emotional incest can be defined as a parent's becoming overly involved with and overly invested in his or her child's life. This may take the form of being overly possessive and not wanting the child to have friends or to begin dating. It may take the form of making the child into a sort of "surrogate mate" by treating the child like a lover or spouse. Or it may take the form of seductiveness and intrusion.

Many parents walk a fine line between emotional and sexual incest. Even though these parents may never touch their children inappropriately, they display an unhealthy interest in their children's bodies by openly staring, by taking seductive pictures, by making inappropriate sexual remarks, or by not allowing their children privacy in the bedroom or bathroom.

Two of the many effects of emotional incest are chronic relationship problems and a curious blend of high and low self-esteem.

When Janette was growing up, she and her father acted more like a happily married couple than father and daughter. They went everywhere together, leaving the mother at home with Janette's little brother. Janette was the one who attended social functions with her father, whether it was a company dance or the movies on Saturday night.

When boys began to notice Janette her father acted more like a jealous boyfriend than a father. He refused to let her date until she was eighteen and then he was critical of each boy she went out with. Janette began to lie to her father and sneak out on dates with men, many of whom were either married or involved with drugs, gambling, or crime.

"I know now that I was just acting out against my father's possessiveness. I needed some space from him and somehow these kinds of men, who were as different from my father as could possibly be, provided me with that sense of space. Unfortunately, my self-esteem was further damaged because I felt so guilty going against my father and because the men I got involved with usually ended up either using me or dumping me."

Sexual problems are common among victims of emotional incest. Because the child and adult are in essence more like intimate partners than family members, it is natural for sexual feelings to arise. This sexual energy then must be either expressed or repressed. The child may choose to express the sexuality in the form of excessive masturbation or promiscuity or repress the sexuality and later pay the price of sexual dysfunction or lack of sexual desire. This is especially true if there are rigid and strict family injunctions against sex.

IF YOU WERE ABUSED BY A FEMALE

If you were sexually abused by a female you probably won't receive the same kind of sympathy or support that some survivors have been fortunate enough to receive from friends or family. Sexual abuse by females is played down, minimized, or laughed at. The reason for this is that most people are extremely uncomfortable with the idea and so do not want to admit that this type of abuse occurs.

Even though you may not receive the same kind of support as other survivors, it is important to remind yourself that you suffer from the same kind of damage and have the same symptoms. In fact, the damage caused by a female perpetrator can be even more devastating.

In addition to symptoms suffered by other survivors, those who were abused by a female suffer the additional symptoms of:

• Being overly attached to their mother.
• Being confused about sexual orientation—often wondering whether they are gay or straight.
• Having an overwhelming fear of getting too emotionally or sexually intimate with a partner.
• Finding it difficult, if not impossible, to trust other females.

SPECIAL PROBLEMS OF VICTIMS OF SIBLING INCEST

In addition to all the symptoms listed earlier, those who were victimized by a sibling will also suffer from additional problems, including:

• An added amount of guilt, self-doubt, and self-blame, because the lines between victim and perpetrator are not as strong, because sibling abuse is often considered to be an unnatural attraction between siblings, because you may have physically enjoyed it.
• Difficulty becoming involved with men or women in your age range.
• Guilt because you may still be sexually attracted to your sibling.
• Difficulty disengaging emotionally from your sibling.
• If you were traumatized by the violence of the situation you may suffer from sexual dysfunctions such as vaginismus (involuntary contraction of the vaginal muscles) or impotency, or a fear of sex.
• A tendency to reenact the abuse by victimizing others less powerful than you (younger siblings, younger children, animals)

either sexually, physically, or emotionally. This behavior may have started when you were a child (introducing a younger sibling to sex or physically abusing or emotionally bullying younger children).

IF YOU ARE A MALE VICTIM OF SEXUAL ABUSE

Some male survivors feel unable to define themselves as sexual beings at all because sexuality became associated with abuse in their minds. Lawrence's case is a good example: "My stepmother began to seduce me from the time she moved into our house when I was thirteen. She would walk around the house with hardly anything on, accidentally walk in on me when I was in the bathroom, and she was always having me rub her back, supposedly because it was sore. This behavior went on all during high school, when I should have been dating girls. I felt both turned on and repulsed by her, and this is how I still feel about women in general, fifteen years later. I can become attracted to them, but if they become the slightest bit aggressive with me, I lose all interest. I feel so ashamed about the feelings I had for my stepmother that I just can't seem to develop any confidence with a woman."

In our society, sexual activity between older women and younger boys is rarely treated as abusive. A boy who comes forward and talks about having been sexually abused by a woman is often greeted by police, doctors, media, therapists, and even his family with disbelief or denial. They may trivialize or even romanticize his story. Faced with this situation, the boy may redefine his experiences to fit in with other people's perceptions, even to the point of bragging or joking about it.

All sexual abuse victims suffer from low self-esteem and feelings of inferiority after having been abused. In addition, male victims of a male perpetrator tend to feel less masculine than other males—or, worse, less human. Feeling branded and irreparably damaged, they believe no female would now want them. To counteract these feelings, many victims go to great lengths to prove their masculinity. They become sexually promiscuous, sexually violent, or overly controlling of women, or they attack other men they view as weaker than themselves. Some become daredevils, risking their lives to prove their manhood.

Because males are so embarrassed at having been sexually victimized, they cannot tolerate the feelings of helplessness that all victims feel. They short-circuit these feelings and instead of identifying with other victims they identify with those who seem powerful—the abusers. This is the beginning of the vicious cycle of sexually abused boys becoming sexually abusing men. (Women are more likely to repeat the cycle of abuse by continuing to be victimized.)

If the perpetrator of the sexual attack was a male and a primary role model, a male victim may well conclude that "being a man" means being abusive: He may believe he needs to inflict pain before it is inflicted on him. He may conclude further that the only way to empower himself is to make someone else a victim. As a result, many males who were sexually abused as children become child molesters themselves. This, of course, adds to the shame they already feel and further discourages them from seeking professional help.

Adult males suffer from a variety of sexual problems as a direct result of childhood sexual abuse. The most common are an inability to achieve or maintain an erection, premature ejaculation or an inability to ejaculate, fears of specific sexual acts (often those performed by the abuser or acts that the victims were forced to perform on the abuser), and painful intercourse. In addition, many male survivors suffer from sexual obsessions and fetishes, addiction to sex, compulsive masturbation, and a tendency to associate sex with humiliation and pain, which is the case with individuals who practice sadomasochism.

If you were sexually abused when you were a child, that experience has probably influenced your sexuality more than any other factor. It is almost impossible for someone who was sexually abused to have a healthy attitude about sex. Survivors of child sexual abuse usually feel a tremendous amount of shame and guilt, not only about the abuse itself, but about sex in general. Sex becomes and continues to be something bad, illicit, shameful, and dirty. Sexual thoughts become evil, sexual fantasies become dark and forbidden, and sexual acts become ridden with guilt, shame, fear, and anger. Sex becomes synonymous with manipulation, exploitation, anger, and violence.

Sexual abuse robs children of their self-esteem. Children who are sexually violated tend to blame themselves, to turn their anger at the perpetrator against themselves until they are full of self-hatred. Children who are abused by a parent or other relative or loved one are especially prone to self-blame, since children have a particularly difficult time recognizing that someone they love can do bad things. Instead, they find it easier to make themselves bad, thus protecting their image of the parent as all good. In addition, sexual abuse causes children to feel like damaged goods. They feel dirty, evil, and rotten inside.

Not only does child sexual abuse affect self-esteem directly due to the tremendous amount of shame and self-loathing the child feels, but just as significantly, it causes the victim to behave in ways that lower self-esteem even further. Examples of this kind of acting-out behavior are:

- An attraction to illicit sex.
- An obsession with pornography.
- Sadomasochism.
- Sexual promiscuity.
- Sexual addiction.
- Drug and alcohol abuse.
- Stealing or shoplifting.
- An inability to remain sexually faithful to one's partner.

Many of the sexual and self-esteem problems we will be discussing in this book were in fact caused by childhood sexual abuse. Keep in mind that, even if you don't remember being sexually abused, if you have many of the symptoms it may be that you were indeed abused and may have blocked out the memory.

RECOGNIZE AND GET HELP FOR CHILDHOOD ABUSE

If you were either emotionally, physically, or sexually abused as a child the scars from that experience will follow you into your adult life, affecting your self-esteem, your sexuality, your ability to trust and to be intimate, and your ability to sustain long-term relationships. In other words, all the issues we have been discussing in this book. You cannot expect yourself to "just put it behind you" without some help.

There are many services for adults abused as children in most communities. If money is a problem there are low-cost support groups as well as individual counseling available. If you discovered while taking your personal sex history that you were sexually abused as a child, for example, you will need to seek help in the form of one-to-one therapy or a support group for survivors of childhood sexual abuse. A combination of the two is considered by most experts to be ideal.

Group therapy will raise your self-esteem in general by helping you to realize that you are not alone with the problems you suffer from and will help you to fully comprehend why the abuse was not your fault. In many group settings, particularly support groups for adults molested as children, there is a lot of discussion concerning how abuse affects sexuality. The feedback and suggestions from others will help you understand how your sexuality has been damaged by the abuse and how you can go about recovering from the damage.

Groups for survivors of childhood abuse should be and usually are led by skilled, licensed therapists who have extensive training and experience working with survivors. Some groups are time-limited and continue for a specific number of weeks, while others are open-ended, with no specific limit to how long the group continues. Most sexual abuse groups consist of five to eight people and most are unisex, although there are co-ed groups.

Individual therapy is particularly beneficial in terms of exploring the effect sexual abuse is having on your present relationships, and for making the changes in your life that your sexual abuse experiences have prevented you from making. Long-term individual therapy can also re-create the parent-child relationship in a healthy way and be a corrective experience to your abusive past.

In addition, there are many books written expressly for survivors of childhood abuse. These books will also help you understand that you are not alone, and include discussions regarding self-esteem, sexuality, intimacy, and trust. There will be a listing of the books I particularly recommend in the back of the book.

Chapter Six

ADOLESCENCE—A CRUCIAL TIME

Even though our attitudes about sexuality begin early in our life based on parental messages and childhood experiences with sex, it is during adolescence that our sexual self-esteem truly begins to be established. Adolescence is a time when our bodies change shape, when our generalized sexual feelings become specific, and when there are new social relationships, an attraction to either the same or opposite sex. Beginning with puberty, our attention becomes focused on how our bodies are developing, how we are seen by the opposite sex, and how we are going to cope with our raging hormones.

As soon as our bodies begin to develop we know that we will never be the same. Some of us looked forward to these changes, while others didn't:

"I remember when I first started getting pubic hair—I felt horrified. My mother had told me about menstruation and I was expecting that, but she didn't tell me about getting hair 'down there.' I thought there was something wrong with me—that maybe I wasn't really a girl at all but maybe a hermaphrodite like I had heard the kids talking about. I thought only boys had body hair. One night my best friend spent the night and we showed each other our 'privates.' She didn't have any hair there and this made me feel even more weird. After that I made sure no one saw my body naked until I got into high school. There, in gym class, I finally saw that all the other girls had pubic hair also. I was so relieved, but the feeling that there was something wrong with me held on for a long time."

Because of a lack of adequate information about sex and the way the body reacts to sexual stimulation, many adolescents become upset and fearful about their bodies' reactions:

"Every time I came home from a date with my boyfriend my underwear would be really wet. When I wiped myself there was always this discharge. For years I thought there was something wrong with me—that maybe I had a disease or something. It wasn't until years later that I found out that the 'discharge' was just lubricant and that it was natural for me to lubricate when I was excited."

For many people, adolescence is one of the most difficult periods to get through. In addition to the confusion and anxiety about our body's development, there are pressures from all sides—to do well in school; to be popular; to date; to compete scholastically, athletically, and socially; to plan for college, a career, and marriage; and to somehow come to terms with our sexuality. Questions like "Am I sexually attractive?" "What is my sexual orientation?" "Do I become sexually active?" plague most adolescents.

During adolescence, more than any other time in our lives, it is vitally important that we "fit in" with our peers. As we walked down the halls at high school we were keenly aware of others and their reactions to us—we worried about whether we were being admired or laughed at, emulated or scorned. During classes that were difficult for us we prayed that the teacher would not call on us so we wouldn't be humiliated. And even in classes where we did well we might not want to be called on for fear of appearing to be an "egghead." In gym class we worried about whether we would be picked when it came time to choose teams or whether we would have to stand there feeling humiliated as everyone else was picked but us. At lunchtime we scurried to our "designated" table, desperately clinging to whatever social group we were accepted in.

It didn't matter how attractive we were—we still worried that our hair looked stupid, or that we would break out in pimples, or that we were too fat, or too skinny, or too tall, or too short. If we did well in school, we worried. If we weren't doing well, we worried. If our parents had money, we worried that others would perceive us as snobbish; and if our parents weren't rich, we worried that we couldn't wear the latest styles or drive a great car.

In addition to the pressures all teens feel, those who do not fit in with the crowd for one reason or another have a particularly difficult time. This was the situation with Paul: "I was only five feet two inches tall by the time I was sixteen years old. Being so short made me feel incredibly unattractive and inadequate. I was teased mercilessly and called names like 'Shorty,' 'Midget,' and 'Pee Wee.' I didn't dare ask a girl out because I just knew she would laugh at me, so instead I just acted like a pal. In fact, I was so insecure about my height that I didn't ask a woman out on a date until I was twenty years old and that was only because she was shorter than I am and she came on to me first."

Sheila told me her story: "When I was a teenager I was overweight. This of course eliminated any possibility of being asked out on a date. Time after time I watched my girlfriends be asked out while the boys just ignored me completely. In fact, I did not have one date during high school."

The need to belong becomes one of the most important things in a teenager's life—so important that if he or she appears to be completely indifferent to group opinion he or she is probably covering up feelings of isolation and estrangement, as was the case with Terence:

"All during high school I convinced myself that I really didn't care whether I fit in or not. I developed a 'screw you' attitude and did the most outrageous things as a way of rebelling against all the group-conformity bull. I held on to this attitude way into my twenties until I finally realized that it was all a facade—I cared deeply what other people thought, especially women. It's just that I am so terribly insecure around them that it is painful."

For all these reasons and more, adolescence is a painful time for most teenagers. Because it is such a difficult time, and because of all the changes going on inside of our bodies, we are extremely sensitive, emotional, and changeable. We often feel as if we are going to explode with emotions.

In the midst of all this upheaval, uncertainty, and worry, we also have to deal with the issue of dating. For girls the problem is whether or not anyone will ask them on dates or whether the *right* boys will ask them on dates. For boys the issue is whether or not they can get up the courage to ask a girl out and then, of course, whether they can handle the humiliation if she says no.

During adolescence we begin to judge ourselves based on who will go on dates with us. If a popular boy asks a girl out she is automatically popular by association. But if no one asks her out except a boy who is not popular, her social standing is spelled out for her. And, of course, those who don't have dates at all are left to come to no other conclusion but that they are not attractive at all and that no one will ever like them.

Once we get past the initial dating jitters we are then faced with another problem—what to do with our sexual feelings.

These are some typical experiences:

"I remember being horny from the time I entered puberty. All I thought about was sex but I just couldn't seem to find a girl who would go all the way. I got a reputation for being a 'lech' and girls wouldn't even talk to me. But I just couldn't help myself. Whenever I was around a girl I would try something with her because I'd become so turned on. Even though I masturbated a couple of times a day it didn't seem to help. I think I spent my entire high school years frustrated."

"I remember making out with my boyfriend in the backseat of his car for hours and hours. Every week he'd try to talk me into 'going all the way' and every week we'd have a big fight over it. He'd tell me he loved me and that if I loved him I'd do this for him. I'd tell him that if he loved me he wouldn't pressure me so much. I wanted to have sex too and I knew that he never really understood how hard it was for me to say no, but I was deathly afraid of getting pregnant."

"My sexuality embarrassed me and made me feel out of control. As soon as I saw an attractive girl I would immediately get an erection. I can't tell you how many times I was embarrassed by getting an erection at the most inopportune times. I'd be dancing with a girl in dance class and all of a sudden I would get this tremendous hard-on. I'd try to hold the girl as far away from me as possible so she wouldn't feel me. I just wanted to crawl in a hole and die."

The decision as to when to begin being sexually active is one that plagues not just girls but boys as well. The factors that influence this decision are often religious beliefs, parental upbringing, and peer pressure. Often, these things are in conflict with one another, as they were with Mack:

"I was raised in a very religious family and I was taught that premarital sex is a sin. I had every intention of waiting until I was married to have sex but I found that this decision was not an easy one to keep. I received a tremendous amount of pressure from the other boys to start having sex. They all talked about their sexual conquests and then would ask me about mine. At first I stood by my convictions and told them I wasn't going to have sex until I was married. But this soon gave me the reputation of being a square, or worse yet, a queer. I was taunted mercilessly by the boys, who began to call me 'Virgin Mary.' Finally, to save face I lied about having sex with a girl I had been going out with. This got them off my back but I felt terrible about lying about the girl. I was afraid that it would get back to her and she'd never speak to me again and I really liked her a lot."

YOUR PERSONAL SEX HISTORY

In the last several chapters I have discussed in detail the significant factors that influence and shape our sexual self-esteem. From this information you can begin to develop an extensive sexual history of yourself and from this sexual history you can begin to develop a plan of action as to how to raise your sexual self-esteem.

Because sex cannot be separated from the rest of our lives, we need to look at the overall picture in order to see which factors have affected us the most. Exploring your personal history, especially in ways that pertain to your sexuality, is the first step to raising your sexual self-esteem, for only by knowing where we come from can we change ourselves. Your personal sex history includes your early childhood upbringing, the sexual training you received within your family, your experiences with sex during your childhood and adolescence, your choice of partners, your first sexual experience, your first romantic relationship, and your first serious relationship. Your sexual history includes events from your childhood, your adolescence, and your early adulthood up to the present, including your sexual behavior in general and your sexual behavior while under the influence of alcohol or drugs. Our sexual self-esteem has been molded and influenced by everything that has happened to us in the past and from all of these experiences our sexual personality was formed. These things affect not only your sexuality but how you feel about your body, the amount of shame you feel about sex, how powerful you feel as a person, and how free you are to express your sexuality.

Everyone reading this book will be in a different place regarding his or her personal history. Some of you may have already done extensive work on uncovering your past, either in therapy or on your own. Others may really be looking at the past for the first time, especially as it pertains to sexuality. But each of you, no matter what your level of self-awareness, will benefit from this personal history taking and the self-evaluation it will require.

TAKING YOUR OWN SEX HISTORY

1. How old were you when you first remember having sexual feelings? Describe the situation and the outcome, including how you felt about having the feelings.

2. Describe the first time you remember having any kind of sexual exchange with another person, including how you felt about the experience.

3. How old were you when you first saw a member of the opposite sex naked?

4. Did you ever take baths with your siblings or other children? How old were you and how did you feel about it?

5. Describe the first time you ever saw one or both of your parents nude or partially dressed.

6. Did you ever see one or both of your parent's genitals? Describe how you felt.

7. When was the first time you saw an adult's naked or partially naked body (other than a parent)?

8. How old were you when your parents stopped bathing you? Did your parent(s) ever take a bath or shower with you? If so, how old were you, how old were you when they stopped, and how did you feel about the experience?

9. Did you ever sleep with your parent(s) or any other adult? If so, how did you feel about it?

10. Did you sleep in the same bed with a sibling? If so, how did you feel about it?

11. Did any other adult or older child ever bathe you or take a bath or shower with you?

12. When was the first time an adult touched you sexually or touched a sexual part of your body?

13. When was the first time you had a sexual exchange with someone of the same sex? How did you feel about it?

14. When was the first time you had a sexual exchange with someone of the opposite sex? How did you feel about it?

Exercise—Sexual Messages

1. Make a list of all the experiences, from the time you were a small child until today, that influenced your sexuality in some way—that were significant in some way in shaping your sexual self-esteem.

2. Next to each experience, write down the message you received from this experience.

Although we all survived adolescence, some of us did it more successfully than others. Many, many people still have horror stories to tell about their teenage years, and some feel so humiliated that they still don't want to talk about it. Unfortunately, all too often our image of oneself as an adolescent seems to stick with us throughout adulthood, no matter how attractive or successful we become as adults. For some people, this old self-image is like an albatross around their necks, influencing their sexuality in a number of ways—from whether they feel sexually desirable to creating questions about their sexual identity.

Chapter Seven

ADULTHOOD—OUR SEXUAL
SELF-ESTEEM IS STILL DEVELOPING

You would think that by adulthood our sexual self-esteem would be fairly well established, and in some very basic ways it is. We carry into adulthood the parental messages we received, our early childhood and adolescent experiences, and our body image, and these things profoundly affect both our sexual relationships and how we view ourselves sexually. But even as adults our sexual self-esteem continues to be strongly influenced by our sexual experiences, feedback from others, and other factors. And even more important, throughout our lifetime we are vulnerable to situations that can lower our sexual self-esteem.

For example, during our twenties we tend to establish certain patterns of sexual behavior. These patterns of behavior can further influence the level of our sexual self-esteem. The most significant patterns are: 1) who we choose as sexual partners and 2) what type of sexual behavior we become involved in. These two patterns, more than almost anything else, can have a continual effect on our sexual self-esteem. Because of their importance, I will discuss each of these patterns in detail.

OUR CHOICE OF SEXUAL PARTNERS

If we are fortunate enough to choose sexual partners who are complimentary, easy to satisfy, affectionate, and giving, the effect on our sexual self-esteem can be uplifting. While a positive experience with a lover doesn't have the effect of erasing our past, it certainly can lessen its impact on us. It is possible, for example, for someone raised in a restrictive environment where sex was never talked about except in negative terms to begin to view sex in a more positive light if he or she is blessed with a loving, patient, spontaneous lover; or for someone with a poor body image as a child to have that body image improved by an experience with a partner who clearly expresses enjoyment of and appreciation for his or her body.

When we have loving, nurturing partners who encourage us to express our sexuality freely, and who love and appreciate our body, it can have a remarkable effect on our sexual self-esteem. When we know we are loved for who we are, when we know our body is accepted and that our partner is satisfied with us sexually, we are bound to feel good about ourselves, our bodies, and our sexuality.

Unfortunately, it is far more likely for us to choose a partner who only reinforces whatever messages we received about sex from our parents and from our early sexual experiences. For example, those who had a philandering father tend to get involved with lovers who are unfaithful; those with abusive parents tend to get involved with abusive lovers; and those who were sexually abused often get involved with sex addicts or child molesters. Even when we vow to fall in love with someone who is the opposite of our parents or other significant caretakers, we tend to repeat the pattern again and again.

Having a partner who is critical of our body, our sexual performance, or any other aspect of our sexuality can definitely lower our sexual self-esteem, as it did with Emily:

"Max was always so critical of my body during our marriage. By the time he finally left me for a younger, thinner, more beautiful woman, my self-esteem was so low I thought I'd never let another man see me naked again, much less make love to me. Max had convinced me that I was so undesirable that no man would possibly want me. He always made me feel like he was doing me a favor to be with me."

Unfortunately, Emily's experience is not unusual. Many, many people find that their sexual self-esteem has been damaged by a critical, demanding, or rejecting partner. The following are some examples of esteem-robbing partners—that is, partners who through their negativity or neglect drain us of whatever good feelings about our sexuality we have.

Esteem-Robbing Partners

THE DEMANDING, PRESSURING LOVER

"I know it sounds funny to say, but my wife was so sexually demanding that I started to lose interest in sex. I know a lot of guys think they would love to be in my place but they would have to be there, if you know what I mean.

"When we were first together and even after we were first married it seemed so exciting to have sex all the time. But gradually, I started feeling smothered by my wife's constant need for sex. I wanted to start going out with friends more and to just have some time alone. But she was always all over me, kissing me, hugging me, trying to stimulate me until I became so aroused I would finally give in, even if I was tired or not interested.

"The only way she would stop would be if I physically pushed her away and then she would cry and tell me that I didn't love her and I'd feel terrible. Eventually, I started staying away from home more often, just to avoid the situation.

"The more I stayed away and the more I pushed her away the more demanding and angry she became. She started accusing me of sleeping around or of being gay. When that didn't seem to work she started telling me that I wasn't all that good a lover anyway and that she was going to start getting her needs met elsewhere if I didn't change. That tactic really got to me. No matter how hard I tried to convince myself that she was just saying that to hurt me, I eventually started doubting my ability to satisfy a woman. I began to wonder if perhaps I was the one who had the problem, that perhaps I was undersexed, or perhaps if I had satisfied her in the first place she wouldn't want sex so often.

"I decided to give it one more try, to be the best lover I could possibly be. I read some books and I asked her to guide me so that I could please her. But it became evident that she was having orgasms and that no matter how often we had sex she still wanted more. Once again, I began to feel smothered and once again she started berating me. We divorced after only one year of marriage.

"By the time the marriage ended, I not only had very little confidence in my ability to sexually satisfy a woman but I was afraid to enter into another sexual relationship out of the fear of being sexually smothered by another woman. I haven't had a sexual relationship with a woman now for over a year and unfortunately I don't seem any closer to wanting one."

THE SEX ADDICT

"Sid always complained that I never initiated sex with him. He said that if he waited for me we'd never have sex and I always suspected he was right. Now I realize he never gave me a chance to find out. He had a tremendous sexual appetite and he could have had sex three or four times a day if I'd been willing.

"Not only was he having sex with me every day but he would masturbate every morning and every night while in the shower. I thought he had to masturbate because I didn't satisfy him enough. I really thought there was something wrong with me until a friend of mine told me that most men don't need to have as many orgasms as Sid did. I didn't discover until years later that Sid was a sex addict and the problem was his and not mine, but that was after years of feeling inadequate."

THE UNFAITHFUL LOVER

Few people can have a relationship with a lover who has been unfaithful and still maintain a high level of sexual self-esteem. Unfaithful lovers make us doubt our attractiveness, our ability to satisfy sexually, and even our value as a person. This is what happened to Gena:

"One of the most damaging events in my life was when I had a three-year relationship with a man who was constantly unfaithful to me. I don't know why I hung in there for so long except that I kept thinking that if I just became a better lover he wouldn't have to be with other women.

"Each time I discovered he was with someone else I would confront him and we'd have a big fight. Then we'd make up and he'd be so incredibly attentive and loving. He'd beg me to forgive him and promise me that he was going to be faithful to me and I would believe him. Then, a few more months would go by and he'd do it again.

"Finally, I couldn't take it anymore and I moved out, but not without a tremendous amount of pain. I felt so terrible about myself that I started eating junk food as a way of punishing myself. I already felt so ugly and undesirable and I just wanted to make myself even uglier so I wouldn't have to bother with men again.

"In six months I gained fifty pounds. Finally the outside of me matched how I felt about myself inside. For years I had felt completely unattractive sexually and now my body actually was unattractive to men. I was filled with not only self-loathing but with anger toward my ex-lover and for all men, for that matter."

THE MARRIED LOVER

Having a relationship with someone who is married can also be devastating to your sexual self-esteem. There are often feelings of guilt and shame associated with the affair, since you are involved in something you know is wrong no matter how much you try to rationalize it. And because your lover is always leaving you to go home to a spouse, there are constant feelings of rejection, abandonment, and jealousy, as Jack discovered:

"I couldn't believe how terrible I felt about myself by the time I finally ended the affair I had last year with a married woman. I thought I was a tough, modern guy and that I could handle anything, but I was just fooling myself.

"Each time she left my apartment to go home to her husband and kids I felt such feelings of rejection and jealousy. I wanted her with me all the time and I didn't want to have to share her with her family. I lay in bed at night, waiting for her to call, imagining her in bed with her husband and comparing myself with him. By the time we would finally get together I was always competing with my fantasized image of *him*, trying to outdo him in bed so that she wouldn't want to be with him anymore.

"Every time she went home to him I felt like she was rejecting me and choosing him, and in essence, she was. That did horrible things to my male ego. I finally had to end it because I was becoming a jealous monster who hated himself for acting so childishly. It's taken me six months to be able to even ask out another woman because my self-esteem is still so low from the affair. Believe me, I'll never get involved with a married woman again."

THE REJECTING LOVER

"My wife and I got married right out of high school and believe it or not, we were both virgins on our wedding night. Both of us looked forward to that first night so much and it was wonderful. I knew she loved me and she knew I adored her. We were both awkward and innocent and that just added to the sweetness.

"As the years went by we learned about sex together and it was a very exciting time for both of us. But once our first baby was born something happened to my wife. She became so totally wrapped up in taking care of the baby that she seemed to forget about me.

"At first she told me she couldn't have sex so soon after the baby's birth. Then she told me she was too tired. As time went on there was one excuse after another for not resuming our sexual relationship and when she would finally consent she just wasn't there emotionally.

"I was devastated by my wife's rejecting behavior. Our sex life had been so precious to both of us—a way of connecting emotionally and renewing our feelings for one another. Suddenly it was all over—the closeness, the intimacy, the sensuality.

"Sometimes I blamed myself. I assumed that perhaps I hadn't been as sensitive a lover as I had thought, or that perhaps I had been selfish all along. I tried to talk to her about it but she just told me that I was being silly and that all married couples go through changes like this.

"After I had tried everything I could think of, I just stopped approaching her. I just couldn't stand to be rejected one more time. I began to doubt my masculinity, my attractiveness, and even my love for her.

"Eventually, I started having affairs, not just because I missed having sex but because I needed to know that I was okay sexually. In many ways though, the affairs have just added to my bad feelings about myself. I feel guilty about being unfaithful to my wife and the affairs only make me miss my wife more."

THE GAY LOVER

Janine recently discovered that her husband of seven years is gay. While she had suspected as much for over a year, her husband finally confirmed her suspicions. Janine is devastated. She loves Dan very much and up until the past year felt that they had the ideal marriage:

"Dan is a wonderful husband and father. He has always been good to me and he's wonderful to the children. I just can't believe he could be gay. I feel so betrayed—by him, but mostly by life.

"I keep thinking I can change him even though everyone, including Dan, tells me that I can't. But I just can't help feeling that if I were sexy enough, or if I had been able to satisfy him sexually, he would want to stay with me. This whole thing has made me doubt everything about myself—my sexual attractiveness, my own sexuality, my reasons for marrying a gay man. It's been a terrible blow to my ego, my sexuality, and to my image of myself as a woman."

THE LOVER WITH A SEXUAL DYSFUNCTION

Sexual dysfunction, as we will discuss later, can be a major problem in a relationship and can lower the sexual self-esteem of not only the one who has the dysfunction but the partner as well, as it did with Jeremy:

"All during my marriage, my wife did not have an orgasm with me. This was devastating not only to my male ego but to our relationship. At first we both just assumed that it was the typical problem that many women have of not being adequately stimulated. But no matter what we tried, she still couldn't climax.

"After a while, she began to blame me. She told me that if I was just more sensitive to her needs and more tender with her she would be able to relax enough to orgasm. But no matter how much time I took with foreplay, no matter how soft and tender I was, she still couldn't climax.

"Eventually, the problem started to affect our relationship. She became overly sensitive about not having orgasms and I started feeling so criticized by her and so inadequate that I didn't even want to try any longer. While there were other problems in the marriage, our sexual relationship certainly was a major factor in our divorce."

While it is devastating enough to have one partner with a sexual dysfunction, some people are unfortunate enough to actually develop a pattern of getting involved with lovers who have a sexual dysfunction, as Kristan did:

"I don't know what it is with me but for some reason I keep getting involved with men who are impotent. Everything seems to start out fine but weeks or months after the affair has begun the man stops being able to function most of the time.

"It's a terrible blow to my ego because I can't help but blame myself. If it only happened with one man that would be one thing, but this has happened to me several times now. Not every man I have an affair with is impotent but enough of them have been to make me wonder about myself. Each time it happens I become less and less secure about my sexuality and my attractiveness."

THE ABUSIVE LOVER

Emotional, physical, or sexual abuse in a relationship is devastating to your sexuality and your self-esteem. When you are being emotionally abused (constantly criticized, dominated, verbally abused, or rejected) it is extremely difficult to feel sexually attractive or desirable. When you are being physically abused the last thing on your mind is sex, especially with the person who just beat you up. In fact, you don't even want to be touched. And if you are being sexually abused (raped or forced to have a type of sex you find repulsive), you have probably had to shut down emotionally and physically in order to cope with the abuse. Over time any kind of abuse systematically drains us of our sexual feelings. As we shut down more and more in order to cope with the abuse, our body becomes increasingly numb until we are either partially or completely disconnected from our sexual feelings.

Often our anger at the abuser also interferes with our sexual feelings, as it did with Juliette:

"Who wants to have sex with someone who has hurt you so deeply, who obviously doesn't care enough about you to stop themselves from losing control and hurting you?

"All the time I was married to Josh I thought something was really wrong with me sexually. I just never felt sexual—never. Josh constantly complained about it and that just made me feel worse about myself because I couldn't please my husband. At first I really worried that maybe something was wrong with me physically, so I went to the doctor. But he told me everything was okay with me physically and referred me to a psychotherapist, telling me that perhaps my problem was emotional. I am so grateful to him now for that referral because otherwise I would have never found out that I was being abused by my husband and that the abuse was the cause of my being shut down sexually.

"As difficult as it is to believe, I didn't realize that what my husband was doing to me was really abusive. My father had always hit my mother and I was raised to believe that a man had the right to do pretty much whatever he wanted to do to his wife and it was her duty to take it. So when my husband started hitting me I thought he had the right to do it because I wasn't performing my duties as a wife properly.

"But that didn't stop me from seething inside. I realize now, through the help of therapy, that I was enraged with him for hitting me and that because I was so angry it was virtually impossible for me to feel sexual toward him at the same time. My therapist told me that many battered women (I can't believe I can actually call myself this now) suffer from sexual dysfunction or a complete lack of sexual desire as a direct result of the physical abuse.

"Now that I am divorced from Josh (another thing I never thought I'd do) I am beginning to get my sexual feelings back and my self-esteem is improving greatly. I really don't think I will ever get involved with an abusive man again but I know I have to be really careful with my choices because of my past."

Whether you are aware of it at the time or not, each sexual encounter does affect your sexual self-esteem. If you end up feeling good about yourself after a sexual encounter because the experience was a positive one, your sexual self-esteem will either be enhanced or at the very least maintained. If, on the other hand, you end up feeling embarrassed, humiliated, ashamed, guilty, or afraid, your sexual self-esteem will be diminished, perhaps not perceptibly, but nevertheless diminished all the same. If you have a sexual encounter with someone and the result is that you end up doubting your sexual or physical attractiveness, your ability to satisfy a lover, or your ability to perform adequately, you may want to question your choice of partner instead of assuming the problem is with you.

It takes only one bad relationship to make us begin to doubt our sexual appeal. Because we are so incredibly vulnerable with our sexual partners, sharing with them not only our bodies but our hearts as well, they have the ability to make us feel either wonderful about ourselves or horrible about ourselves. The experience and the feelings attached to it then follow us to our next relationship, and so on. By the time we have had several relationships, our sexual self-esteem has probably been through the ringer because by that time we have probably experienced rejection and criticism as well as a broken heart or two.

SEXUAL PRACTICES THAT LOWER SEXUAL SELF-ESTEEM

In addition to choosing esteem-robbing sexual partners, we often get involved with sexual practices that can lower our sexual self-esteem. An esteem-robbing sexual practice is any sexual activity that causes us to feel bad about ourselves, either because the act is something that goes against our values and belief system, or because the act itself is emotionally (or even physically) damaging to us.

Sex should cause us to feel attractive, stimulated, excited, sensuous, and, ultimately, relaxed and appreciated—if not loved (often in this order). In short, it should make us feel good about ourselves. Esteem-robbing sex may make us initially feel many of the same things, but ultimately we end up feeling remorse, shame, guilt, and humiliation.

After we have engaged in esteem-raising sex we tend to want to repeat the act because it makes us feel so good about ourselves and our body. Esteem-robbing sex, on the other hand, may cause us to feel a tremendous amount of remorse and may make us promise ourselves we will never do it again. Unfortunately, esteem-robbing sex can become addictive and we find that we continue the behavior even against our better judgment. Time after time we repeat the behavior and time after time we promise ourselves we will not. A vicious cycle is created wherein the more we engage in the negative behavior the worse we feel about ourselves, and the worse we feel about ourselves, the more we engage in the behavior. The following are but a few of the kinds of esteem-robbing behaviors I am referring to.

Promiscuity

Sexual promiscuity is generally defined as instant and indiscriminate sex. Those who are promiscuous tend to have shallow relationships where there is little or no emotional involvement. Instead the focus is almost entirely on sexuality. Those who are sexually promiscuous generally live for the moment, engaging in sexual activity with multiple partners. Unfortunately, this type of sexual lifestyle leaves the individual feeling empty and alone and can lower both self-esteem in general and sexual self-esteem in particular. And, in the age of AIDS, it can even endanger one's life.

Pia came into my office with a bounce to her step and a big smile on her face. As soon as she sat down she announced, "Boy, did I have a close call!" She then went on to tell me that she had recently heard that a man she had had a one-night stand with two years before had just died of AIDS and how worried she had been that she had contracted it from him. "But I just got my AIDS test back and it was negative! I lucked out this time."

As our session continued, though, Pia's bright smile faded and the lilt to her voice was replaced by sadness. "I am so frightened that I won't be so lucky next time. I just can't keep being so reckless with my life. One of these days it is bound to catch up with me."

What Pia was referring to and the reason for her beginning therapy in the first place was the fact that she was sexually promiscuous. She promised herself over and over that she wouldn't have sex with a man until she really knew him, and yet she repeatedly broke that promise by going out to a club, getting high on alcohol and sometimes drugs, and ending up having sex with a man she had met that very night and would probably never see again.

Pia would feel tremendously ashamed the next day, when she would realize that once again she had done things with a stranger that she even had a hard time doing with someone she loved. "I feel so dirty, so cheap, when I think about the things I've let guys do to me. I'm losing all sense of self-respect."

In addition to the shame she felt, she also recognized what danger she was putting herself in. "I don't know these guys—one of them might end up being a mass murderer or something. Not to mention the fact that one of them could have a venereal disease, or worse yet, AIDS."

Sexually promiscuous people use sex to work out more fundamental problems—ones unrelated to sex. They seldom get the warm satisfaction they really seek but instead invariably create new, more complicated problems. Promiscuity can stem from a number of sources: sexual abuse, unmet emotional needs, negative reactions toward parental values, overcontrol, or an overly permissive parental example.

The evidence suggests that the best insulation against indiscriminate sexual behavior is a high degree of personal worth. A sense of personal worth insulates a person from selling himself or herself short and lessens interest in irresponsible sexual behavior. The person who likes himself seeks relationships that nourish self-esteem rather than meaningless ones that tear it apart. The person with low self-esteem has had negative experiences with love and, once burned, prefers fly-by-night arrangements that permit him to remain uncommitted, irresponsible, and uninvolved. Such a person may marry, but he usually chooses a person who also shies from psychological intimacy. He cannot grow and flourish, of course, without genuine intimacy, but he prefers this hunger to the proven danger of closeness.

Excessive Masturbation

Roger reported to me that he felt compelled to masturbate at least three or four times a day and often masturbated for hours, causing himself to lose sleep at night or to be late for work in the morning: "I realize I am completely out of control. I've tried to stop or at least cut down, but nothing seems to work."

Many people, like Roger, use masturbation as a tension reducer. When someone masturbates excessively, it usually indicates that he or she is addicted to sex—or, rather, addicted to the release he or she feels after an orgasm. Much like those who are addicted to food, alcohol, drugs, or gambling, those addicted to masturbation use their addiction to avoid deeper problems such as the effects of childhood sexual abuse, feeling empty inside, and repressed anger, among others.

Excessive masturbation often indicates that the person is unhappy, under too much pressure, or has too few meaningful relationships. The person's tensions may come from holding in negative feelings, having unrealistic expectations, feelings of inadequacy, or feelings of loneliness.

Extramarital Affairs

Extramarital affairs can have a devastating effect, not only on a marriage but on a person's sexual self-esteem as well. While we tend to think about affairs as steamy interludes that raise our sexual self-confidence, it is not always the case, as Preston found out:

"I started my affair with Ricki almost two years ago. Even though I was happily married I just couldn't resist her. She was so young and so beautiful and she thought I was wonderful. After eleven years of marriage my sex life with my wife had gotten stale and Ricki turned me on the way I used to feel when I was a teenager.

"But shortly after I began seeing her I began to feel terribly guilty around my wife. I started having a difficult time looking her in the eye when we talked and I began to avoid any intimate contact with her for fear that she would somehow sense the difference in me. While our marriage and our sexual relationship had become somewhat routine, sex had always been fairly frequent and satisfying. After I started having sex with Ricki, though, I stopped wanting to have sex with my wife. Consequently, she began to feel rejected and started assuming that I didn't love her anymore. I tried to reassure her that I did indeed love her but words alone were not going to satisfy her. I knew I needed to shower her with affection and passion but I just couldn't bring myself to do it.

"Since I couldn't have sex with my wife, I started feeling even more guilty about having sex with Ricki There was my wife, devastated because she thought I no longer desired her, and here I was having sex with someone I didn't even love. I guess I just couldn't take all the guilt, because it wasn't long before I couldn't make love to Ricki, either. I had become completely impotent with both my wife and my mistress. I felt about as low as a man can get. My affair ended shortly after I became impotent and this was a terrible blow to my ego. My marriage also came terribly close to ending but my wife hung in there with me and we were able to work things out."

Sadomasochism

Sometimes when we are young and impressionable we are introduced to types of sexuality that we wouldn't have thought about or become interested in on our own. These activities may at first seem exciting, and our natural curiosity may get the better of us, or we may go along with such activities in order to be accepted or in order to hold on to a sexual partner, as was the case with Marta:

"When I was just twenty-two an older man I was madly in love with introduced me to sadomasochism. The whole idea of it scared me and he had to do a lot of persuading to get me involved, but he gradually got me over my fears and I tried it. We started out doing some really mild things, like having him tie me up and blindfold me. This was kind of exciting since I could fantasize that he was forcing me and not have to feel guilty about having sex like I sometimes did. But gradually, things kind of got out of control. He started hitting me with a whip while I was tied up and putting clips on my nipples.

"You have to understand that I was really crazy about this guy and he was really exciting to be around. He had lots of interesting friends and we were always going to these really neat parties and sometimes even meeting celebrities. A lot of his friends were into the same kind of thing so it seemed almost normal at the time.

"When he started to get rougher with me and actually hurt me I tried to tell him that I really didn't like it. But I wasn't very forceful about it and he was very persuasive, telling me all about the fact that I was increasing my ability to experience sexual pleasure and what an exciting lover I was and how he didn't need anyone but me. And so I let it go on even though I was sometimes really frightened and was often physically hurt.

"After a while, the experience started taking its toll on me, not only physically, but emotionally. I started to dislike myself for letting my boyfriend treat me as he did and for not standing up to him. And he started treating me like a slave or a whore outside of the bedroom as well. He'd order me around and expect me to do whatever he wanted. Gradually, I stopped hanging out with my friends because I knew they wouldn't understand what I was into. I felt ashamed of myself when I was around my family so I stopped seeing them very often too. I became more and more isolated until I only associated with my boyfriend and his friends.

"As I became more and more dependent on my boyfriend he became more and more abusive to me in and out of bed. I wanted to leave him but I didn't feel strong enough to. Eventually, he left me for another woman. It has taken me three whole years to recover from that relationship and to be able to hold my head up with people and not feel horribly ashamed."

Swinging

We don't have to be young to be naive, nor do we ever become exempt from letting our hearts rule our lives. Amy was thirty years old by the time she got married and had had several relationships before that, and yet she became involved with something against her better judgment, just to hold onto her marriage:

"We had only been married for two years when my husband brought up the idea of swinging. He said it would help our marriage by guaranteeing that we wouldn't get bored with each other and that neither one of us would betray the other by having an affair behind the other's back. I was dead set against the idea and I told him so. But my ex-husband was a clever and manipulative man and I loved him very much and desperately wanted to please him, so gradually, he talked me into it.

"The first time we went to a swing party I was absolutely devastated. We weren't there thirty minutes before my husband wandered away from me, started talking to a woman, and went into one of the bedrooms with her. I just sat there on a couch, feeling like a fool, getting sick inside thinking about my husband being with another woman.

"It wasn't long before a very nice man came over and started talking with me. I was feeling so ugly and so rejected by my husband that I welcomed the attention. But soon I realized he wasn't just being understanding and nice to me, he wanted to have sex with me. He started putting his hands all over me and kissing me.

"I broke away from him but just then my husband came out of the bedroom with the other woman. He smiled at me as if to say, 'Boy, did I have fun.' I felt so humiliated and so angry my head was spinning. In my head I was talking to my husband; 'Okay, this is what you say you want. How will you feel when you see me walk into a bedroom with another man?' So when the man I was with stood up and held his hand out for me to follow, I found myself getting up and going into a bedroom with him.

"Once inside the room the man started taking off my clothes and before I knew it we were having intercourse. I don't even remember what happened exactly, it was like I had checked out or something. All I could think about was my husband being with that other woman and wondering if he liked her better than me.

I remember the man I was with kept telling me how good I was and this gave me a feeling of satisfaction and a sense of getting revenge on my husband.

"Afterward, I wanted to lie in the man's arms a little while and have him reassure me that I was beautiful and sexy but he had better things to do. We were up and dressed in no time and he was off with another woman within minutes of depositing me back on my couch. I felt so used. Having sex with this man obviously meant no more to him than having a dance with me.

"Even though my first experience was so horrible for me, I continued going to the swing parties for several years with my husband. Eventually, I convinced myself that I was really enjoying it but deep down inside I knew the truth. I hated myself for being so weak that I would do something I didn't believe in just to hold on to my husband. And I despised my husband for wanting other women and still wanting a normal marriage in all other respects. By the time I finally got up enough courage (with the help of two years of therapy) to leave him, I had very little self-esteem left. I've been divorced now for two and a half years and I have yet to accept a date. I feel so cheap for having slept with all those men."

Pornography

"I started out like so many boys did, sneaking pornographic magazines into my bedroom and masturbating to them late at night when everyone else was asleep. But because I felt so unattractive I continued using the magazines far into my twenties, while my friends were dating women and having sexual relationships. I guess you could say I was addicted to them.

"I'd look at women all day long but because I felt so unattractive and insecure I never asked anyone out. Instead, I would come home from work and masturbate using porno magazines or videos. During the day, I'd often sneak off to a porno movie house at lunchtime or to a peep show. I felt so slimy sitting there with all those other men, people that I would be ashamed to associate with socially, and I was always afraid someone from the office would see me as I came out of the movie house.

"The more I got involved with pornography, the worse I felt about myself. I became more and more isolated from others and I began to rely on it so much that it began to interfere with my work. I felt so much shame that I knew no decent woman would ever want me. Finally, I consulted a sex therapist because I wanted to stop relying on pornography and find out why I was so afraid to ask a woman out.

"I found out a lot about myself and why I was so afraid of women, but I also found out that pornography had a lot to do with my low sexual self-esteem. Because sex for me was always associated with secrecy, shame, degradation, and illicitness, my image of myself as a man was that of someone who was slimy, filthy, shameful—a 'dirty old man.' "

Voyeurism

My client Mitchell told me this story on his first visit to me: "I started peeping in my neighbors' windows when I was thirteen years old. At first it just seemed exciting to see half-naked and naked women parading around the house. But when I was sixteen, a neighbor set a trap for me and I got caught. He had tied a rope across his yard which happened to be the path I used to get to some of the houses where I peeped. I felt so humiliated when he came running out and I felt even worse when two neighbors pressed charges against me. Fortunately (or maybe unfortunately, now that I think of it), I got off with only probation. I realized that what I was involved with could have some serious consequences, but that didn't stop me.

"I continued peeping; I just went farther from home. It got so bad that I would go out nightly, looking for houses where I could get a good look without being seen. There was always an excitement to it but over time there was also a sick feeling that would come over me when I realized what could happen to me if I got caught.

"When I went away to college I continued peeping on campus and finally got caught again. This time I didn't get off so easy. I was expelled from school and my parents were notified. That was beyond a doubt the worse day of my life up to that point. I can still see the look on my mother's face when I returned home. She looked so hurt but also disgusted. My father was furious, and if I had been younger I know he would have beat me. Instead, he just ignored me for weeks and never really forgave me.

"After that I really tried hard to stop and for a while I was successful. I got married to a wonderful girl, got a great job, and things seemed to be going my way. But it wasn't long before I started having urges to peep, even though my sex life with my wife was really good. I thought that if I increased our sexual activity, or if I asked my wife to walk around in lingerie, I might be able to resist the temptation to peep. But no such luck.

"Before long I was making excuses to leave the house at night to go peeping. I'd say I had to go get something at the store, or I wanted to go for a run. Eventually, though, my wife started getting suspicious because I was going out more and more. So I started just going into the backyard to see what I could see. There was a single woman who lived next door who sometimes left her shade open so I started looking over there every night.

"Then my worst nightmare came true. One night while I was intensely engaged in watching the next-door neighbor, my wife came out into the backyard and caught me red-handed (I was masturbating). She told me she had suspected for quite some time and that she just couldn't take it any longer. She cried and told me that it made her sick to think that her husband was a pervert and, believe me, I felt like one at that moment.

"She told me that if I didn't go to therapy she would divorce me, and I guess this is what I needed all along to get me on the right track. I know there is something wrong with me and I am willing to do anything in order to be able to stop this behavior. It's tearing my life apart."

Exhibitionism

This is what Leonard told me when I asked him why he had come into therapy: "I first started exposing myself when I was a teenager. I'd stand in my living room and masturbate in front of the picture window. I'd feel so horrible afterward, so full of guilt and remorse. I'd even pray to God that if I got away with it this time, if no neighbors reported me to the police or told my parents, that I would never do it again. But the next time I got the urge I forgot all about my promise until after it was all over, and then once again I'd feel awful and make another promise.

"By the time I moved out of my parents' house I had graduated to exposing myself in parking lots, alleyways, and movie theaters, and I had stopped praying and making promises to God. I just figured my days were numbered before I would get caught, and sure enough, by the time I was twenty-one I had been arrested for indecent exposure and required to register as a sex offender.

"This scared me so much that I stopped exposing myself for a long, long time. But even so I found that my image of myself did not change. I still perceived myself as a demented pervert because I found exposing myself so sexually stimulating, and because I was afraid to actually be with a woman in a sexual relationship. Recently, the urge to expose myself has become so intense that I knew I better get help or I'd do it again. That's why I'm here."

Homosexual Behavior

While the majority of people have either had a homosexual relationship or been attracted to someone of the same sex at some point in their life, this does not make them homosexuals. Many people fear that just because they have had such an experience or attraction they are latent homosexuals and this affects their sexual self-esteem immensely, as it did with Forest:

"When I was thirteen I had a homosexual affair with one of my best friends. It only lasted for a few months but it has haunted me since, even though I have had many relationships with women. I feel such shame about the affair and I am desperately afraid that somehow one of the women I am involved with will find out about it. I don't have any attraction to men today but I feel like a fraud sometimes when I am with a woman, carrying around this big secret."

While being a homosexual is certainly not anything to be ashamed of, nevertheless, many people who are homosexual are ashamed of their sexuality. This is understandable since many people in our society still view homosexuality as a perversion even though most experts feel strongly that it is not a perversion or a mental illness but a natural phenomenon that just happens to occur to about ten percent of the population. Generally speaking, homosexuals who suffer from low sexual self-esteem benefit by associating with other gays or lesbians, by becoming more educated about homosexuality, and by learning to accept themselves as they are.

Sexual activities that cause us to feel ashamed, guilty, fearful, or humiliated can be extremely damaging to our sexual self-esteem.

We risk losing all pride in ourselves, our ability to satisfy someone we really love, our sense of physical attractiveness, and our good feelings about ourselves and our sexuality. When sexuality becomes associated only with the forbidden, with secretiveness, pain, or humiliation, which are esteem robbing, there is no room for true intimacy, love, affection, and joy, which are esteem enhancing.

The patterns or issues that we have discussed in this chapter—our choice of sexual partners and the types of sexual activities we become involved in—are both extremely important influences on our sexual self-esteem as adults. Taking a closer look at how our choices and behavior affect us and an even closer look at the reasons for our particular choices and behavior will be an important topic that will be discussed in Part II of this book.

CONCLUSION TO PART I

In a perfect world we all would have been given all the nurturing and positive touch we needed as infants and as children. We would have been given permission to explore our own bodies without being made to feel guilty or shameful, and we would have been free to satisfy our curiosity about other children's bodies as well. We wouldn't have grown up in a culture where sex is seen as sinful and forbidden but rather in one in which sex is the beautiful, natural thing that it was meant to be. In this perfect world no child would ever be sexually abused because all adults would have high self-esteem and be healthy sexually and thus have no need to exploit the innocent. Our value would not be predicated upon how our body looks but rather on how big our heart is. No one would be criticized for the way he or she looks because there would be no "ideal" look. No one would be rejected because his or her sexuality didn't fit the "norm" because there wouldn't be a "norm." Instead, differences would be respected and seen as part of what makes the world so fascinating.

But alas, this is not a perfect world, and so we all grow up confused, or in some way messed up about our sexuality. We all have hang-ups, insecurities, and fears about this most delicate aspect of ourselves.

Now that you have a better idea about what actually caused your low sexual self-esteem we will turn our attention to the task of raising it.

PART II

CHANGING THOSE THINGS ABOUT YOURSELF THAT YOU CAN CHANGE

Introduction to Part II

Discovering what caused your low sexual self-esteem, as important as it is, is only half the answer. Now you must learn what you can do given whatever negative beliefs, images, or handicaps your personal history has thrust upon you.

There are basically two ways of raising your sexual self-esteem:

1. Changing those things about yourself that contribute to your low self-esteem.
2. Learning to accept yourself the way you are.

Both methods are equally effective. Some causes of low sexual self-esteem can be eliminated by focusing your attention on them and by following my recommendations and those of other experts. On the other hand, no matter how much time and attention you give, there will be things about yourself that you simply cannot change and instead will need to begin to accept.

We will begin in Part II by focusing on how to change those things about yourself that you can and must change in order to raise your sexual self-esteem. In Part III we will discuss the option of learning to accept those things about yourself that are perhaps more difficult or even impossible to change in order to raise your sexual self-esteem.

When it comes to looking at what you *can* change about yourself, there are four areas to focus on:

1. Work on counteracting the negative messages and experiences that have tainted your sexuality. This includes recognizing and then releasing the emotions that interfere with your becoming emotionally and sexually intimate with others.

2. Begin to make esteem-enhancing choices. This includes discontinuing sexual behaviors and fantasies that cause you to feel shame and guilt.

3. Change the way you interact with your sexual partners.

4. Get help for your problems.

Chapter Eight

WORK ON COUNTERACTING THE NEGATIVE MESSAGES AND EXPERIENCES THAT HAVE TAINTED YOUR SEXUALITY

By reading Part I and taking your own personal sexual history you learned many of the causes of your low sexual self-esteem. The negative messages you received about sex or your body, and any traumatic or disturbing experiences you had regarding sex, will continue to affect your sexuality in negative ways unless you work on finding ways to either counter them, replace them with more positive messages or experiences, or release the negative emotions attached to them.

COUNTERACTING NEGATIVE MESSAGES

Although your sexual self-esteem has been greatly influenced by the negative messages you received regarding sex and your body, you do not have to continue to replay these messages to yourself for the rest of your life. It is possible to counteract these negative messages with healthier, more positive ones. Sometimes it just takes some education to counteract negative messages that are based on false information or old wives' tales. If you feel that you are still suffering from a lack of accurate information concerning sex, it may be time to crack a few books on sexuality. I have listed a number of authoritative books on human sexuality in the back of the book that will help you to this end.

Sometimes we only have to go as far as turning on the television or reading the newspaper to be informed about sexuality. Celebrity experts such as Dr. Ruth Westheimer and even our old standbys Ann Landers and Dear Abby have attempted to counteract the misinformation that has plagued us. Just as you were "programmed" into believing the negative messages about sex that you received as a child, you can now "reprogram" yourself with more positive ones. Counteracting negative messages with positive ones, as I will have you do in the following exercise, can sometimes be extremely effective.

• Retrieve the list of negative messages that you made in Part I, or write a list now of all the negative messages concerning sexuality and your body you remember receiving from your parents and other authority figures when you were a child.

• Notice which of these messages you tend to still believe today even though you may know intellectually that they are not true.

• For each of these particular messages, work on turning the negative statement into a positive one. For example, the message "Good girls do not have sex until they are married" could be made into the statement "It doesn't make me a bad person because I am unmarried and I enjoy sex" or "I am a good person and I enjoy sex."

• Keep your list of positive statements or affirmations handy and refer to them often, especially whenever you find yourself slipping back into believing an old negative message about sex.

Although these positive statements usually don't counteract our erroneous, deep-seated beliefs about sex entirely, they are an important first step toward changing our belief system.

Under the Influence

It sometimes takes a tremendous amount of work to counteract negative messages regarding sex, particularly if they were given by our parents or other influential adults. Even when we rebel against our parents' messages or determine that we are not going to be like them, their beliefs about sex can influence us anyway, as was the case with Jennifer:

"The messages I received from my mother about sex probably had the most devastating effect on my feelings about sexuality. My mother's message was not only that sex is bad but that sex is unimportant and that people make too big a deal out of it. In her eyes, anyone who focuses on sex is sick.

"When I was young I rebelled against my mother's messages about sex not being important. In fact, in my attempt to counteract her messages I went to the other extreme and made sex *overly* important. I became very outspoken about sex, talking about it frequently and behaving in a very overtly sexual way.

"Interestingly, by the time I reached my mid-thirties I found that all that sexual bravado and innuendo was an overreaction to my mother's insistence that sex was not important. I was trying so desperately to prove her wrong that I didn't know how I really felt about sex. When I started to discover that much of my sexual behavior had been inappropriate and a reaction to her messages, I found that I was not interested in sex at all for a while. During this time I was desperately afraid that I was going to end up like her—alone and sexless from the age of forty on."

Jennifer sought help for her lack of interest in sex. In therapy she was able to emotionally separate from her mother and her messages about sex. She found she didn't need to rebel against her mother in order to discover her own particular sexual values and reconnect with her sexual desire.

Sometimes talking to other people about your beliefs about sex, particularly those people you trust, can help to counteract early negative messages. Hearing how others struggle with the same conflicts regarding what they were told as a child, and what they now want to believe, can help you to feel less alone with your conflicts and validate your perceptions that indeed these early messages are not just erroneous but damaging.

In fact, sharing your feelings with others about the beliefs you were raised with can do more to counteract negative messages than almost anything else. Unfortunately, although there are all kinds of support groups available for almost every kind of problem, we don't as yet offer support to those who suffer from low sexual self-esteem due to negative indoctrination regarding sex. But this doesn't mean you can't start your own formal or informal support group or that you can't take the risk of opening up with friends to bring sexuality into your conversations.

DISPELLING ESTEEM-ROBBING MYTHS ABOUT SEX

Some myths about sex or about a particular gender are so derogatory that believing them can rob us of our self-esteem. By continuing to buy into these myths we are continuously whittling away at our sexual self-esteem.

Some of these myths are:

- All women prefer a large penis to a small one.
- All men prefer large breasts to small ones.
- All women can have "vaginal" orgasms and these are superior to clitoral ones.
- All women can have multiple orgasms and these are preferable to just having one orgasm.
- Most people like to experiment with lots of different positions and the person who knows these various positions will be more pleasing to a sexual partner.
- All men prefer thin women.
- All women prefer muscular men.

Chapter Nine

LEARNING TO RECOGNIZE AND RELEASE EMOTIONS THAT AFFECT YOUR SEXUALITY AND ABILITY TO BE INTIMATE

Aside from our early upbringing and our first adventures into the world of sexuality and intimacy, the next most influential factors affecting our sexuality are our emotions. The emotions of shame, guilt, anger, fear, envy, and jealousy affect our sexuality and our sexual self-esteem in profound ways—ways that are insidious, cumulative, and intense, and are often outside of our awareness. This lack of awareness of how these emotions can shape and continually influence our sexuality is exactly what gives them their power.

Repressing negative emotions holds down positive, loving ones as well. The person who is cut off from her emotions, who is guarded in her interpersonal relationships, doesn't set aside her controls when she hops into bed. Her sex life will lack the quality of openness and spontaneity that the rest of her life does and it will remain primarily physical.

Feelings of anger, guilt, shame, fear, envy, and jealousy can contaminate your sexuality and your sexual relationships in a multitude of ways, one of which is to cause you to lose your sexual desire. It is vitally important that these emotions be recognized and then released so they do not continue to undermine your sexuality.

SHAME AND GUILT—MAJOR CAUSES OF LOW SEXUAL SELF-ESTEEM

None of our other emotions affects our sexual self-esteem more than shame and guilt. Single-handedly these two emotions can wipe out the excitement and rapture of sexuality and the joy and luxurious pleasure of sensuality. They can rob the child or adolescent of his sexual curiosity; the young adult of his ability to be intimate, and thus to find appropriate sexual partners; the middle-aged man or woman of the contentment and fullness of a compatible, loving sexual relationship with a partner; and the elderly person the pleasure of guilt-free fantasy.

We carry shame and guilt with us from childhood into our adult life and these feelings tend to contaminate our sexuality. Those who have sexual shame and guilt tend to experience their sexuality in negative ways, such as viewing it as something that should be hidden, secretive, or forbidden. This sets the climate for illicit sexual activities such as extramarital affairs, prostitution, voyeurism, and exhibitionism.

For this reason, we need to understand what causes both guilt and shame. While they operate in similar ways, especially concerning our sexuality, it is important to define them separately.

Shame

Shame is sometimes difficult to define. It is a normal, healthy emotion intended to remind us that we are human and thus limited. Healthy shame provides us with the structure we so badly need, which in turn helps us to develop a boundary system within which we can safely operate. Healthy shame keeps us grounded, reminding us that we have made and will continue to make mistakes, that we are not invincible, and that we need the help of others. It allows us to know our limits, to not waste our energy on goals we cannot reach or on things we cannot change.

Healthy shame may come in the form of feeling embarrassed over a mistake, a shortcoming, or a failure, or it may come as a feeling of timidity or shyness in the presence of strangers.

Unhealthy shame, on the other hand, causes us to feel that

there is something wrong with us personally that we cannot change. Unhealthy shame causes us to feel that we are no good at our very core. This feeling is so horrifying that we become secretive about our shame. We don't want anyone to know how bad we are and we live in fear that someone will find out.

THE EFFECTS OF SHAME

Those who were shamed in childhood suffer in numerous ways, many of which are directly related to sexuality and sexual self-esteem:

1. Fear of being vulnerable, of exposing oneself to other people.

2. Extreme shyness and feelings of inferiority.

3. Fear of intimacy, a tendency to avoid real commitment in relationships.

4. Feelings of being worthless and unlovable.

5. Sense of being ugly, flawed, and imperfect. (May lead to overattention to clothes, makeup, etc., in an attempt to hide imagined or real flaws in personal appearance and self.)

6. Difficulty being spontaneous.

7. Feel they must do things perfectly, which often leads to performance anxiety.

How Shame Affects Intimacy

Shame affects our ability to form loving relationships. This is true for several reasons. First of all, when we are full of shame it is impossible to feel good about ourselves, and unless we feel good about ourselves we will not be able to love another person in a genuine way. A healthy love relationship requires that we be able to both give and receive affection. Those who are full of shame cannot really take in love and affection. Because they feel so unworthy, they feel they do not deserve to be treated well and will push away love in one way or another, sabotaging any good relationship they have, as Barbara did:

"No one had ever treated me as well as Randy did. He was so kind and considerate. But I just couldn't believe he was for real. I kept thinking he wanted something from me, or that he was a phony or something. Finally I started interpreting his kindness as weakness and I began to despise him. I became so cruel to him that I finally drove him away. Now I know the problem was with me, and I lost the best person I have ever known."

Like Barbara, those who are full of shame will very likely distrust their lover's motives when he or she is affectionate or loving. Shame eats away at their self-esteem and prevents them from even taking in compliments. While most people respond positively to compliments and kindness, a person who is full of shame tends to push them away because they do not match how he or she feels inside.

Eventually, those involved with a person who is full of shame get tired of trying to convince the shame-ridden person that indeed they do love him or her, as was the case with Sly and Megan:

"I realized that Megan had very low self-esteem when we first got involved but I thought that somehow I could make her begin to appreciate the good qualities that I saw in her. Unfortunately, it seemed like I was pouring water down an endless hole. The love, attention, and kindness I gave her didn't seem to do very much good. In fact, the more I loved her, the more she pushed me away."

And last, if you are full of shame about your sexuality—either because you were sexually abused as a child or because of negative messages you received as a child concerning sex—this shame will contaminate your sexual relationships. You will either numb your body to the point where you are unable to enjoy your sexual feelings or you will tend to enjoy sex only when it is forbidden, illicit, or abusive.

How Shame Affects Self-Esteem

In order to have high self-esteem and to be a self-actualized human being, you must be able to feel both shame and power. Unfortunately, most people can feel only one of these powerful emotions at a time. To many it is as if one of these emotions cancels out the other. If they are feeling shame they feel excessive shame—they feel as if they *are* shame. In this extreme form, shame immobilizes people, causing them to go into a deep depression in which they lose all sense of personal power.

Shame tends to drain us of our power. When you are full of shame you lack energy or hope for change. In time a vicious cycle is created wherein the more shameful you feel, the more you are robbed of your drive and initiative. You become more and more isolated, and therefore you have fewer positive and affirming experiences.

Some people stay in this state of unhealthy shame most of the time and are thus unable to initiate any positive action, including either beginning a new relationship or ending an unhealthy one.

Others can tolerate their feelings of shame for only so long before they bury them completely and connect instead with an exaggerated feeling of power. This decision to deny the shame and compensate instead with feelings of power is an unconscious one and few people are even aware that they have made it. Unwittingly, they shift into a state of nonfeeling in which they feel overly confident, come to believe in unrealistic goals, and even believe they are infallible. Caught up in this illusionary world, those who deny their shame in this way are susceptible to becoming abusive of others.

One of the first steps toward ridding yourself of your core of shame and taking back your power is to discover the source of your shame.

SOURCES OF SHAME

Those who grew up in dysfunctional families experienced humiliation, ridicule, abandonment, and self-hate. They were made to feel ashamed by their parents, both intentionally, as a form of control, and unintentionally, out of the parents' own shame-based childhoods. Such parents don't reassure a child that he or she is okay though his or her behavior is upsetting, but instead brand the child as a failure. The child learns to feel that there is something irrevocably wrong with who she or he is—something that cannot be fixed—and it is around this core of shame that the child forms an identity.

Shame as a Form of Discipline

Feelings of shame begin early in a child's life. Developmental psychologists have discovered that feelings of shame begin as early as two years of age. These feelings of shame trouble children much more than most adults realize. When shame is used as a means of discipline it is more likely to produce anger and resentment than to change behavior.

Children have a deep sense of shame, and most adults don't

realize that their deepest fears involve being shamed or made to look foolish or stupid. Because young people's egos and their sense of self are poorly formed, they need parents and other adults to support them and to help in building their self-esteem. Shame digs into a person's sense of self, leaving a feeling of embarrassment and humiliation. This can linger long after childhood.

Shame is often used with toilet training and as a way to discourage bed-wetting. Children are often humiliated, laughed at, taunted, or made fun of when they make mistakes in this area, to the point that the child's self-esteem is horribly damaged.

In an attempt to force Ramone into remembering to come into the house to go to the bathroom instead of having an accident in his pants, his mother would continually go out into the yard while he was playing with other kids and pull down his pants to see if he had soiled them. Instead of helping, this practice caused Ramone to be so anxious that he continued soiling his pants until he was five years old and started kindergarten. To this day he remembers feeling horribly humiliated about having his body exposed to the other children and from being laughed at by them.

In fact, Ramone felt so exposed and embarrassed as a child that today he has quite a few problems with sex. He is unable to undress in front of anyone, even his girlfriends, for fear of their laughing at him. Unfortunately, this behavior has caused women to tease him about being shy, reinforcing his shame. They do not realize, of course, just how serious Ramone's problem is or that their taunting makes him feel even worse.

Micky's mother also used shame to discipline him. Micky's problem was that he continued to wet the bed well into his teens. No matter how hard he tried he just couldn't make it through the night. Much to his dismay, he would awaken to discover that once again he'd had an accident in the night. In an attempt to make him get up in the night, Micky's mother tried taunting him by calling him a baby, and even forced him to wear diapers to bed.

This kind of shaming can be terribly damaging to a child's self-esteem, and in Micky's case it caused him to feel a level of shame that carried over into his adult sex life. Ironically, because Micky experienced some sexual arousal when his mother would diaper him, he now has a fetish for wearing diapers and for wanting women to put diapers on him.

This fetish has become an obsession to the point that unless a woman agrees to do this with him he cannot become sexually aroused. (We will discuss fetishes later on in Part II.) Since most women are repulsed by the idea or just laugh at him, he has experienced a tremendous amount of rejection, which, of course, just adds to his shame and low self-esteem.

Shame and Your Body

Every normal human being has sexual feelings, and a positive attitude toward sex means accepting these urges as vital, healthy, and appropriate; it also means not perceiving sensual or sexual feelings as shameful. But as we discussed in Part I, parents often pass on the message to their children that the body, especially the genitals, is something to be ashamed of. As a child you may have repeatedly been told to cover your body, and you may have been made to feel ashamed for having sexual feelings. In addition, many people are traumatized by shame when their parents catch them masturbating or involved in sexual play or exploration, as Lucille was:

"One day my mother walked in on me and my best friend Judy while we were undressed. We were both eleven years old and had just started to develop and we were curious about how we each looked. When my mother saw us she started yelling at me and accused us of being lesbians. She made us stand there naked while she lectured us about lesbians and what kind of a life they lead. Then she sent Judy home and told her to never come back. I was so humiliated that I never talked to Judy again, nor have I been able to have another close female friend.

"I worried all during high school that I was gay and never allowed any girls to get close to me. Instead, I started having sex with boys when I was in junior high school just to prove to myself that I wasn't gay. By high school I had a reputation with all the boys for being fast and was treated horribly by nearly everyone in school. I had lost all self-respect. I grew to hate myself and my body. I felt that it had betrayed me, first by making me feel 'lesbian' feelings and then by making me feel so cheap."

In order to have self-respect we need to wholeheartedly accept our body and its sexual feelings. Unfortunately, this is difficult to do when we are discouraged from it starting when we are small children.

The Shame of Childhood Sexual Abuse

As I mentioned earlier, those who were sexually abused as children often experience conflict and have difficulty with sexual pleasure and orgasm. For these people, sexual pleasure is often associated with guilt and shame. In addition, their capacity to trust is severely damaged. Sex and sexual impulses may even feel dangerous for survivors of sexual abuse.

If you were sexually abused as a child you didn't know that you were not responsible for the abuse. You probably felt that you should have stopped it, or could have stopped it, and that somehow it was all your fault. If you experienced sexual pleasure, appreciated the attention and affection you received, or were especially close to the offender, you probably feel particularly ashamed and guilty.

In order to rid yourself of this debilitating type of shame you must come to know—not just intellectually, but deep inside of you—that you were not to blame for your sexual abuse. This, of course, is easier said than done. Reading books on the subject of childhood sexual abuse will certainly help you to understand from an intellectual, logical point of view that you were not responsible, but it doesn't usually take care of the deep, nagging feeling that you are, in fact, the one person who *was* responsible for his or her own abuse. Books also don't necessarily take care of the feeling of shame that comes with the realization that you might have experienced physical pleasure during the abuse, or explain to you sufficiently why you kept going back for more.

In order to quiet these nagging doubts you will probably need to join a support group with other survivors. Listening to others tell their stories and share their feelings will help you come to understand that *all* survivors feel responsible for the abuse on some level, that many experienced physical pleasure during the abuse, and that many "went back for more" because they were so desperate for attention and affection. In the group you will be encouraged to connect with and express your feelings of anger toward the perpetrator and to put the blame where it belongs.

Individual therapy can also help rid you of your shame by helping you to deal with your core of shame and to connect with a sense of personal power.

SHARING SECRETS

After you have discovered the source or sources of your shame the next step is to begin to share your secrets, to look into your past, to explore all the painful circumstances and bring them out into the open. You may do this with a close friend, a lover, or a therapist.

Taking the shame out of sex begins with unlearning much of what we have learned about sexuality. By sharing your experiences, learning to talk about sex openly with those you are close to in an authentic way, you take the shame out of sex. But when you don't talk about it but instead keep your sexual feelings, thoughts, and experiences secret, you continue to feel ashamed of them. As long as you feel ashamed you will feel that there's something wrong with you and will be unable to fully experience the joy and pleasure of sex. It is only when we take ourselves out of that hidden, silent, secret place that we begin to feel a healthy sexuality.

All of us have sexual secrets, whether they are about embarrassing experiences in our childhood and adolescence, childhood sexual abuse, sexual fantasies, or sexual practices and experiences we interpret as abnormal or unacceptable. The shame we feel about keeping such sexual secrets lowers our self-esteem. The hiding and secretiveness remind us of our childhood experiences of sneaking around and breaking rules. Everyone who keeps secrets feels, at times, like a "bad child."

Hiding who you are, what you want sexually, how you feel, or what happened in the past prevents you from creating the relaxation, trust, and enthusiasm that satisfying sex requires. Sexual secrets compel you to hide your body, worry about your performance, fear that your partner is getting bored, or hope that you won't be discovered or rejected.

When you withhold information about yourself, you invite your partner to withhold as well. Withholding information from someone you care about breaks an unspoken agreement that most relationships have—"we won't keep anything important from one another."

On the other hand, sharing your secrets with those you trust or should trust offers you the opportunity of being accepted for who you really are—something we all long for and need in order to establish true intimacy.

This is especially true of those who were sexually victimized. Keeping the secret from those you are close to helps maintain your belief that there is something wrong with *you* because you were traumatized. Speaking out and seizing the *choice* of how to run your life—including whether, and whom, to tell—will help you to let go of the victim role.

When you share your sexual experiences with other people good things begin to happen: You discover that the sexual feelings, thoughts, and fantasies that you previously thought were sick or perverse and thus only entertained by you alone are shared by many, many people. You begin to recognize that you are not all that different or perverse after all and that what you are doing and feeling is common to many. And you come to have compassion for yourself as having had few choices and living in a far less than healthy climate for feeling good about yourself.

Guilt

Like shame, there is healthy guilt and unhealthy guilt. And like shame, guilt serves a purpose in our lives but is often misused. Guilt feelings serve to prevent us from repeating an act. We need to be able to know when what we are doing is morally wrong and we need to be able to know and acknowledge our guilt.

It is important to distinguish between neurotic guilt and real guilt. Neurotic guilt is felt when you have done nothing to feel guilty about. Real guilt, on the other hand, is a necessary social emotion. It is our conscience's way of preventing us from doing things we will later regret. Our society would fall apart if we were incapable of feeling real guilt. Real guilt is felt when we have violated our own moral code, when we have gone against our own value and belief systems, when we have gone against who we think we are or should be.

An important aspect of guilt is that it frequently works upon us without our knowing about it. We can suffer the consequences of unconscious guilt and not even realize it. Among the signs that may attest to the presence of unconscious guilt is a powerful need to injure oneself or a persistent need to get or to give oneself punishment. Thus, we get into unhappy marriages, lose all our money, or become ill as an unconscious punishment for crimes we may or may not even have committed. A man who begins to cheat on his wife may punish himself by becoming impotent with his lover, a woman who believes that sex should be confined to marriage may punish herself for premarital sex by not allowing herself to have an orgasm.

The purpose of guilt is to prevent, not to punish. And yet many people punish themselves after they have committed a "forbidden" act, but then go on to commit the same act again and again. Although their conscience acknowledges that what they did was wrong, and punishes them for their sins, their guilt never functions for them as a warning signal.

Healthy guilt is appropriate—in quantity and quality—to the deed. A healthy conscience produces guilt feelings commensurate with the act. Healthy guilt leads to remorse but not self-hatred. It discourages us from repeating our guilty act without shutting down a wide range of our passions and pleasures.

SOURCES OF GUILT

The Guilt of the Innocent

Children who were abused or neglected often try to avoid feeling their *helplessness* and *powerlessness* by blaming themselves for the abuse or neglect. This is often reinforced by the fact that abusive or neglectful parents often tell the child that he or she is to blame for the parents' behavior. Many an abusive parent yells at, beats, or punishes a child in cruel and severe ways and then blames the child for his or her own behavior. But even when a parent doesn't blame the child, the child will automatically assume he or she was at fault, as Byron did in the following example:

Byron was severely neglected as a child. His parents would leave him alone for long periods of time with no food in the house. At other times he would be put outside in the backyard and told to stay there all day long, again without food. But Byron did not feel angry at his parents for this behavior, either as a child or as an adult. Instead, he held fast to the belief that if he hadn't been a "bad" boy his parents would not have neglected him so.

If you were a victim of emotional, physical, or sexual abuse, you were powerless to change the situation. But it may have felt just too frightening to allow yourself to feel this powerlessness. You may have preferred instead to feel guilty, since at least then you had the *illusion of control* over what was happening to you. As Rod explained: "While my stepfather was beating me I would just lie there. Afterward I would feel tremendously guilty. I would chastise myself for not having fought back—for just taking it. Now, I understand that I was too afraid and too powerless to fight back, but at the time all I could feel was guilt."

Even today, as an adult, you may still prefer to feel guilty and to blame yourself rather than to feel how helpless and out of control you really were as a child. As Judith Viorst, in her book *Necessary Losses*, stated: "By blaming ourself, we can believe in our life-controlling powers. By blaming ourself, we are saying that we would rather feel guilty than helpless, than not in control."

You also may be choosing to feel guilty rather than to admit the truth about what really happened to you as a child. It may feel less painful to blame yourself for the abuse or neglect than to face the fact that someone you love could have hurt you or neglected you in such a way.

Guilt can also be caused by the withholding of your anger that should have (but could not have) been directed toward those who hurt you as a child. Victims often direct their anger against themselves, often in the form of guilt.

Other victims feel so guilty, ugly, and dirty inside from sexual and other kinds of abuse that they believe they were and are being punished by God for being "bad." Otherwise, why would such a horrible thing happen to them? They believe that terrible things happen because they deserve it. This belief adds to their guilt.

Work on distinguishing your *real* guilt from your *neurotic* guilt. If you are feeling guilty rather than accepting your helplessness as a child—holding on to the illusion of control—then you are suffering from neurotic guilt, not real guilt. If you refuse to believe that someone could have harmed you or neglected you in such a way, not because you did anything wrong but simply because they wanted to, because of their own selfishness or sickness, then you are choosing to hold on to neurotic guilt rather than face the truth. If you continue to believe that God caused the bad things that have happened in your life in order to punish you for being a bad child, you are also refusing to admit the truth and holding on to neurotic guilt.

SOURCES OF SEXUAL GUILT

Sexual guilt comes from several sources: negative childhood messages, including those regarding masturbation; having "forbidden" sexual thoughts and fantasies; violating your own sexual values; and sexual violation.

Negative Messages

Feelings of sexual guilt often begin in childhood. They may begin when little children are scolded for handling their genitals, or when a six-year-old is given rigid rules about nudity, or when a ten-year-old's questions about sex are met with embarrassment.

The word *masturbation* is emotionally charged for many people. In the 1970s, researcher Shere Hite asked three thousand women whether they masturbated regularly, and eighty-two percent answered affirmatively. More than ninety percent of men reported they masturbate at least weekly. And yet while most people masturbate, many feel guilty about it. Both women and men have received many negative messages about masturbation. Many religions teach that any sexual activity not aimed at reproduction is a sin and that masturbation is a carnal activity that debases our moral character.

"Forbidden" Thoughts and Fantasies

One form of unhealthy guilt is indiscriminate guilt—a failure to distinguish between forbidden thoughts and forbidden deeds. Thus, we feel as guilty about what we have *thought* about doing as we would if we had actually done it. An example of this might be our sexual fantasies. To someone who suffers indiscriminate guilt a "wicked" wish is as bad as a "wicked" act. Their conscience cruelly condemns them for their fantasies.

Certainly, thoughts are not the same as deeds and we should not condemn ourselves for our thoughts and fantasies. On the other hand, if your thoughts and fantasies are causing you a great deal of guilt you will need to explore those thoughts and fantasies more closely. We will discuss fantasies much more comprehensively later on in the book.

Going Against Your Own Value System

At some point in your life you may have engaged in sexual activities that you now feel guilty about or you may have become involved with sexual partners that you now regret. You may have done these things because you were young and impressionable, because you were rebelling against parental messages or rules, because you were intoxicated or under the influence of drugs, or as a way of acting out due to childhood trauma such as sexual abuse. Or you may feel guilty due to the fact that you have used sex as a weapon or a manipulation to get things you wanted, such as attention, money, alcohol, or drugs.

Instead of becoming obsessed with what you have done in the past, or beating yourself up for engaging in activities that you now regret, you will need to begin to forgive yourself and move on. But before you can forgive yourself you will need to do the following:

• Come to an understanding of why you engaged in a particular activity.
• Take responsibility for your actions.
• Make amends and acknowledge behavior that has hurt others as well as behavior that has hurt yourself.
• Work on making wiser choices in the future.

Guilt Caused by Being Raped as an Adult

Society tends to blame the victim of a crime, and this is never more prevalent than in the case of rape. Rape victims consistently receive the message that they "asked for it" because they were dressed provocatively, because they were in the wrong place at the wrong time, or because they were being seductive. With all of this blaming going on it is important to remind yourself of the following:

• No circumstance justifies rape. You did not have anything to do with the rape—no matter what you were wearing, no matter what led up to the rape, and no matter what you didn't do to prevent it. It was not your fault.
• Rape is a crime of violence, power, and aggression—not sex. Although the instrument of assault—the penis—is sexual, the act is not. Men rape to express rage, dominance, or ownership, not to express sexual feelings.
• Every six minutes in the United States, another woman is raped. Forty-four percent of all women report having been the victim of a rape or an attempted rape during their lifetime. You are not alone.

Date Rape

When a woman is date-raped her feeling of guilt is even stronger than when she is raped by a stranger. This is because she will believe that she should have used better judgment. Although she has been betrayed by someone she trusted, she will blame herself for not being able to recognize what the man expected or what kind of person he was—for not being able to judge the man's character. It is important to remember that those who are date-raped are no more responsible for their victimization than other rape victims.

Guilt Caused by Childhood Sexual Abuse

Victims of child sexual abuse feel a tremendous amount of guilt. They feel guilty for the abuse itself, for the things they did as children as a result of the abuse, and for the things they have done as adults to hurt themselves and others. If you were sexually abused as a child, in order to raise your self-esteem in general and your sexual self-esteem in particular, you must free yourself from the guilt by acknowledging what you are responsible for and what you are not.

You may not be aware of your guilt. It can be working on you without your knowing it. Unconscious guilt can cause you to be self-destructive, abusing your body with food, alcohol, drugs, cigarettes, self-mutilation, or by being accident-prone, sabotaging your success, or eliciting punishment from others.

This unconscious guilt may cause you to tenaciously hold on to your problems and your pain because they give you the punishment you feel you deserve. You may have spent your life punishing yourself with one bad relationship after another, or one illness after another—including, as we have mentioned earlier, sexual dysfunction. In the words of Judith Viorst in *Necessary Losses*, you may be "sentencing yourself to a lifetime of penance for a crime you didn't commit."

Guilt Caused by "Acting Out"

If you were abused as a child you will also need to forgive yourself for things you did in childhood as a consequence of being hurt by the abuse.

Unable to express your anger toward those who abused you, you may have vented your anger at those who were smaller and weaker than yourself. Since you hated yourself for being weak and helpless, you hated others who were weak as well. This behavior may have begun in childhood and continued into adulthood.

If you were introduced to sex too early, you may have initiated sex play with other children in an attempt to deal with the reality you experienced. It is also common for victims of sexual abuse, because they were already sexualized, to have sexual feelings toward other children. They may initiate sexual play and even sexual intercourse with children younger than themselves as a way of feeling powerful or as a way of acting out their pain and anger. Many victims fondled their siblings' genitals, or the genitals of other children. Fran confessed: "I remember feeling appalled at myself one time when I was baby-sitting a little toddler. I was twelve, and it was right after I had been molested. While I was changing his diapers I was suddenly overwhelmed with the desire to suck his penis. I felt sexually excited and also angry. I wanted to hurt him like I had been hurt. I felt so afraid and disgusted with myself, but I just couldn't seem to stop myself."

Memories like these can make you feel horrible about yourself. You suddenly feel no better than the perpetrator. The guilt and shame can become overwhelming. You may torment yourself with questions like "How could I do such horrible things?" There are several things to remember so that you can begin to forgive yourself:

1. You were a confused, disturbed child or adolescent who was acting out your pain.

2. You had been sexualized too early, before you were emotionally and physically equipped to handle it.

3. You are different from the abuser because you are trying to change so that you won't hurt anyone like that again.

Just as you are not *bad* because of what someone else did to you (the abuse), you are also not *bad* because of the sexual and cruel acts you committed *as a child* as a consequence of the abuse you sustained. You may feel you are responsible for these actions, but in fact you are no more responsible for them than for the abuse you endured. These acts are as much of a symptom of the abuse as are all your other symptoms. Try to be forgiving of yourself for being a disturbed child.

Stop blaming yourself for the things you did as a child. You were not old enough to be held responsible. On the other hand, if you feel you *were* old enough to be held responsible (because you were a teenager, for example), then take some control over your guilt and shame now. It does no one any good for you to continue blaming yourself and punishing yourself, including the people you may have hurt.

If you feel you were old enough to be held responsible for your actions, ask yourself the following questions:

• Are you feeling guilty about something that you chose to do, on your own volition, without being coerced?
• Did you do this act when you were old enough to have developed a moral code?
• Were you of an age when you had learned all of society's rules and values?
• Did you commit this act with another person?
• Was it an adult of your own age or were you a child acting with an adult?
• Was this an act against another person or against your own moral code?

The chances are high that after answering these questions you will realize that you cannot be held responsible for your actions.

WHEN SELF-FORGIVENESS ISN'T ENOUGH

If you still consider yourself responsible for your actions as a child, if you believe you were old enough to be held accountable for your actions (under sixteen is *probably* not old enough), and if you believe you acted freely on your own accord, you may be suffering from real, healthy guilt. If you have done something against your value system, if you have broken your own rules, then you feel real guilt. While real guilt can serve a positive function in our society, *holding on to* your guilt feelings does *not* serve a positive function. If you have decided that you are indeed feeling real guilt about something, it will be important to follow these steps:

1. Learn from your mistake or transgression so that you do not repeat it. Why was it a mistake to do this? Did you hurt someone

else? What were some of the other consequences? Get therapy if
you need it to stop hurting others. If you have learned from your
mistake, and do not wish to repeat it, then you no longer need to
feel guilty about it. Let it go.

2. You will now need to find some way to atone for what you
have done before you can rid yourself of your guilt. It is important
to be *accountable* for your actions and behavior. Being accountable
can take the form of:

- Admitting your transgression to yourself and the person
or persons you hurt or deceived.
- Apologizing to the person or persons you hurt.
- Making amends or restitution to the person you hurt.

All people make mistakes as part of being human. You don't
need to continue to be critical of yourself, to suffer or punish yourself. You do need to learn from your mistakes, to be accountable
for your behavior, and to forgive yourself.

MAKING A NEW START

After you have worked to alleviate the core of shame and guilt
that you have carried forward from childhood and earlier times in
your life, you will need to make a new start. Making a new start
means that you don't continue to engage in sexual activities that
add new shame and guilt to your life. This requires that you take
a long, hard look at your personal choices regarding your sexuality
and decide whether these choices are good ones as far as your sexual self-esteem is concerned. For example, are you engaging in sexual activities that either reinforce the shame or guilt you felt as a
child or provide you with new shame or guilt each time you engage in them because they go against your value system? We will
discuss making healthier choices in later chapters.

By beginning to make changes in your sexual behavior and by
discovering and then honoring your own personal value system
when it comes to sex, you can achieve a sense of sexual dignity.
This will empower you to express your sexuality without violating
or coercing others and encourage you to become accountable for
your sexual self. Working with the issues that have kept you from
empowerment and responsibility—shame, guilt, and sexual violation—will enable you to experience intimacy with yourself and
with those you love.

ANGER—THE DESTROYER OF SEXUAL INTIMACY

Sex and anger do not mix. Normally, when we are angry, sex is the last thing we want. Anger is a defensive emotion, causing us to feel protective, closed up, and distant from others, particularly those we are angry with. The last thing most people want to do when they are angry is to have sex with the person they are angry with.

When we are angry we generally feel distrustful, tense, and consumed by our anger and what caused the anger. Typically, in order to feel sexual we need to feel open, trusting, vulnerable, and to be focused on our partner and our sexual desire. Anger causes us to be distracted and removed from our partner, even when it is not our partner we are angry with. While some people, especially men, can have sex when they are angry, there certainly is no intimacy or emotional closeness involved.

The emotion of anger affects our sexuality in many ways—the most potent being that of destroying the emotional and sexual intimacy between two people. There are several ways in which this occurs: by suppressing or repressing our anger, or by displacing our anger.

When we *suppress* our anger we are consciously choosing to ignore it, put it aside. But no matter how deeply we try to bury our anger, it always manages to remain just under the surface. Long-term suppressed anger can damage relationships because it inhibits us from being joyous, loving, and sexual.

Suppressed anger almost always blocks a desire for sex and intimacy with the person we are angry with. This is especially true when one or both partners won't discuss differences. Instead, they simply attempt to ignore or bury them, with the result that mountains of resentment start to build and the lines of communication become even more disrupted.

Although the event that created your anger may have been quite some time ago, you may still be angry with your partner and thus feel unwilling to be vulnerable and open with him or her. This was the case with Bree and her husband. Bree had discovered that her husband had had an affair two years ago but has been unable to let go of her anger and go on. Consequently, she no longer feels sexual with him at all.

Whereas suppressed anger is anger we consciously choose to ignore, *repressed* anger is anger we have unconsciously denied, "forgotten," or buried. Repressed anger can be dangerous because it can build up inside of us until it finally reaches a "boiling point." We can "keep the lid on" for just so long before the pressure has to be released, all too often causing us to become abusive and violent toward ourselves or others.

The person who represses his feelings of anger often uses sex as an outlet for his pent-up rage. For example, Bailey got back at his wife for going back to work against his wishes by becoming a premature ejaculator. Although he did not do this consciously, his repressed anger was at work nevertheless. At the other extreme, repressed anger can cause us to become numb to our feelings altogether, so that we are no longer in contact with how we feel. We lose our enthusiasm and aliveness, we feel tired much of the time, and we lose our sexual desire.

Both suppressed and repressed anger slowly eat away at a relationship, causing partners to distance from one another, distrust one another, and eventually begin to lose any feelings of love or sexual attraction.

When we *displace* our anger we direct it to where it doesn't belong. Instead of focusing our anger where it is appropriate, we blame innocent people and become irrationally angry at circumstances or even at inanimate objects, often for no good reason. Since displaced anger does not offer a release to the appropriate target, the anger itself seldom dissipates. This results in a cycle of constantly blaming others, which in turn makes relationships difficult.

Repressed anger from the past, even when it is not about your current relationship, can affect your sexuality today and your current sexual relationship. We often *displace* our *repressed anger* by directing it toward someone or something that is not the real cause. Carl was unaware of how very angry he was until his wife, Amy, finally refused to have sex with him anymore. He was completely surprised when Amy told him that she had gone to the doctor because she was in such pain. The doctor told her that her vaginal walls had been torn and were so damaged that she needed to abstain from intercourse for several weeks in order to let them heal, and that she should not allow her husband to be that forceful.

When Carl realized how much he had hurt his wife he vowed to be more gentle. After several weeks, Amy felt that she was ready to resume having sex with Carl, especially since he was determined to change. But Carl soon discovered that change was not so easy. He would start out being gentle but before he realized it he was being rough again. Amy was beginning to be more assertive and would tell him now when he was hurting her. It got so bad for Carl that he didn't even want to try to have sex with Amy for fear of hurting her.

Carl realized that he needed some help and came to me for sex therapy. As it turned out, Carl was not really angry with his wife but with his mother and sisters, who had dominated him when he was a boy. Determined to never allow another woman to control him, throughout his dating years Carl always chose women he could dominate, in and out of bed. Amy was no exception. From the beginning she had passively allowed Carl to run things and their marriage seemed from all outward appearances to be a good one. But Amy was so passive that she had allowed Carl to nearly rape her each time they had sex and she never complained.

Once Carl was able to pinpoint the source of his anger he was halfway there. "I've been taking all my anger at my controlling mother and sisters out on Amy, who has never tried to control me. It just isn't fair. She is such a sweet person, she doesn't deserve this kind of treatment."

Carl still needed to express his long-repressed feelings of anger and rage toward his mother and sisters. We did some of this work in my office, with Carl having an imaginary conversation with first his mother and then his sisters. After Carl had said the things he had always wanted to say to them he found he was far less angry.

Unexpressed rage can affect our sexuality in other ways as well. John came to see me because at twenty-five he had been sexually impotent all his life. I suspected he was extremely angry from the first moment I saw him. His tense jaw, his clenched teeth, his rigid posture, and his clipped, short way of talking all showed anger. In fact, he seemed so tense and angry that I was a little concerned about my own safety at first.

After several difficult sessions, I was finally able to discover that John was very angry with his mother. Although he wouldn't go into too many details, he did say that she was an alcoholic and that he blamed her drinking for his parents' divorce. John had loved his father very much and never seemed to get over being away from him.

As time went by John was able to tell me more and more about his feelings toward his mother. It turned out that John hated his mother and was so enraged with her that she was lucky he hadn't tried to hurt her. They did have some battles, both verbal and physical, when he was a teenager, but John had stopped fighting with her entirely after a very upsetting experience.

John had come home from school one afternoon to find his mother drunk as usual and in a particularly foul mood. She started arguing with him and they ended up in a knock-down, drag-out fight. During the battle, John got on top of his mother to hold her down and to his absolute shock he got an erection. He was so horrified that he got up and ran out of the house. That was the last time he even argued with his mother. Instead, he completely withdrew from her and became extremely passive in her presence to avoid any kind of altercation.

Afraid of what he might do if he were to express any of his angry feelings directly toward his mother, John became emotionally and physically impotent. He clearly needed to find a safe, constructive way of releasing his anger toward his mother in order for him to feel safe enough to express his sexuality. Although he initially resisted this idea, eventually John was able to talk openly with me about his anger toward his mother. With some of his anger unleashed, John felt less and less afraid of what he would do with his pent-up anger. As time went on and more and more of John's anger was expressed, he was able to take back more of his power—which, in turn, caused him to feel less resentful and less victimized by women in general. Before John ended therapy he was able to not only have a successful sexual relationship with a woman but an intimate, caring one as well.

SOURCES OF ANGER

Parental Modeling

Children sense the kind of relationship their parents have and form impressions about love relationships from what they see lived out in front of them day after day. As a result of such experiences, they can conclude either "Marriage is rewarding" or "Marriage is destructive."

When parents model constructive ways of resolving conflicts and encourage open discussions, the child learns that confrontation doesn't wipe out love and commitment. When a child is encouraged to express his anger he doesn't grow up repressing his anger and then channeling it through sex.

On the other hand, if a child's parents had heated, prolonged, or destructive arguments that frightened or overwhelmed him, he is likely to not only repress his anger but to believe that marriage and relationships are frightening and should be avoided.

Childhood Abuse and Neglect

When a child, adolescent, or adult is victimized, that person is full of rage at having been violated, betrayed, or neglected. As we have seen, sometimes this rage is then turned against all future sexual partners in the form of domination, force, and aggression.

Sometimes, as in Carl's situation, the need to dominate takes the form of always choosing a passive sexual partner who allows the more dominant one to dictate exactly when and how they will have sex. At other times the person who was abused actually rapes those he or she dates—or even those the person supposedly cares about. At still other times the abused person seeks out relationships with those who are involved with sadomasochism. All of these forms of domination are reenactments of earlier childhood abuse.

On the other hand, sometimes anger is expressed by withdrawal or passive-aggressiveness. Those who are still angry at their parents for being neglectful or abusive may grow up to silently resent their partners, viewing them more as parents than as mates. This kind of displaced anger can cause sexual dysfunction or lack of sexual desire.

Exercise—Who Are You Angry With?

If you are to successfully clear up your repressed and suppressed anger you will need to first become aware of what you are still angry about. This exercise will help you to discover this.

1. Make a list of all the people you feel anger toward. Include those from your past as well as those in your present life.

2. Now assign a number to each person on your list, number one being the person you are most angry with. Those people numbered one through three are the ones you need to work on releasing your anger toward first.

GETTING PAST YOUR FEAR OF YOUR ANGER

The reason we tend to either suppress, repress, or displace our anger is because we have been raised to believe that anger is a negative emotion, capable of causing us to hurt others and ourselves. For many, anger can be the most threatening and frightening of all the emotions. And yet anger in itself is not a negative emotion at all. It is what we choose to do or not do with our anger that makes it positive or negative.

For many people, expressing anger means losing control. They are afraid that once they start venting their anger they will "go crazy" or hurt someone. Ironically, it is the person who represses his anger who is much more likely to lose control, to become destructive, or to have his rage erupt in inappropriate ways and at inappropriate times. The following exercise will help you with your fear of losing control of your anger.

Gradual Release Exercise

1. Get into a comfortable position, take some deep breaths, and close your eyes.

2. Visualize your anger as steam that has built up in some pipes. Imagine that the steam (anger) has filled the pipes almost to the bursting point (losing control).

3. Slowly let some of the steam out of the pipes by carefully and gradually opening a valve. Allow only a small amount of steam out at a time. Eventually all the steam will be released and no pipes will burst. Your anger is the steam building up inside of you. If you release your anger a little at a time, you will not lose control.

Sentence Completion Exercise

Without planning your answers, complete the following sentences until you have no more responses:

- Losing control means . . .
- I am afraid to release my anger because . . .
- I don't want to release my anger because . . .

WAYS OF CONSTRUCTIVELY RELEASING YOUR ANGER

Learning to release your anger will prevent the buildup of resentment and help release the physical and emotional tension that has sapped you of your energy—energy that could otherwise be used to feel and express love, compassion, and sexuality.

There are many, many ways of releasing anger constructively. Below are just a few examples of effective anger-release techniques.

Verbalizing Anger

- Have an imaginary conversation with the person you are angry with. Tell that person exactly how you feel; don't hold back anything.
- Pretend the person you are angry with is sitting in a chair across from you. It may help to put a picture of the person on the chair. Now talk to the empty chair or the picture and "tell off" that person.
- Express your feelings of anger into a tape recorder.

Anger Letters

One of the most effective ways of releasing suppressed anger is to write letters to those you are angry with. This letter is intended for releasing anger, not for mailing, although you may choose to do so later. Here are some tips to help make your letters as effective as possible:

- Make statements in your letters instead of asking questions such as "How could you . . . ?" or "Why did you . . . ?" It is too easy to hide your anger behind the questions and they tend to help maintain your role as a victim. Instead make "I" statements such as "I'm angry with you for what you did" or "I don't like what you did."

• Be assertive and direct. Don't censor yourself by trying to be "nice" or reasonable. State how you really feel.

Dealing with Your Everyday Anger

Of course, the more effective way to release suppressed anger that has built up in a relationship is to express it to your partner directly. If you have been reluctant or afraid to do so, the above exercises can serve as a "rehearsal," preparing you for the real thing.

Your anger need not be about big things in order for it to affect your relationship negatively. Sometimes little things, like habits that your partner has that bother you, or inconsideration on the part of your partner, can continuously irritate or hurt you to the point that it begins to affect your feelings for your partner.

Certainly if there have been acts of betrayal, neglect, or abuse on the part of your partner it is vital that you find a way to communicate your anger and any other feelings you have about the incident or incidents in order for you to regain the sense of trust necessary for closeness.

FEAR—THE PARALYZING EMOTION

I refer to fear as the paralyzing emotion because more than any other emotion it tends to immobilize us and cause us to become so tense and rigid that we sometimes cannot function sexually. For example, newcomers to sex are often so terrified of the act itself that they are unable to function. Boys as well as girls have been known to be so frightened of pregnancy that their sexual feelings become deadened. Those who have been sexually abused or raped become immobilized with fear when even the slightest suggestion of sexuality is foisted upon them. And those who have been hurt in love often become numbed to their sexual feelings—so afraid are they of being hurt again, as it was with Iris:

"After my divorce I couldn't feel anything sexually for over two years. I had been so devastated by my husband leaving me that I was afraid I could never trust another man again. After about six months I started to date a little, but I could never bring myself to become sexual with any of the men."

When we begin to fear sexual encounters instead of looking forward to them, we begin to censor ourselves. Instead of letting our sexuality flow freely we begin to focus on performance more than pleasure. Our feelings about our sexuality become tainted and overshadowed by our fears.

SOURCES OF FEAR

Parental Influence

It is not surprising that parents would pass on to their children information about sex that is based on their own sexual experiences. Joellen shared with me the following:

"My mother had told me such horror stories about sex—about how men are rough and insensitive to their wives and about how horrible the wedding night is. Because of these stories I was scared out of my mind on my wedding night. My husband, who is actually the opposite of all the men my mother told me about, had to hold me all night while I cried, I was so scared. For weeks he kept reassuring me that he would be gentle but I couldn't even unlock my legs I was so frightened. Fortunately, my husband is a very patient and kind man and in time I finally relaxed enough to get over my fears."

Sebastian's father had been extremely wild when he was a young boy. He had to quit high school and join the navy when he was only seventeen because he had made two girls in the town pregnant and he was afraid of their fathers. While in the navy he became infected with gonorrhea and syphilis from his continual escapades.

When Sebastian entered puberty, his father sat him down and warned him about what could happen to him if he wasn't careful. His intention, of course, was to prevent Sebastian from suffering the way he had, but the end result was that Sebastian became afraid to have sex. He was so afraid of having the horrible things happen to him that happened to his father that he kept putting off having sex until he became self-conscious about still being a virgin. When he first saw me he was twenty-three and convinced that if he tried to have sex with a girl now she would laugh at him for being a virgin or for being so inexperienced.

The therapy I provided Sebastian consisted mostly of providing him accurate information regarding sex—including methods of contraception, ways to protect himself from contracting venereal disease, and distinguishing between recreational sex and sex as part of a caring, intimate relationship. With this information under his belt, and with the freedom to talk openly about his fears, Sebastian was finally able to get over his fears of sex.

Old Wives' Tales

Many people's fear of sex begins because of the misinformation they are told by their friends as they are growing up. These are some of the many stories I have heard through the years:

"When I was a teenager some friends told me that females have teeth inside of their vagina and they can bite off your penis if you don't please them. Needless to say, my first sexual experiences were incredibly frightening for me. And even though I finally cleared up this misconception, to this day I still focus too much attention on pleasing the woman."

"My friends told me that you can get stuck inside of a woman if you get too excited—like dogs do. I lived in fear of this for about four years until someone finally set me straight. Even so, I still tend to hold back and not get too sexually aroused. Incredible, isn't it?"

Fear Based on Religious Messages

Some children who are raised in highly religious families are given the message that sex is evil and should never be engaged in except for procreation. They are lectured to about the "wages of sin" and about the "evil of sex" so much that they begin to connect sex with sin. When they first begin to feel sexual feelings, instead of welcoming them, they view them as temptations by the devil and therefore try to ignore such feelings.

Over time, these repressed sexual feelings can become distorted and exaggerated and can actually cause people to act out sexually in ways that are dangerous, harmful, or against the law, as Hugh did:

"I was raised to believe that sex was a sin and so when I began to have sexual feelings and became interested in girls I became very afraid. I was fearful that if I allowed these feelings to take over I would lose control and become a sinner, so I held these feelings in check. All during high school I distracted myself from my sexual feelings by being very active in school activities, sports, and church.

"I married my college sweetheart and she and I were both virgins on our wedding night. I felt proud of both of us for living a healthy, Christian life and thought our lives together would be blessed. Unfortunately, somewhere along the way something had happened to me as a result of all that sexual repression.

"As an adolescent, I developed a rich and exciting fantasy life as a way of controlling my sexual urges. While I felt somewhat guilty about these fantasies, I felt that as long as I wasn't engaging in sex I was not sinning. My sexual fantasies always involved the forbidden—whether it was having sex with a married person, a child, or an animal.

"I assumed all these fantasies would go away once I was married and actually having sex. For the first months of my marriage I was so excited to actually be having sex that the fantasies did subside. But actual sex with my wife never seemed as exciting as my fantasies were, so I reverted back to them. Eventually, neither sex with my wife nor my fantasies were satisfying me and I began to act out my fantasies.

"I began by picking up young prostitutes along Hollywood Boulevard. The more illegal and illicit the sex was, the more exciting it was for me. I was finally arrested one night for picking up a girl who turned out to be only sixteen years old. This finally made me realize that I needed help. I had risked my marriage, my family, my job, and even my health because of my constant need for more and more exciting sex."

Fear of Rejection

Misinformation is not the only cause of sexual fear. Some people are so afraid of rejection that they are unable to make a move toward someone sexually, as it was with Roberto:

"When I was eighteen years old I fell madly in love with a young woman I was dating. I thought I wanted to spend the rest of my life with her. She was so beautiful, so intelligent, and so talented that I was intimidated by her. We dated for several months but I just couldn't bring myself to do anything more than kiss her good night. I guess she finally got tired of waiting for me to make my feelings clear and she stopped seeing me. Looking back on it, I realize now that she was giving me every indication that she wanted me to go further but I was just petrified she would reject me."

The fear of rejection is a common fear affecting our sexuality. Men and women alike are afraid that they will disappoint their lovers and then be rejected. This performance anxiety is partly due to the enormous amount of pressure put on both sexes to be sexual gymnasts as well as to be perfect physical specimens. But often fears of rejection go deeper than our attempts to meet the expectations presented by the media. Sometimes a fear of rejection can come from having experienced rejection when one was a child or adolescent, as it did with Todd:

"By the time I reached the age when I was supposed to begin dating I already felt so rejected by my parents and peers that it was literally impossible for me to ask a girl out. I simply did not have the self-esteem necessary to take such a tremendous risk. My father was an alcoholic who spent more time in the bar than he did at home and my mother was the kind of woman who just shouldn't have had kids. She resented having to take care of us and made it very evident by her attitude toward us. We were just a burden to her—just another chore to get through.

"Because I felt so rejected by both my parents, I had no confidence at school. Of course, this made me a sitting duck for ridicule by the other kids. I guess when you know your parents don't care about you it's pretty difficult to think that anyone else would, either. Even when someone was nice to me I was so afraid of rejection that I was afraid to trust their intentions."

Todd's experience is not uncommon. Children who experience continual rejection, especially by parents, grow up assuming they will be rejected by others and are often unable to become close to others.

Fear of Intimacy

And finally, there is the opposite problem—that of being afraid of intimacy. This fear also tends to go back to early childhood, to a child's first intimate relationship—the relationship with one's parents, most notably one's mother. If your parents were overly controlling, possessive, or smothering, your fear may be that if you become intimate with someone you will be smothered by her or him as you were as a child.

Those who were abused as children will be terribly afraid of intimacy, especially those who were sexually abused. To survivors of abuse, intimacy means intrusion or abuse.

And last, but certainly not least, those who have "lost themselves" in past relationships by giving up their interests, friends, and dreams in order to please their partner will be fearful of future relationships.

HOW TO COPE WITH FEAR

Unfortunately, unlike our other emotions, there are no ways to "release," "ventilate," or "let go of" our fear. Instead, we can only recognize it, own it, and—above all—not hide from it. Fear, perhaps more than nearly any other emotion, must not and cannot be ignored. But by facing it, looking for its causes, and acknowledging it, you will, in fact, be going in the direction of alleviating it.

Sometimes, of course, we can talk ourselves out of being afraid by trying to be logical and by giving ourselves information that will counter our fears. But at other times, nothing will soothe or diminish our fears. Instead we may need to focus our energies on discovering the reasons for our fears. This is especially true of our sexual fears.

ENVY AND JEALOUSY
Envy

When we are feeling envious we are, in fact, expressing a deep longing for and despair at ever receiving the good things of life. It grows out of the fear that we will never possess the things we admire or want. Envy begins with the recognition of something good—another person, a material object, the beauty of nature, a personality trait. The very thing that attracts us makes us feel the absence of it in our own lives.

This lack of hope then leads to envy. This means that if you lack any hope of ever having what someone else has you are bound to become envious. Once you are envious of someone you can't help but become angry because to envy someone is to begrudge what he or she has and to look at the person with malice or resentment.

Tess fell in love with Wylie because he possessed those qualities that she lacked or imagined she lacked. He was assertive, successful, gregarious, and physically strong. Tess, on the other hand, tends to be passive, has been unable to find or explore her talents, is shy around others, and is physically weak. They got married and Tess went about the task of pleasing Wylie and making him happy, the way she had been raised. She continually built him up, admiring him for his success and strength and telling others how wonderful he was. Sexually she admired his assertiveness and his physical strength.

But after the newness of the relationship wore off Tess found that she felt bored and empty just being a good wife. She wanted to do more with her life but she didn't feel competent enough to explore her talents. The more hopeless she felt about ever becoming successful and actualized herself, the more she began to resent the very traits in her husband she had once admired. Sexually, she began to resent his assertiveness and began to experience it as aggressiveness, his strength as abusive. She no longer received any sexual pleasure out of being submissive and instead began to complain that Wylie was being too rough, that he was hurting her, or that he was being insensitive. Secretly, she wanted to become more aggressive sexually; she wanted to be on top but she was too afraid to say so.

In time Tess began to feel repulsed by her husband and didn't want to have anything to do with him sexually. While she still submitted to his advances from time to time she became deadened to any sexual feelings. Instead she just "serviced" him and despised him all the more.

All of this was caused by the fact that Tess wanted to experience the freedom her husband experienced in the world and possess the qualities he possessed but felt hopeless about ever attaining them. Instead, her envy caused her to hate him for having what she wanted.

Tess's case is not unusual. Envy often interferes with our sexual feelings toward our lover or mate, as it did with Jim:

"My girlfriend and I are both aspiring singers but lately she has begun to get a few breaks while I am still struggling to make it. Recently I've noticed that I don't feel as turned on to her, especially right after she has had a gig."

After talking about it for a while, this client began to realize that his envy of his girlfriend's success was the cause of his lack of sexual desire for her. Once he was able to admit this to himself, and eventually to talk it over with his girlfriend, he was once again able to feel sexual with her.

While it is tempting to say that more women envy men than men envy women, this is not necessarily true. Men certainly do have more power and influence and women certainly have and still do feel hopeless at ever achieving the amount of freedom, wealth, and power that men possess. And women do, in fact, envy the amount of power men have. But I have been surprised at the number of male clients I have had who envy women in spite of their obvious handicaps in this and most societies.

Jared was a case in point. He believed that "the hand that rocks the cradle rules the world," an expression that he often heard from his mother as he was growing up. Jared saw women as all powerful. He perceived them as being far more intelligent than men and as able to manipulate men into getting whatever they wanted. On the other hand, Jared saw men as weak, powerless to women, and so stupid that they allowed women to control them. Time after time Jared would tell me, "Women have all the control because men will do anything to get a woman in bed and the women know it. They can get anything out of a guy if they just smile seductively or flirt a little." It was clear that Jared didn't want to give women this power over him.

How did Jared deal with the fact that he saw men in this way, especially given that he himself was a male? He became completely impotent. His relationships with women were confined to "friendships" even though he secretly fell in love with each of his close women friends. Because he felt so hopeless about ever being able to perform sexually, he saw himself as more and more inadequate compared to his women friends. He allowed them to use him, to take advantage of him financially—in other words, to walk all over him. In turn, he became more and more envious of their power and more and more enraged with them.

HOW ENVY CAN BECOME A CATALYST FOR CHANGE

Envy reveals our own emotional wounds to us. If we can begin to recognize that at its core envy is a rejection of the self, we can begin to make a major shift in our attitude. This shift in attitude needs to include the following ideas:

1. We must see envy for what it is and begin to allow our envy to reveal to us those needs and desires within us. What needs within you long for satisfaction? Direct your needs to positive and constructive action.

2. We must recognize that as humans we will always be incomplete.

3. We must see how envy plays itself out in daily life and recognize the signs.

4. We must refocus from seeing good as always being "out there" to seeing good inside ourselves.

5. We must learn to forgive our envy so we can be more open to seek the good things that are already within us and to feel gratitude even if we don't have all that we want. Envy is the dark side of gratitude. If gratitude is absent, envy is always present. As our experience and appreciation of good expands, envy will decrease.

Jealousy

Jealousy differs from envy in several ways. First of all, when we are feeling jealous there are three parties involved (the subject, the object whom the subject loves, and a third party who threatens to take away the loved one). On the other hand, when we are feeling envy there are only two parties—the subject and the object.

Envy is the pain you feel when you see someone else with what you want. Jealousy is the fear that you will lose what you have.

People with low self-esteem and a poor self-image are more likely to be jealous lovers. Since they see everyone else as being more attractive and more worthy, they can't understand why their mates have chosen them or how those mates could possibly remain faithful when there are so many more worthy (beautiful, sexy, rich, talented) people to choose from.

This is the struggle that Lee Ann had. Her husband, Bob, was an extremely attractive man who tended to be friendly toward everyone. Although Lee Ann was also attractive, she had very low self-esteem and so no matter how often she was told she was pretty, she just couldn't take it in and really believe it. Instead, she focused on her faults and saw every woman as a potential threat to her marriage. Since Bob tended to be so friendly, they were constantly fighting. She would accuse him of flirting and he would become angry at her accusations. Although he tried to reassure her over and over that he didn't want anyone else, that he was happy with her, Lee Ann just couldn't be reassured.

Eventually, Lee Ann's jealousy began to seriously threaten her marriage. By the time they began marriage counseling, Bob had already left Lee Ann twice. "I feel like I am in prison," he told Lee Ann at their first session. "I feel as if I can't even be friendly to another woman without you having a fit. I just can't live this way."

While some couple sessions did help Lee Ann and Bob to vent their feelings, Lee Ann really needed individual therapy in order to discover the cause of her jealousy and low self-esteem. If you also suffer from jealousy, it would be wise for you to try to continue to gain insight into the causes for your lack of self-esteem and self-confidence. This self-focus will be the key to overcoming your problems with jealousy.

Unfortunately, because sex has always been and will continue to be forbidden, because most of us are not allowed to explore our sexuality freely and develop sexually at our own pace, but are either strongly criticized by parents for being sexual or are thrust into the adult world of sexuality before we are emotionally and physically able to handle it, most of us have a distorted view of sexuality. Sex has become all mixed up with sin, power, anger, fear, guilt, and shame. When we express ourselves sexually we are often also expressing another emotion along with it, when we experience sexual release we are often also experiencing the release of an emotion—whether it be anger, fear, or a need to feel powerful.

Chapter Ten

BEGIN TO MAKE
ESTEEM-ENHANCING CHOICES

If you really want to raise your sexual self-esteem you must begin to make esteem-enhancing choices—that is, choices that make you feel good about yourself and your sexuality and thus raise your self-esteem rather than choices that rob you of your self-esteem because they make you feel bad about yourself. Some examples of esteem-enhancing choices are:

- Choosing partners who make you feel good about yourself.
- Choosing to have equal relationships.
- Choosing sexual activities that are fulfilling, erotic, and sensual without making you feel shame or guilt afterward.
- Examining the effects pornography has on you and your relationships.
- Choosing sexual fantasies that are esteeming, not degrading.

CHOOSING PARTNERS WHO MAKE YOU FEEL GOOD ABOUT YOURSELF

As we discussed in Part I, if the people you choose as sexual partners do not treat you with respect and caring, but instead are critical, demanding, controlling, or even abusive, you are likely to feel bad about yourself afterward. And when you are with someone who criticizes your body (either directly or by implication) or your sexual performance, who blames his or her sexual inadequacies on you, or is rejecting afterward, you will end up feeling bad about yourself sexually.

Because of your low self-esteem you may have tended in the past to allow others to select you instead of actively choosing those with whom you wish to get involved.

For example, many women believe that they are supposed to remain passive, waiting for a partner to select them. The very idea of being the one to actively select a potential partner seems foreign to them and suggests that if they have to go looking it is because no one wants them.

In fact, we do choose our sexual partners, whether we do it consciously or unconsciously, actively or passively. Assessing the characteristics of those partners you have chosen in the past can be very revealing. As you take the time to go over your personal history of relationships you will notice that certain patterns are revealed. Often the unresolved issues we have with our parents or other significant caretakers get played out in the adult relationships we establish.

Getting to the Core of the Problem—Problem Parents

Some people unconsciously choose partners who are very much like their neglectful or abusive parents, who emotionally deprived them, were overly critical of them, or were extremely controlling or possessive of them.

While there isn't room in this book for an in-depth exploration of the different types of emotionally abusive parents, the following brief descriptions will help you to discover whether one or both of your parents are models for your attraction to those who treat you poorly.

THE POSSESSIVE PARENT

The possessive parent wants to control, own, and consume the child. She or he begins when the child is an infant, overprotecting her, holding her so close that the child may feel suffocated. When the child reaches the age where she wants to begin exploring the world separate from her parent, the possessive parent feels threatened and clings to the child even tighter. This behavior continues

162 · RAISING YOUR SEXUAL SELF-ESTEEM

throughout childhood, with the parent feeling jealous of anything and anyone that threatens to take away the child.

For example, the parent may discourage the child from making friends by always finding fault with each of the child's playmates. Instead of beginning to loosen the reins a little bit as the child becomes older and more mature, the parent may become even more strict, insisting on knowing at all times where the child is going and with whom. When the child begins to take an interest in dating the parent may become especially threatened and may either forbid the child to date or make her feel that no one is good enough for her.

Many fathers find having a daughter a very satisfying and rewarding experience until she reaches adolescence. Then he must deal with his daughter's sexuality and curb any incestuous thoughts he may have. Oftentimes a father is possessive of his daughter because he is sexually aroused by her and wants no other man to have her. He will forbid his daughter to date or will be horrified when she wears anything that is the slightest bit revealing.

Some parents' possessiveness comes from a need to protect their children from harm. Perhaps because they themselves were sexually abused as children, they may assume that all men are capable of sexually molesting their daughters. Some men who have these impulses themselves or who have been promiscuous or used women sexually assume that every boy who dates their daughters is going to use them sexually.

Other parents do not want their children to grow up because they want them to be available to take care of their needs. These parents may not have gotten their needs met by their mothers or spouses and may in turn expect their daughter to meet those unmet needs. Others become too attached to their children because they are widowed, divorced, or having difficulties with their spouse. If a father treats his daughter like a confidante or friend, he is being abusive. It is not a daughter's role to make her father feel good, or listen to his problems (sexual and otherwise).

THE OVERCONTROLLING PARENT
Overcontrolling parents will attempt to control not only their children but their spouses as well. They behave in inflexible, even cruel ways, expecting everyone in the family to bow down to them and do as they say. These parents believe strongly in rules and obe-

dience and that parental authority should never be questioned—no matter what. They attempt to dominate their children completely, needing to feel in control over others in order to feel powerful and important. Often raised by overcontrolling parents themselves, they are often ventilating the anger they could not express to their own parents onto their children.

A child growing up with an overcontrolling parent hears a barrage of commands, orders, and suggestions about anything and everything—what foods to eat, how to eat them, what clothes to wear, what classes to take in school, what boys or girls to date. She or he will not be allowed to make independent decisions and any that they do manage to make will always be considered wrong.

Shannon's father had to be in control of everything that went on in the household: "My mother and I couldn't do anything without checking with Dad first. We had to ask permission to buy clothes and then when we returned from a shopping trip he had to see all the receipts. He always had to meet all my friends and when I got older he would interrogate my boyfriends before he'd let me go out with them. He was the one who decided what college I went to and even what I majored in."

THE ABANDONING, REJECTING PARENT

Parents can abandon their children *physically* (leaving them solely in the care of baby-sitters, leaving the child home alone, having the child wait in the car for hours at a time, forgetting to pick up a child at the movies, or, because of a divorce, leaving the house and seldom seeing the child again) or *emotionally* (being emotionally unavailable to the child, depriving their children of the necessary attention, affection, and encouragement they need).

Parents who escape into alcohol, drugs, sleep, television, or books also abandon their children because they are essentially not there for them emotionally. Nathan told me the painful story of how it felt to be raised by a mother who was detached from him. "My mother is just never present, if you know what I mean. You just can't connect with her. When I was a child it was extremely painful to be around her because I always felt so empty and alone even in her presence. She didn't take an interest in anything I did or listen to anything I ever said. She reminded me of a ghost sometimes, kind of floating around, never really touching ground. Most of the time she had her head stuck in a book, off in some fantasy world. In many ways I feel like I never had a mother. Instead I had this robot who would cook for us and clean the house and do the laundry but couldn't really talk to us or hold us."

Many fathers, while physically present in the home, are passive and not actively involved with their children. Marta describes her relationship with her father as a "nonrelationship": "He was there, but he seldom talked to me except to say good night or to nod if my mother told him something about me. He just wasn't interested in me or what I was doing. I knew I wasn't important to him, I was just a mouth to feed."

In addition to being unresponsive, some parents are also unaffectionate. Carly shared with me: "I can't remember my father hugging or kissing me. Even to this day he seems very uncomfortable with affection. I hugged him at my graduation from college and he stiffened up so much that I felt terribly rejected and embarrassed.

"I loved my father and couldn't understand why my love for him wasn't returned. I kept wondering what was wrong with me and I kept trying to be a better daughter so he'd love me." Not having her father's time, attention, or direction, Carly felt worthless and assumed that there was something wrong with her, otherwise her father would have wanted to be with her.

Exercise—Discovering Your Patterns

• Divide a piece of paper into thirds by making two vertical lines and thus creating three columns.

• Head the first column with the name of your most recent relationship, the second with the word *Mother* and the third with the word *Father*. (If you were not raised by your mother or your father substitute the name of the person who raised you, or other significant caretakers.)

• Under each column list the most significant characteristics of each person. You may include personality traits and physical characteristics.

• Now compare your three lists. Does the person you have most recently been involved with share many of the characteristics of one or both of your parents? The chances are very high that there are many similarities between your recent partner and one of your parents, most likely the parent that you least admire or have had the most difficulty with.

• Now repeat this exercise with a new piece of paper and the names of three of your most significant relationships. Once again you'll probably find two things: some similarities between the people you have been involved with and similarities between each partner and one or both of your parents.

Who Do You Tend to Get Involved With?

ABUSERS

Those with low sexual self-esteem often become involved with those who abuse them emotionally, physically, or sexually. Feeling that they do not deserve any better, those with low self-esteem tend to put up with abusive behavior from their partners far longer than those who value themselves and perceive themselves as deserving of kindness, consideration, and respect.

There are several reasons why you may seem to repeatedly find yourself in abusive situations—and why you stay in them too long. The most notable reasons are these:

• You are used to being treated poorly.

If you have been consistently treated poorly in your life, either by parents, other caretakers, previous lovers, or friends, you may have come to the conclusion that this is the way life is or that you do not deserve to be treated well.

• You had poor modeling by your parents and other caretakers.

As we discussed earlier, if you saw one parent treating the other poorly, showing little respect or caring, you may have grown up repeating their pattern, believing that that is the way all men/women treat their partners, or reenacting their drama.

• You are reenacting earlier abuse.

If you were abused or neglected as a child, the ensuing damage to your self-esteem has more than likely caused you to underestimate your abilities and desirability; created difficulties with intimacy and closeness in your relationships; or made you overly dependent, possessive, and smothering; *and* has given you a problem with control to the point of aggressivity or passivity. Those who were abused or neglected as children tend to grow up to be either victimizers or victims, either repeating the pattern of their childhood abuse by abusing those who are close to them or by letting others abuse them.

Whether you are the victim or the abuser your relationships will tend to follow a pattern that closely resembles your original abuse. Survivors of sexual abuse even tend to choose partners who resemble their abuser both emotionally and physically, often getting involved with someone who is of the same age, in a similar occupation, and has some of the same mannerisms and similar behaviors of their abuser. Or they may find lovers who resemble themselves as a child and proceed to treat them as they were treated by the abuser. These abusive relationships tend to confirm the survivor's belief that relationships must be abusive.

What Is Abusive Behavior?

Oftentimes we are being abused without knowing it or being abusive without realizing that we have actually crossed over the line. Since we all have a tendency to deny our own or a loved one's abusive behavior, the following descriptions can help you to recognize your own or your partner's abusive behavior, perhaps for the first time.

Emotional Abuse

Emotional abuse is any kind of abuse that is emotional rather than physical in nature. It can include anything from verbal abuse and constant criticism to more subtle tactics, such as intimidation, manipulation, and refusal to ever be pleased.

Emotional abuse is like brainwashing in that it systematically wears away at the victim's self-confidence, sense of self-worth, trust in her perceptions, and self-concept. Whether it is done by constant berating and belittling, by intimidation, or under the guise of "guidance" or "teaching," the results are similar. Eventually the recipient of the abuse loses all sense of self and all remnants of personal value.

The following is a description of many of the types of emotional abuse. You will readily recognize many of the behaviors on the list as abusive, but it may surprise you to discover some that you may not think of as abusive.

DOMINATION

People who dominate others need to be in charge, and they often will try to control another person's every action. They have to have their own way, and they will often resort to threats to get it.

When you allow yourself to be dominated by someone else, you begin to lose respect for yourself and you become silently enraged. Someone else is in control of your life, just as assuredly as if you were a slave doing what you were ordered to do. You are no longer the master of your own destiny.

VERBAL ASSAULTS

This set of behavior involves berating, belittling, criticizing, name-calling, screaming, threatening, blaming, and using sarcasm and humiliation. This kind of abuse is extremely damaging to the victim's self-esteem and self-image. Just as assuredly as physical violence assaults the body, verbal abuse assaults the mind and spirit, causing wounds that are extremely difficult to heal. Not only is this kind of abuse demeaning, it is frightening as well. When someone yells at us, we become afraid that they may also resort to physical violence.

ABUSIVE EXPECTATIONS

Here the abuser places unreasonable demands on you, and you are expected to put aside everything to satisfy his needs. This abuser demonstrates a constant need for your undivided attention, demands frequent sex, or requires you to spend all of your free time with him. But no matter how much time or attention you give, it is never enough; this person can never be pleased, because there is always something more you could have done. You are subjected to constant criticism, and you are constantly berated because you don't fulfill all of this person's needs.

EMOTIONAL BLACKMAIL

Emotional blackmail is one of the most powerful ways of manipulation. An emotional blackmailer either consciously or unconsciously coerces another person into doing what he or she wants by playing on that person's fear, guilt, or compassion. Women, in particular, are easily exploited because they tend to place others' wishes and feelings ahead of their own. They can be made to feel guilty simply for thinking of their own needs and feelings first.

You are being emotionally blackmailed when someone threatens to end a relationship if you don't give him what he wants, or when someone rejects you or distances himself from you until you give in to his demands. If someone gives you the "cold shoulder" whenever they are displeased with you, threatens to stop having sex with you if you don't do what they say, or uses other fear tactics to get you under control, they are using the tactic of emotional blackmail.

UNPREDICTABLE RESPONSES

In this type of abusive situation, the abuser has drastic mood swings or sudden emotional outbursts for no apparent reason, or gives inconsistent responses. Whenever someone in your life reacts very differently at different times to the same behavior from you, tells you one thing one day and the opposite the next, or frequently changes his or her mind (one day liking something you do and hating it the next), you are being abused with unpredictable responses.

The reason this behavior is damaging is that it causes you to feel constantly on edge. You are always waiting for the other shoe to drop, and you can never know what is expected of you. You must remain hypervigilant, waiting for the abuser's next outburst or change of mood.

An alcoholic or a drug abuser is likely to be extremely unpredictable, exhibiting one personality when sober and a totally different one when intoxicated or high. Living with someone who is like this is tremendously demanding and anxiety provoking, causing the abused person to feel constantly frightened, unsettled, and off balance.

CONSTANT CRITICISM

With someone who is unrelentingly critical of you, always finds fault, and can never be pleased, it is the insidious nature and cumulative effects of the abuse that do the damage. Over time, this type of abuse eats away at your self-confidence and sense of self-worth, undermining any good feelings you have about yourself and about your accomplishments or achievements. Eventually, you become convinced that nothing you do is worthwhile, and you may feel like just giving up.

CHARACTER ASSASSINATION

Character assassination occurs when someone constantly blows your mistakes out of proportion; gossips about your past failures and mistakes; tells lies about you; humiliates, criticizes, or makes fun of you in front of others; and discounts your achievements. In addition to the pain this behavior causes you personally, character assassination can ruin your personal and professional reputation, causing you to lose lovers, friends, and jobs.

GASLIGHTING

As in the movie of the same name, using a variety of insidious techniques, your antagonist makes you doubt your perceptions, memory, or your very sanity. He or she may accomplish this by continually denying that certain events occurred, by denying that they said something when in actuality they really did, or by insinuating that you are exaggerating, lying, or that you are a hypochondriac. The person may use gaslighting techniques as part of a deliberate plan to gain control over you, or it may just be a way of keeping you off balance, shifting the blame, or avoiding responsibility for his or her own actions.

CONSTANT CHAOS

Characterized by continual upheavals and discord, this behavior includes deliberately starting arguments, being in constant conflict with someone, and being "addicted to drama." Creating chaos provides excitement in such crisis-oriented people, and the "chaotic person" seems unable to enjoy harmony and peace. Instead he or she breaks forth with constant disruption and continual negative moods.

Physical Abuse

Any physical show of force for the purposes of intimidating, threatening, or controlling another person is physical abuse. Physical abuse includes slapping, hitting, punching, kicking, pushing, tripping, burning, biting, or pinching whenever it is done in anger.

Other acts of physical abuse include throwing objects at the person, using an object to hit a person, holding someone down, forcing someone to sit or lie in a certain position, forcing someone's arms behind his or her back, and pinning someone down. Face slapping, hair pulling, head banging, ear pulling, or shaking are also abusive.

No one has the right to physically abuse a partner *no matter what he or she has done to them*. It has been estimated that fifty percent of American women have been physically abused by their husbands or lovers, and many of these women were victims of either physical, sexual, or emotional abuse when they were children.

Women who are physically abused by their lovers or husbands usually turn off sexually. It is almost impossible to be physically hurt and emotionally terrorized and then get into bed with your abuser and enjoy a sexual relationship.

Men can also be physically abused by women, although this certainly does not occur as often as the other way around, mostly because of the superior physical strength of men. Those men who are physically abused by a female partner are also likely to have been abused as children, therefore having been set up for further abuse. These men, with damaged self-esteem, a fear of being alone, and a feeling that they deserve to be mistreated, often put up with physical abuse and do not fight back even though they may have the physical strength to do so.

Men are also physically abused by male partners with much the same dynamic occurring as in heterosexual couples. Again, even though the abused male may have the physical strength to fight back, he doesn't have the emotional strength.

Lesbian women have also been known to physically abuse one another. Sometimes the abusive partner is physically stronger than her victim, but at other times the inequality of power is emotional rather than physical.

Sexual Abuse (by a Partner)

We don't normally think of "sexual abuse" as applying to adults abusing other adults, but, in fact, that is exactly what occurs in some circumstances. It is not uncommon, particularly with a dominant male and a more passive female, for sexual abuse to occur in the relationship without either party actually defining it as such. It also occurs with alarming regularity in dating situations. Date rape, which is getting so much attention lately, is but one example of how sexual abuse occurs within the dating arena.

Sexual abuse can occur between two adults under the following circumstances:

1. When one person pressures the other into having sex by continual harassment.

The term "sexual harassment" is used most often with regard to work settings, but a woman or man can be sexually harassed by anyone, including a lover or spouse. Sexual harassment is defined as unwelcome sexual advances or physical or verbal conduct of a sexual nature. Whenever your partner pressures you into becoming sexual against your will, whether it is because you don't feel like being sexual at the time or because you don't want to engage in a particular sexual activity, you are being sexually harassed.

2. When one person physically forces another to have sex against her or his will.

Physically forcing a woman or man to have sex is called rape. This is true even if it is your spouse or lover who is doing the forcing. When you say no or don't consent to sex and your partner forces himself or herself on you by either holding you down or by forcing his or her body into yours—you are being raped. The same is true if you are gay or lesbian and your partner forces you to have sex.

3. When one person pressures the other into engaging in sexual acts that she or he finds distasteful or repulsive.

If your partner suggests a type of sexual activity to you and you express a lack of interest or are turned off to the idea, he or she should drop it. It is abusive for your partner to hound you or try to make you feel guilty for not doing what he or she wants.

4. When one partner treats the other as if she or he were a child or engages in "playacting"—pretending that their partner is a child and he or she is the adult.

While sex can certainly be fun, and being playful during sex can be a very healthy thing to do, pretending that one of you is a child and the other is an adult can be abusive, especially with a survivor of sexual abuse. It is a replay of the sexual abuse she or he sustained as a child and should be avoided.

UNAVAILABLE OR DISTANT PARTNERS

If you continually get involved with those who are un-available—because they are married, because they are incapable of intimacy, because they are gay, or because they are unwilling to commit to one person, you are constantly lowering your sexual self-esteem. Other types of distant or unavailable lovers are those who are depressed and unable to meet your needs or those who are profoundly narcissistic and refer everything back to themselves.

Unavailable or distant partners are not partners in the true sense. They do not and cannot bring equal sharing, intimacy, and commitment to the relationship.

A common response to having a distant partner is to pursue him or her, as Consuela did: "My boyfriend was terribly afraid of closeness. Each time we began to get close he would back away from me. I in turn would go after him, trying to bring him back. This happened time after time, until I finally decided I just couldn't take the merry-go-round anymore."

Once again, the source of your attraction to unavailable or dis-tant partners will more than likely be one or both of your parents.

ALCOHOLICS AND ADDICTS

If you have a pattern of being involved with alcoholics or those who are addicted to drugs, gambling, sex, or food, you will need to look closely into your own family history for the reason for your attraction. For example, a very high percentage, as much as eighty percent in some studies, of those raised in alcoholic homes will become chemically dependent themselves or will marry alco-holics or addicts. In addition, those who grew up in dysfunctional families were well trained to see dysfunctional ways of relating to others as being normal.

In addition to looking into your family history, you will also need to look at your own behavior in the present. Alcoholics, ad-dicts, and codependents tend to choose alcoholics or other addicts as partners.

Active alcoholics and addicts are simply not emotionally available for an intimate relationship and are incapable of meeting your emotional needs. The focus of their attention will always be on their addiction—whether it be the bottle or the drug, work or gambling, sex or eating.

You deserve a partner who treats you with kindness, respect, and consideration. And you deserve a partner who likes and appreciates your body, enjoys touching you and being touched by you, is sexually excited by you, wants to be with you, and wants to be both affectionate and sexual with you.

In the next section we will talk further about how you can work toward achieving such a relationship.

CHOOSING TO HAVE EQUAL RELATIONSHIPS

True intimacy is based on mutuality and equality. When there is a lack of equality in a relationship, one person has more power than the other. Equality means that neither partner has more power than the other.

Sources of Difficulties with Power

DISCIPLINE AND POWER

As we have discussed earlier, the way a child is disciplined has a tremendous impact on his or her sexual development. When a child is raised in an environment where discipline is fair, nonabusive, and intended for setting limits and teaching proper behavior, not as an outlet for parents' anger and need for control, children learn commitment, involvement, a respect for others' boundaries and limits, and mutual respect that carries into their sex life. A dominated child, on the other hand, may grow up to use sex to control others, making intercourse more like rape than something that is mutually enjoyable. Conversely, if a child is crushed by authoritarianism, he or she may become a sexual doormat.

Clint and Babette came into therapy because they were having terrible marital problems. As it turned out, Clint had been raised in an overly permissive household, which caused him to think only of his own needs. All during his dating years he "loved 'em and left 'em," never considering the girls' feelings either during an affair or when he broke it off. When he married Babette she loved him so much that she tolerated his selfishness, but as time went on, she began to get back at him by devious devices. By the time they entered therapy, their marriage bed had become an arena for ploys, counterploys, selfish victories, and hurtful defeats.

Hilary, on the other hand, grew up in the opposite kind of household. This is what she shared with me about her need to now be in control: "It's fun to get a guy going. It gives me a feeling of power over a man if I can get him aroused. Then I basically can make him do anything for me or give me whatever I want. I like that. I never had any control when I was a child and I guess that's why I need it so much now. My father ruled me with an iron thumb, controlling my every move. I guess in some ways I am getting back at him, doing the things I do with men. I guess I am saying, 'You aren't in control anymore, Dad, I am,' to every man I meet."

ROLE MODELS AND POWER

Many of us grew up watching one of our parents dominating the other. You might have seen and heard your father constantly putting your mother down while your mother silently took it. Or you might have heard your mother constantly complain to your father that he wasn't ever going to make anything of himself, that he was a lazy good-for-nothing who couldn't even support his family properly. Whatever it was that you grew up watching and listening to, your parents were your role models and thus provided you with a picture, however distorted, of what it is like to be in a relationship.

Take a good look at the way you and your partner interact. Are you treating her or him the way your father treated your mother, or vice versa? From what you know of your partner's parents, does it look like she or he is treating you the way her or his parents treated each other? Is there a pattern in the relationship, with one of you consistently being in control over the other one, or one of you being too critical of the other?

ABUSE AND POWER

Unfortunately, when one or both partners in a relationship

were victimized as children, there is seldom equality in the relationship. One person almost always has more power and is thus more in control than the other. If you were victimized as a child or if you are involved with someone who was abused as a child, the chances are very high that you have an unequal relationship with your partner.

A common reaction survivors of childhood abuse have is to be overly controlling and domineering. Because they had so little control in their childhood they tend to overcompensate and now need to be in control of others. Some survivors deliberately choose partners whom they can control or have power over.

Many people, especially males, who were sexually abused as children cope with that abuse by utilizing a form of denial called "identifying with the aggressor." When a young child refuses to acknowledge that he or she is being victimized at the time, but instead justifies or minimizes the behavior of the abuser, he or she will often grow up to be very much like the abuser, behaving in the same abusive ways.

Out of touch with their own feelings and with their own victimization, some survivors have in turn chosen to play the role of the victimizer in their relationships. Other survivors, extremely angry for having been victimized but afraid to confront those who victimized them, take their anger out on their partners. Still others are angry at the perpetrator but have generalized their rage to include "all men" or "all women."

Power Plays—Who Has Control in Your Relationships?

ASSESSING THE BALANCE OF POWER

Any good relationship is a relationship of equals. This means that both parties contribute equally to the relationship and that each is seen as an equal in the other's eyes. On the other hand, unhealthy relationships demonstrate an inequality of power created because one person feels superior to the other.

Which do you tend to be? Do you tend to be controlling, domineering, and critical, or do you tend to be more passive, less demanding, and more on the receiving end of criticism than on the giving end of it?

In some cases, we are talking about overt, extreme domination and abuse, but more than likely we are talking about more subtle forms of domination and control. Up to now, you and your partner might have settled into a rather comfortable and familiar way of dealing with one another. This does not mean, however, that your way of relating has been a healthy one for either one of you.

The following questions will help you examine just who has the most power in your relationship. This alone does not necessarily establish that you have an abusive relationship but answering the questions can help you spot any inequality that exists. Take some time to think seriously about the questions before you answer them.

• Who has the most personal power in the relationship, you or your partner? By "personal power" I mean who do you feel is the stronger of the two—in terms of being able to ask for what you want, in terms of being able to take care of yourself emotionally?

• Which one of you has the strongest need to be in control? Who usually gets his or her way in terms of choosing what you will do at any given time?

• Who has control over the finances?

• Who is most in control in your sexual relationship?

• Which one of you seems to be the least satisfied with your partner and with the relationship? Which one of you has the most complaints about not getting your needs met in the relationship? Which one of you is the most critical of the other one?

• Which one of you has the most self-confidence? Which one feels the best about himself or herself?

• Which one of you is the most successful in your career?

• Who makes the most money?

• Who would you say loves the other one the most?

• Who is the most emotionally dependent on the other? Which one of you would have the hardest time going on without the other one?

• Who would you say feels superior to the other one in the relationship?

If the answer to most of these questions was "me," you have the most power in the relationship and therefore probably control the relationship far more than your partner does. On the other hand, if you answered "my partner" to most of these questions, then your partner has the most power.

If You Tend to Have More Power in Relationships

If you've answered "me" to most of these questions you have more personal power than your mate. Are you abusing your power by controlling someone who is weaker than you? Did you choose your mate so you could feel powerful and in control? This was, in fact, the case with Ivan:

"I realize now, much to my dismay, that I chose to get involved with Teddy in the first place because she seemed so weak and helpless. Being around her made me feel great because it made me feel so much stronger than I really am. I was the strong one in the relationship, I was the one in charge for a change. Unfortunately, I didn't realize that I would begin to hate her for her weakness, just as I hate myself for my own. Once I was in the position of power I slowly began to misuse that power by demanding more and more from her, and by becoming more and more critical. In the meantime, I wasn't dealing with my own weaknesses and problems but compounding them because I was liking myself less and less the more abusive I became."

There are several reasons why people get involved with someone who is not an emotional equal:

- So they can control or have power over the other person.
- Because they have low self-esteem and they don't think a healthier, stronger person would want to be with them.
- Because they are afraid of rejection and so choose a person they don't think will reject them, who is either more needy than they are or has more problems.
- Because they can get away with being abusive—they know that a less powerful person will put up with their behavior.
- Because they are afraid of being alone.
- Because a less powerful partner is a reflection of how they really feel about themselves.
- Because they are repeating a pattern from their childhood of either treating their partner like one of their parents treated the other, or by treating their partner like they were treated by their parents.

THE PRICE OF TYRANNY

Whenever you try to control another person you are taking a

tremendous risk, and that risk is that the person you are controlling is going to resent you and eventually become enraged with you. Tyranny always has a price, either because the person you tyrannize will eventually rebel and retaliate, or because you will eventually come to hate yourself for using your power over someone.

Sex is a force that must be respected. It can be a creative and nurturing life urge—a way of expressing love, responsibility, and commitment—or it can be a weapon for control and exploitation. Sex is a very powerful force of and in itself. But when it becomes a way of handling other emotions, when it becomes a vehicle for other powerful forces, the energy behind it can become not only powerful but manipulative and abusive. When we channel our need to be in power through our sexuality we run the risk of becoming abusive.

THE PRICE OF PASSIVITY

It is as destructive to both yourself and your relationships to allow someone to dominate you as it is to be the one who is dominating. When you get involved with someone you perceive as being "better" than you are in some way—because he or she seems more intelligent, stronger, more successful, more attractive, or more powerful—you are setting yourself up to be controlled by that person.

Work Toward Becoming Sexually Assertive

If the adults in your life emotionally, physically, or sexually abused you as a child, you may now, as an adult, behave as if you have no rights over your own body, allowing others to touch you when you do not want to be touched or even to physically abuse you. You have the right to choose who can touch you and when, as well as what type of touch is acceptable to you. This does not refer to sexual touching only. If you do not like having your boss put his arm around you while he is talking to you, for example, you have the right to say something about it. Do it diplomatically at first, taking him aside and quietly telling him that it bothers you. But if he continues to do it, you have the right to tell him more firmly. No one, under any circumstances, has the right to touch you if you do not want to be touched! This includes doctors and nurses and even your partner. If a person's touch is bothering you, ask the person to do it differently.

You may also need to continue working on setting emotional boundaries. You may have allowed others to take over your life or otherwise control you, or you may have virtually "lost yourself" in others by becoming enmeshed in their lives. All of your energy and focus may have gone outward, toward others, so that you could anticipate and meet their needs.

Break Your Pattern of Being Either Abusive or Abused in Relationships

If you have come to realize that your relationship is indeed an unequal one and that you are either too aggressive or too passive with your partner, you will need once again to look to your child-hood for the answers. In an unconscious or sometimes even a con-scious attempt to undo or rewrite the past we come to believe that since we didn't get it right in the first place we must keep trying. We develop patterns of relating to people based on our futile at-tempts to master and change what has already happened.

Freud called this tendency to reenact the past the *repetition compulsion*, since we seem to be compelled to repeat our past—to do again and again what we have done before. Judith Viorst, in her classic book *Necessary Losses*, talks about this repetition com-pulsion: "Thus whom we love and how we love are revivals—unconscious revivals—of early experience, even when revival brings us pain . . . we will act out the same old tragedies unless awareness and insight intervene."

Misused, sex destroys human relationships; used responsibly, it can nourish and enrich. Continue to look at your own behavior for signs of dominance and submission. A healthy relationship is one between two equals, not one in which one partner is dominat-ing and controlling the other. If you find that you are either being abusive or being abused, don't judge yourself too harshly. Remem-ber that the chances are very high that you were either abused as a child or that you observed abusive behavior in your formative years and are thus repeating a pattern. Sometimes, just discovering that we are repeating such a pattern can help us to break it. While it will be difficult, catching yourself when you are being abusive or controlling, or when you are allowing your partner to abuse or control you, can help you change your behavior little by little.

For some, seeking professional help may be the answer. Changing patterns of behavior that are rooted in childhood abuse can often be a very difficult process unless you have some help.

The important thing is that you are honest with yourself and that you come out of denial about your behavior and its relationship to childhood abuse. With this connection in mind you can then work toward having equal relationships.

CHOOSING SEXUAL ACTIVITIES THAT ARE FULFILLING, EROTIC, AND SENSUAL WITHOUT MAKING YOU FEEL SHAME OR GUILT AFTERWARD

It makes sense that if you continue negative or esteem-robbing behavior it will only serve to make you feel worse and worse about yourself. This is especially true when it comes to participating in sexual activities that cause you to feel shame or guilt.

When you become involved in sexual behavior that causes you to feel bad about yourself you are both creating and perpetuating low sexual self-esteem. This kind of esteem-robbing behavior can be something you do only with yourself, such as excessive masturbation or having particular sexual fantasies, or it can involve another person or persons, such as extramarital affairs or sadomasochism. In either case, no matter how pleasurable a particular sexual behavior may be, if it goes against your own personal value system you will end up feeling guilt or shame and will thus lower your sexual self-esteem.

There is a big difference between avoiding a sexual activity because it is unacceptable to those who raised you, or it was deemed sinful by the leaders or rules of the religion you were raised in, and avoiding a sexual activity because you have personally come to believe that it is unacceptable. For example, while you may have been raised by either your parents or your church to believe that sex before marriage is wrong, if you have grown up to believe that premarital sex is not wrong for you, you are free to engage in premarital sex without guilt or shame. Having premarital sex does not go against your own personal value system and thus is not esteem-robbing for you.

Sex is esteem-enhancing (meaning that it shows respect, honor, and appreciation for the self) if it is done for any of the following reasons:

- To bring pleasure to yourself and your partner.
- To express affection and love.
- To explore new avenues of sensual and sexual pleasure.
- To express intimacy and connectedness.
- To release tension.

On the other hand, sex is esteem-robbing if it is used for any of the following purposes:

- As a tool of aggression (control, power, punishment, submission).
- As a way to punish yourself.
- As a reenactment of prior sexual abuse.
- As a means of manipulation or coercion, or as a way of earning money or favors.

In short, a sexual activity is a healthy, esteem-enhancing one if it makes you feel good about yourself, and it is an esteem-robbing one if it makes you feel guilty, ashamed, or disgusted with yourself.

The rule of thumb concerning consensual sex—that is, the idea that a sex act is acceptable as long as all parties consent to it and as long as it doesn't hurt anyone (including yourself)—can also be applied here. No matter how sexually stimulating a particular sexual practice is, no matter how intensely erotic, if the act involves harming another person in any way, you are eventually going to have to pay a heavy price for the activity in terms of your self-esteem.

Let's suppose that you are an exhibitionist, someone who becomes sexually aroused by exposing one's naked body or genitals to others or performing sexual acts in front of others. While this behavior may be extremely exciting to you and may seem harmless enough, it can in fact cause emotional damage both to yourself and those you expose yourself to.

While there is a double standard when it comes to whether it is a male or a female who is exposing the body, there is nevertheless a cloak of shame that covers the practice of exhibiting one's naked body to others for the purpose of sexually arousing them. Women who strip for men—whether they do it in a bar, in a pornographic movie, or in a magazine—are often doing so to get the attention they didn't get as children or because they were sexually abused as children. While they will defend their right to expose their bodies, particularly when they are being paid to do so, many of these women are completely out of touch with the fact that they have extremely low self-esteem and that by exposing their bodies to men, they are further lowering their self-esteem. While they may get a temporary feeling of excitement and gratification from knowing that so many men desire them and appreciate their bodies, this feeling is short-lived compared to the feelings of shame that gradually build up within them.

Male exhibitionists also suffer from low self-esteem but they, unlike most female exhibitionists, often have a psychological need to witness the shock on someone else's face when they expose their penis. This both validates their "maleness" and is a source of sexual arousal. Later, when the exhibitionist is safe from being caught, he will recall the pleasure he felt from the person's reaction and either masturbate or have sex with a partner while he is thinking about that reaction.

Unless you are a male stripper, it is against the law to expose yourself in public and so you are risking arrest each time you engage in the activity. This, coupled with the fact that you know you are going against society's rules, will almost guarantee that you will feel guilt or shame whenever you engage in this behavior. Second, it is against the law for a reason—namely, it can traumatize those who are forced to witness your behavior. Exhibitionists seldom realize just how traumatic it is to have someone suddenly expose himself to you against your will. At the very least it can be a shock to the person, causing a tremendous amount of anxiety and fear, and at the most it can actually traumatize a person to the point of needing psychological counseling for the incident, particularly if the person was sexually abused or raped in the past.

How to Stop Engaging in Esteem-Robbing Sex

There are several reasons why people engage in esteem-robbing sex. A common reason is that many people participate in certain sexual activities as a way of acting out, or rebelling against parental, societal, or religious beliefs and standards. Others are trying to get the attention they never got as a child. Still others are reenacting the abuse they experienced as a child. Sexual promiscuity, sexual addiction, and an attraction to illicit sex can be common symptoms and long-term effects of childhood sexual abuse.

In the following pages I will explore the causes for some of the most common esteem-robbing behaviors and present case examples showing just how these behaviors can develop. If you relate to the examples they may, in fact, help you better understand the causes of your own behavior.

PROMISCUITY

While the sexual revolution did much for bringing us out of the dark ages by giving us permission to freely express our sexuality—many believe that it also brought us too far in the other direction. For many, free love didn't turn out to be quite so free. Not only are we paying the price with such diseases as AIDS, herpes, and other STDs, but we are paying the price of lowered self-esteem caused by years of disrespecting our bodies, our personal integrity, and our self-respect.

What we are learning is that while we needn't protect our sexuality as if it were a prize to be awarded only to our bride or groom—we do need to honor it and not throw it away on anyone who desires it. Having sex with anyone and everyone is like giving little pieces of ourselves away.

There are several causes for sexual promiscuity. Those who indiscriminately have sex with many different partners sometimes do so because they are rebelling against parents or other authority figures who were extremely strict, rigid, or zealously religious, as in the following case:

Suzanne came into therapy because once more she had found herself in a bad situation because of her promiscuity. Even though she was happily married, she was having an affair with her husband's best friend and was frightened that her husband was beginning to suspect something was going on between them. "I don't know what I'd do if my husband found out. And I don't know what *he'd* do. He's very jealous and has a bad temper. I'm afraid he might try to hurt either me or my lover. You've just got to help me get out of this mess and help me to not get into any more situations like this."

As Suzanne told me her history it became apparent that she was unconsciously rebelling against her father's rigid rules and beliefs by "acting out" sexually: "My father is a devout Catholic who believes that sex should only occur in a marriage. He didn't allow us to date until we were seventeen and then we had to be home by ten. He'd practically make a date sign in blood that he wouldn't touch me sexually. It was so humiliating that I didn't date as much as I could have.

"I couldn't wait to leave home but my father wouldn't allow me to live on my own. I had been dating Ron for about six months when he proposed and I know I married him so I could get out of the house.

"I wasn't married for long before I started having affairs. I told myself it was because I was so sexually inexperienced, having married so young, and that I wanted to find out what I was missing. But after a few years and a few dozen affairs I have come to the conclusion that something else is going on here."

I confirmed Suzanne's suspicions and we talked about her feelings toward her father: "I love him very much but he is so controlling—even today. I can't stand to be controlled in any way. I don't let my husband tell me what to do—why should my father be able to? I am a grown woman. It's time he recognized that and let me go!"

It was apparent that Suzanne was very angry with her father. As we continued to work together and she was able to express more and more of her anger toward her father, first with me and finally to him directly, Suzanne's need to rebel against him began to diminish.

One day several months after starting therapy, Suzanne came into my office looking very happy. She immediately announced that she had ended her affair and that for the first time in her marriage she felt like being faithful to her husband. "I appreciate my husband more than ever and I don't want to ever do anything that will jeopardize our relationship again. I realize now that I somehow had him all confused with my father. It was my father I was angry with, my father I was rebelling against, but I ended up rebelling against my husband instead. I feel so much clearer now that I have confronted my father and I no longer let him control me. I don't need to continue rebelling now because there is nothing to rebel against!"

Another reason for sexual promiscuity is a deep need for approval and acceptance, as it was with Courtney:

"My father ignored me when I was a child. Whenever I tried to sit on his lap or hug him he would push me away. I know that my need for male approval now is because of my father's rejection. I want every man I meet to approve of me, to like me, and I've found that being sexy is a surefire way to get positive male attention. When a man desires me sexually it is a real ego trip for me. And each sexual experience I have feels like a conquest."

Shawna had different reasons for needing the approval of males so much: "When I was a teenager I was really ugly. I was skinny with buck teeth and pimples. No boy would even look at me, except perhaps to make fun of me. After I left home I worked to be able to afford braces and a dermatologist. Now, even though my teeth are fixed and my skin is clear and I've gained a few pounds, I still feel unattractive. Every time a man notices me I am surprised. And if a man comes on to me sexually I am flattered—so much so that I almost always go to bed with him. When I'm with a man sexually and he is turned on, I feel so good about myself. I feel pretty and sexy and desirable—all the things I never felt growing up. Unfortunately, the feeling doesn't last."

Many people, like Shawna, use seduction as a way of proving to themselves that they're worthwhile and attractive. Although they might appear to be conceited, they're usually insecure. Their deep feelings of inadequacy and inferiority are what drive them. If you suspect that you use sex in this way, you may need counseling in order to gain insight into the cause of your compulsive need for reassurance. With the proper treatment you will be able to build your own sense of self-esteem and will no longer need to use sex as a cheap fix to solve your inner turmoil.

And last, but certainly not least, a very significant cause of promiscuity can be childhood sexual abuse, as we have mentioned before. Sexual abuse causes children to feel so much shame and guilt that they have little or no respect for their bodies, their feelings, or their reputations. They already feel like "damaged goods" and therefore allow people to do whatever they want to them. Children who are sexualized early on may learn to rely on sex as a way of getting the attention, affection, and comfort they are so desperate for. Having sex with someone seems like a small price to pay in order to be held and nurtured.

No matter what your reason for being promiscuous, it is a behavior that most certainly lowers your self-esteem. And whether you are a man or a woman, continuously having empty sex will eventually catch up to you one way or another, whether it causes you to dislike yourself, to tire of sex, or to feel lonely and unfulfilled. Additionally, in the age of AIDS and other venereal diseases, you are risking your health and your very life by continuing this behavior. If you feel out of control and cannot stop on your own, please consider seeking professional help.

SADOMASOCHISM

Sadomasochism is a type of sexual activity that was once confined to only a small portion of our population. Today, celebrities such as Madonna have brought this practice into the limelight and made it popular with a much larger segment of society, most notably young people in their twenties and thirties, gays and lesbians, and those in the avant-garde.

Until recently, researchers had estimated that five to ten percent of the U.S. population engaged in sadomasochism for sexual pleasure on at least an occasional basis, with most incidents being either mild or staged activities involving no real pain or violence.

It appears that many more individuals prefer to play the masochist's role than the sadist's. It also appears that males are more likely to prefer sadomasochistic activities than females. This means that male sadists may have difficulty in finding willing masochistic females to be sexual partners.

If partners are located, an agreement is reached about what will occur. The giving and receiving of actual or pretended physical pain or psychological humiliation occurs in most cases only within a carefully prearranged script. Any change from the expected scenario generally reduces sexual pleasure.

Most often it is the receiver (the masochist), not the giver (the sadist), who sets and controls the exact type and extent of the couple's activities. In many such heterosexual relationships, the so-called traditional sex roles are reversed—with men playing the submissive or masochistic role.

A true sadist or masochist is not just someone who engages in this activity because it is a fad, but is someone who requires this activity in order to become fully aroused and satisfied.

Simon was a client of mine who was a true masochist. The

only way he was able to become sexually aroused was to be dominated sexually or to have fantasies about being dominated. Unfortunately, this behavior caused him a great deal of distress and shame.

Simon was a high-powered attorney who was extremely dominant and forceful in his day-to-day living. He had many wealthy and prominent clients who he imagined would be completely repulsed if they knew that he was a masochist. Simon was married to a woman whom he adored but was completely bored with sexually. Since he could not bring himself to share with her his sexual inclinations, he could not become aroused with her. He went through the motions of being with her sexually but was able to achieve erections only by fantasizing about being dominated. It was becoming more and more difficult to achieve erections and rarely was he able to ejaculate. His wife wanted to have a baby and was pressuring him to get some help for what she thought was a sexual dysfunction. This is what brought Simon into therapy. Once in therapy Simon shared with me the shame he felt at being dependent on the services of prostitutes to meet his need to be sexually dominated.

After many sessions aimed at learning Simon's family and sexual history, we discovered the cause of his masochism. Simon's mother was an extremely domineering woman who insisted Simon toe the line with her. She would punish him by pulling his pants down, turning him over her knee, and spanking his bare butt with her hand. When Simon was very small this form of punishment would make him feel very ashamed and would hurt his behind. But as Simon got older and his mother continued to use this form of punishment, Simon began to feel a new sensation as his mother spanked him. He began to feel sexually aroused. This arousal, coupled with the shame he felt, was the beginning of his sexual masochism.

When Simon first discovered this connection he was terribly embarrassed and blamed himself for his "perversion": "How could I be sexually aroused with my own mother—how sick can I get?" he asked me. But Simon was to learn that he in no way was responsible for this arousal and that, in fact, his mother, either consciously or unconsciously, might have been seducing her son all along. As I explained to Simon, it is inappropriate for a mother to take down the pants of an eight-year-old boy in order to spank him. It was unnecessary and it would have caused him to feel shame and, later on, arousal. By the time children are eight they have a natural modesty and are embarrassed to have their mothers see them naked. In addition, it was unnecessary and extremely inappropriate for his mother to continue spanking him in this manner as he got older. Last, but certainly not least, Simon remembered that at times his mother would be wearing shorts or would hike her skirt up so that his bare skin was touching her bare leg. What boy would not become aroused at having his penis come in contact with the skin of another person? Perhaps inadvertently, perhaps deliberately, Simon's mother had done things to him to sexually stimulate him. If that wasn't bad enough, she did this at the same time that she was shaming him, setting up a connection between sexuality and shame, sexuality and punishment, and sexuality and submission that had created Simon's masochism.

Just learning about how his masochism was formed was a tremendous relief to Simon. He was also able to understand not just intellectually but emotionally that he'd had no choice in the matter and that indeed it was thrust upon him against his will. In addition, Simon was finally able to feel and express his anger toward his mother for causing his masochism and in so doing was able to begin to free himself from his shame and guilt.

In time, Simon was able to "wean" himself from masochism and masochistic fantasies and begin to enjoy other sexual activities. And once Simon discovered that he had unconsciously withheld his feelings toward his wife because of his misdirected anger toward his mother, his sexual relationship with his wife was greatly improved.

PARAPHILIAS

Paraphilia (the Greek word *para* means "beyond" or "outside of the usual," and *philia* means "love") is the scientific name for what many people would call perversions. Some paraphilias are similar to behaviors most of us would not find unusual and are, in fact, perfectly normal, such as a husband's greater arousal when his wife wears black, lacy underpants. This kind of behavior only becomes a problem (and is then called a paraphilia) if it involves the *necessity* of a particular object or behavior for the person to achieve arousal and satisfaction. In addition, the behavior must interfere with the development or maintenance of an intimate relationship between two individuals.

For example, most of us find certain kinds of clothing more sexually arousing than others. The difference between that and fetishism (a type of paraphilia) depends on whether the clothes are absolutely necessary for sexual arousal. It would not be unusual, for example, for a man to be more sexually aroused if his wife came to bed wearing a sheer, black nightgown than if she appeared wearing her usual flannel nightgown.

But if the man is not interested in his wife *unless* she is wearing that particular nightgown, or if he prefers seeing the nightgown alone (without his wife in it), the man is said to have a sexual fetish.

Other paraphilias involve more dramatic behaviors that most people find incomprehensible and about which sexual partners are likely to object (such as a husband's not being able to become aroused or have intercourse *unless* his wife ties him up and treats him like a slave). The most extreme of these behaviors include some that are truly physically and psychologically harmful to others, such as some forms of sadomasochism.

Experts know very little about paraphilic behaviors. It is even difficult to estimate how many people engage in these specific behaviors, because only those who get into trouble legally or have marital difficulties are brought to the attention of researchers, therapists, or legal authorities. It is, however, generally agreed that many more males than females have a paraphilia as part of their sexual behavior pattern.

Although we don't always know why some people have paraphilias, the beginnings of these behavior patterns are thought to become a part of an individual's arousal pattern very early in childhood, and a few may be related to hormonal or developmental factors that influence brain development before birth. In rare instances, paraphilic behavior does not emerge until later in life, perhaps due to physical changes in the brain such as an injury, tumor, or other disease.

What we do know is that paraphilias are not acquired from exposure to the content of books, movies, or magazines—or from others with the behavior.

Paraphilias involve behaviors, not fantasy. There is a considerable difference between having a specific fantasy one uses for arousal and actually needing to act out the fantasy in order to perform sexually, as we will discuss later. There are also differences between individuals in terms of how each uses the paraphilia. Some are aroused only while the paraphilic behavior is actually taking place, while others replay the act in their minds (like a videotape) in order to perform sexually later. But even when a person can use this recall mechanism to carry on what seems to the partner a normal sex life, eventually the paraphilic behavior must be repeated—it is as though the mental videotape wears out or gets stale and isn't arousing anymore.

Many of the same paraphilias can be present whether a person is heterosexual, homosexual, or bisexual—so acquiring a specific paraphilia is not necessarily related to a person's sexual orientation.

Regardless of whether the specific behavior by itself or as viewed by others is just mildly odd, objectionably "kinky," or violently dangerous, in order to be a paraphilia the following must be true:

• The person did not voluntarily "choose" the behavior.
• Punishment does not prevent recurrence of the behavior.
• The person cannot voluntarily control the behavior by willpower.

Help for Paraphilias

Most people who have a paraphilia feel extremely ashamed of it. In fact, it is rare for someone to be able to feel good about himself or herself while engaging in such behavior, since most paraphilias are viewed as unacceptable, "sick," or "kinky" by the majority of people. For this reason, most of those with a paraphilia feel so uncomfortable with their sexual preference that they hide it even from those they are the closest to. In Part III we will discuss the importance of learning to accept yourself the way you are, particularly the importance of accepting those things about yourself you cannot change. If you feel hopeless about changing your preference for certain sexual activities because you have tried and failed so many times, and you want to work on accepting your behavior, by all means do so.

In addition, as I also mentioned earlier, often just finding out that one's specific behavior is shared by others is helpful since many paraphiliacs fear that their problem is unique to them. Reassurance can be gained by finding a magazine or newsletter devoted to a particular paraphilia and then writing to the magazine. For example, the Kinsey Institute collections include a magazine published by individuals who have the paraphilia infantilism—needing items such as rubber sheets, rubber baby pants, sleeping in a crib, being fed from a bottle, and receiving other attention usually associated with infant care, such as being diapered, in order to become sexually aroused. The publication includes editorials, letters to the editor, articles, and a classified section.

But if you would like to work on changing your sexual pattern with the help of a professional it is important to know that there is that option available to you. You can locate a qualified therapist or psychologist who has experience in treating paraphilias by contacting a university or medical school which operates a sex dysfunction clinic and then asking to be referred to an appropriate specialist.

Often the root of a particular paraphilia lies in early childhood development and experiences. Woody came to me because he had a shoe fetish, meaning that he needed to be in contact with a particular kind of shoe in order to become sexually aroused. His preference was women's high heels, particularly black ones, and unless a woman wore high heels he wouldn't get aroused. Woody was so ashamed of his fetish that he was unable to establish a long-term intimate relationship. Instead he had to rely on prostitutes in order to express his sexuality. After each experience with a prostitute he would end up feeling very ashamed and "sleazy."

For several sessions, I had Woody recall his childhood. What was revealed was that Woody was a very lonely little boy who did not receive much attention from either his mother or his often absent father. He had no siblings and would have to spend his days playing by himself. Often, he would go upstairs to his parents' bedroom because he liked the feeling of comfort he got from being there.

In one session Woody told me that he would often go into his mother's closet and play with her shoes. "Sometimes I would try them on and other times I would just sit and hold them. I liked the feeling of the leather and the smell reminded me of my mother. Being close to her shoes was like being close to her. Do you think this has anything to do with my shoe fetish?"

I did indeed. I had heard similar stories from several male clients who liked to wear women's lingerie or who had foot or shoe fetishes. It seemed that when these males did not receive enough love and attention, particularly from their mothers, they would do anything to receive some comfort—whether it was wearing their mother's clothes, sleeping in her bed, or sitting and holding her shoes. But I had also discovered that sexuality was often combined with the comfort experienced by the object. I suspected that there was more to the story than Woody was telling. I pursued the subject by asking: "Do you remember ever becoming sexually aroused by your mother's shoes?" Woody, encouraged by the question, answered, "Yes, I do. In fact," he said shyly, "I used to masturbate while holding or looking at her shoes."

Now we had the complete answer to Woody's paraphilia. Shoes became not only an object of comfort but an object of arousal for Woody at a very early age. He had, in fact, "paired" or connected sexuality with shoes to the point that when he saw shoes that reminded him of his mother he became sexually aroused.

With this insight, Woody was eventually able to work through many of his feelings toward his mother—including his anger at her for neglecting him emotionally. As he did this his attraction to shoes lessened until finally he was able to become sexually aroused by just the presence of a woman he found attractive.

It isn't normally as easy to discover the cause of a paraphilia, nor are all paraphilias eliminated as easily. The most successful treatment found so far for severe paraphilias or those that endanger others is a combination of treatment with injections of medroxyprogesterone acetate (which reduces or eliminates sex drive and sexual fantasy, thus reducing the compulsive need to engage in the paraphilic behavior) and skilled counseling. Once the person is calmed by this specific hormonal drug, it is possible for him or her to begin to work on changing the problematic sexual pattern. If the person has a partner, participation by the partner in counseling has also been found to be helpful.

When it is clear that the individual has learned to be sexually satisfied by behaviors that do not include the paraphilia, the injections can be stopped; this hormone has no known irreversible effects. If after treatment it is clear that the behavior cannot be eliminated or controlled, then the individual can elect to continue the hormone treatment indefinitely.

You should seek professional help if your paraphilia dominates your life and relationships or causes anxiety, guilt, shame, or stress. If it affects your social life, your schoolwork, or your relationships with friends, family, and lovers, therapy will be helpful.

Instead of allowing yourself to continue a sexual behavior that could potentially harm others and that continually damages your self-esteem, consider taking some action that will help you stop this kind of compulsive behavior.

• Look for the origin and meaning of your attraction to this activity.

• Confine your activity to the privacy of your own home (that is, playing games with your partner *if he or she consents*).

• Experiment until you discover some sexual practices that are esteem-enhancing but which are still stimulating to you and slowly begin to substitute them for some of your esteem-robbing practices.

• Consider psychological counseling to help you get to the root of your problem.

CHOOSING SEXUAL FANTASIES THAT ARE ESTEEMING, NOT DEGRADING

The issue of sexual fantasies is far more complicated than most people understand. What we fantasize about can have a great deal to do with our sexual self-esteem and our self-esteem in general. Our sexual fantasies can make us feel good about ourselves or can make us feel ashamed, guilty, or frightened.

In the past ten to fifteen years, particularly since the book My *Secret Garden* by Nancy Friday came out, the general attitude has been that sexual fantasies are positive, that we should give ourselves permission to have them, and that we should even become as creative as possible in inventing new ones. This attitude, which was rather revolutionary at the time, has generally been accepted as the final word on the subject. But it is far too simplistic to say that it is good to have sexual fantasies or that sexual fantasies should be encouraged. There are many aspects of the issue of sexual fantasies that need to be examined more closely.

While sexual fantasies certainly can be a healthy outlet and we should give ourselves permission to fantasize in *most* circumstances, there are some people and some fantasies that should be *discouraged* rather than *encouraged*. Some of the fantasies that should be discouraged are:

• Fantasies that cause you to feel shame, guilt, or fear.
• Fantasies that encourage *any* behavior that you are working on eliminating from your life (for example, the paraphilias or other behaviors we discussed in the previous sections).
• Fantasies about having sex with a child.
• Fantasies about forcing someone to have sex.
• Any fantasy where violence and sex are combined (fantasies about stabbing someone while having sex with them, sex with a bloodied or injured person, and so on).

Experts have discovered that allowing yourself to fantasize about these things can desensitize you to them and actually encourage you to take action. For example, many child molesters report that they fantasized about being with children sexually long before they ever crossed the line and actually committed the act. Once the fantasies began they then moved on to masturbating while fantasizing. Gradually, the idea of actually acting on the fantasy became less and less repugnant to them and at the same time they were developing a stronger and stronger urge to be with a child. Eventually, they acted on their fantasy even though originally it would have been something they could never imagine themselves doing.

Generally speaking, except for the extreme cases listed above, it is difficult to determine whether a particular sexual fantasy should be considered a harmless release or a potentially harmful fantasy that is actually a rehearsal for the real thing. Since fantasies can be either a release or a rehearsal, a much closer look needs to be given to each individual fantasy, the person who is doing the fantasizing, and his or her emotional state while fantasizing; then the fantasy must be put into the context of the person's life.

For example, the fantasies of being dominated sexually by another person or of dominating another person are rather common ones. Determining whether they are fantasies that should be encouraged or discouraged depends upon who is having them and what purpose the fantasy is serving.

Those who were sexually abused, for instance, tend to have fantasies about dominating others or being dominated far more than those who were not abused. For an abused person, domination fantasies can be a way of reenacting their abuse. In essence, they are reliving the sexual abuse they experienced as children, either from the perspective of a victim or as the perpetrator. From this perspective, these fantasies either act as an experience of reabusing themselves or as a rehearsal for abusing others, a form of role reversal that can turn deadly.

The types of fantasies we have actually have more to do with what is going on with the rest of our lives than they do with our sexuality. For example, when we have fantasies about being in control of someone sexually it may indicate that we do not feel in control of our lives or we feel someone is controlling us. Conversely, when we fantasize about being controlled it may indicate that we are too much in control in our daily lives.

Instead of acting out your fantasies or letting them run rampant, examine them the way you would a dream. Our fantasies can tell us a lot about ourselves since, like dreams, they are expressions of our subconscious.

For most of us, sex is not just the rubbing together of bodies. Sex also involves our minds, and our minds can sometimes play tricks on us, bringing themes and images of things we disapprove of or are ashamed of.

For example, Marshall was very upset because he was having homosexual dreams and fantasies. He was worried that he might be a latent homosexual. This troubled him because he was so violently antihomosexual.

I explained to Marshall that fantasies, whether homosexual or heterosexual, cannot be used as an indicator of a person's sexual orientation. Mark Schwartz and William Masters reported in an issue of the *American Journal of Psychiatry* that homosexual fantasies among heterosexuals and heterosexual ones among homosexuals are not unusual. After surveying one hundred twenty men and women, half of them homosexual and half of them heterosexual, they discovered that people's sexual fantasies are often at odds with their sexual orientation. For instance, among both men and women who are homosexual, heterosexual sex ranks as the third most common sexual fantasy, and for heterosexual men and women, homosexual encounters rank fourth and fifth, respectively.

As we worked together it became apparent that Marshall was probably not homosexual but that his intolerance toward homosexuals indicated that he needed to come to terms with the fact that all humans are both male and female. By totally denying the feminine side of himself, he had created tension and anxiety which was expressed in the form of dreams about homosexuality.

Ask yourself the following questions concerning your typical sexual fantasies:

- How do you feel after you have this fantasy? (Guilty? Ashamed? Fearful? Or content? Relaxed?)
- Do you masturbate to this fantasy? When you do, how do you feel afterward?
- Can you reach orgasm during masturbation without using this fantasy?
- Do you have this fantasy when you are having sex with your partner? If so, how do you feel about using it? How do you feel afterward?
- Can you reach orgasm with your partner without using this fantasy?
- Would you feel ashamed to tell someone about this fantasy? If so, why?
- Would you be afraid to tell your partner about this fantasy?
- Is this fantasy something you'd actually like to experience? If yes, why are you not doing it? If no, why do you think you have it?
- What makes this fantasy so exciting to you?
- Why do you think you have this fantasy?

THE NEGATIVE ASPECTS OF FANTASIZING

Fantasy as a Deterrent to Intimacy

Today we find the advice that sexual fantasies don't hurt anyone and that they can indeed spice up a relationship was not all that helpful after all. Sexual fantasies can indeed hurt a relationship since they can create a wedge between a couple and entice people into situations outside the marriage. When a couple is in bed together they should ideally be there alone—not continually share their bed with the inhabitants of each other's fantasies. Fantasizing about someone else when you are having sex can cause you to be disconnected from your partner and can prevent intimacy and true sharing.

While fantasizing about someone else may indeed enhance your sexual feelings, it can also get in the way of true intimacy. If you tend to continually fantasize about someone else while with your partner you may want to ask yourself the following:

- Why do I need to think of someone else?
- Do I find my partner physically attractive?
- After I have fantasized about someone else, how do I feel about my partner?
- Does my fantasizing prevent me from connecting with my partner emotionally?
- Can I have an orgasm only while lost in a fantasy about someone else?
- What would happen if I stopped using fantasy while with my partner?

Fantasy as Distraction

Some fantasies draw us away from what is actually happening in sex and can be a deliberate attempt to block out the reality of the sexual partner. A woman may fantasize about having sex with a stranger because she finds her lover impatient, rough, insensitive, or interested only in his own sexual release. She may let fantasies take the place of a dull or unhealthy reality, or may use them as a way of remaining a compliant sexual partner and keeping the marriage together. A man may use fantasy to keep him aroused when his partner is no longer attractive to him.

Fantasy as an Indicator of Real Problems

It is also important to know that fantasies *can* indicate problems in our real lives. For example, if a man constantly fantasizes about rape, forceful sex, or sex with a child, this is a strong indication that there's a problem of some kind. Also, when people use a fantasy to maintain or increase the distance between themselves and their partner or if they can enjoy sex only when fantasizing about someone else, then counseling or some kind of help is needed.

Fantasies as Replays of Sexual Abuse

Some people are able to have orgasms only while lost in a fantasy, because feeling connected to their partners or becoming too intimate may be far too threatening. Unfortunately, these fantasies may sometimes be unhealthy ones, such as those of being forced to have sex, being overpowered by strangers, or even being with a sexual abuse perpetrator. While no victim of sexual abuse enjoyed being violated, betrayed, damaged, manipulated, or controlled, they may indeed have fantasies about these things. What is occurring is an arousal factor based on the body's having responded to the stimuli during the abuse.

This is particularly true if the sexual abuse was your first sexual experience. Our first experience with sex is highly charged and therefore intensely erotic and strongly remembered. Even though you may have been forced to do things against your will, there may have been erotic elements present, such as your body's feelings of physical pleasure or the perpetrator's expressing sexual pleasure. These memories stay locked in the mind and body long after the abuse, and can cause some survivors to become aroused even while feeling a great deal of shame about them.

If the only way you can have an orgasm is to replay an experience of abuse in your mind, you may opt to do this, either because you want to relieve the sexual tension you have built up or to please your partner. Unfortunately, you are out of control and are in a real sense being revictimized by your own erotic fantasies. Not only are you reexperiencing the trauma of your childhood each time you use such a fantasy to bring yourself to orgasm, but you are damaging your already low self-esteem by doing something you are ashamed of. You may end up thinking that you are perverted or that you must have encouraged the perpetrator. Thus a vicious cycle is perpetuated: The more you use these forbidden fantasies, the worse you feel about yourself; the worse you feel about yourself, the less likely it is that you are going to be able to get close to someone else.

If you are a survivor of sexual abuse you need not have a sexual fantasy that is a replay of the actual abuse (in which you imagine your perpetrator having sex with you, for example) for your fantasies to be damaging to you. Any sexual fantasy in which you are being forced, dominated, overpowered, humiliated, or hurt by anyone is likely to be a consequence of the sexual abuse and thus, in essence, is a replaying of the experience.

Fantasy as Addiction

Sexual fantasies can become an addiction. For example, those who call the phone sex lines frequently become addicted to them, as Reverend Brown did:

Reverend Brown became aware of the phone sex lines from the advertisements on television. While the ads intrigued him he resisted them for a long time. Finally, late one night after his wife had gone to sleep, he gave in to his impulses and made a call. He felt horrible afterward and made a promise to God to never do it again but unfortunately he was already hooked. Like any other addiction, Reverend Brown's phone sex addiction began to control his life. The more calls he made the more he wanted to make. The more calls he made the more guilt and shame he felt. He became more and more secretive and withdrawn, distancing himself from everyone in his life—his wife, his children, even the people in his congregation.

Before he knew it he had run up a debt of five thousand dollars on his credit cards from making the calls. Eventually his wife discovered the credit card bills. Mortified, she left him. This is when he agreed to begin therapy with me.

Although he said he had no problem with his wife before the calls began, Reverend Brown confessed to me that he had begun to have fantasies about being with other women. The more he fantasized the more he liked it. When he heard the ads on television he began to think, I can do more, I can have new experiences without really being unfaithful to my wife.

THE POSITIVE ASPECTS OF FANTASIZING

Studies reveal that at least fifty percent of women and seventy-two percent of men have sexual fantasies. But rather than producing feelings of guilt and anxiety, sexual fantasies should be used to enhance enjoyment.

Some experts think that people who fantasize during sex show more creativity, independence, and nonconformity than those who do not. They also believe that their attitudes toward sex are more accepting, erotic, positive, and uninhibited.

Fantasy can, in fact, enhance a person's sex life. Allowing yourself to fantasize may actually be good, especially if you have been married for many years. Fantasy and the sharing of sexual fantasies can add zest to a relationship and help keep boredom away, especially if you include your partner in your fantasies.

Fantasy can also be used to blot out reality in a rather different way, to enhance a relationship by changing its setting and helping you to concentrate on lovemaking and forget problems at work or in other aspects of your life. When fantasy is used in this way it does not mean that there is anything wrong with your sex life. No one has thrilling and passionate sex all the time, but the dividing line between using fantasy as an anesthetic so that you don't have to take action to change the circumstances in which you find yourself, and using it to enrich reality is a hazy one, and what feels right to you depends a lot on where you see that line drawn.

Fantasy as Compensation

As I mentioned above, we don't necessarily fantasize about what we actually desire to happen. For example, rape fantasies are not uncommon in women, but this certainly doesn't mean that these women want to be raped. In reality, women find the crime of rape horrifying and repellent. But even though rape itself is an act of violence that produces serious and long-lasting trauma, fantasies about it can serve a positive purpose.

According to researchers at the Masters and Johnson Institute in St. Louis, the fantasy of rape or seduction helps to reassure some women that they are being sexually passive rather than aggressive; for others, it gives "permission" for sexual activities that these women have been taught are strictly forbidden. The fantasy might serve to release some inhibitions.

Many women have fantasies which they find exciting at the time, but afterward feel ashamed and guilty about because they degrade the female body and make women the victims of male brutality, such as bondage, cruelty, or rape. These women fear that they must be "perverted" or "oversexed" for having such thoughts and feel at the mercy of their imaginations and fantasies that come without bidding.

Many women are embarrassed to admit to thoughts they consider immoral, exhibitionist, or "dirty." But there is a startling gulf between what a woman is really seeking in a sexual relationship and her fantasies.

Laurel was extremely reluctant to tell me her sexual fantasies and yet she had a need to at the same time: "I almost always end up having a fantasy about being overtaken by a gang of thugs or some criminal who just escaped from prison. I am tied up and gagged and then they do every conceivable thing you can imagine to me. This excites me tremendously and I have one orgasm after another while thinking about this scenario. I know I must be really sick for getting excited by something like this."

But I thought no such thing. One significant element in many sex fantasies is that something is done to you for which you cannot be held responsible because you could not see or you were bound, held down, overpowered, or it happened by "accident." Although violence plays a large part in many women's fantasy lives, having a fantasy of being forced into sex while blindfolded, gagged, and tied to a bed does not mean that you want to actually be treated this way or even that you want your partner to be rough with you. This kind of fantasy may be how you, like Laurel, try to make peace with your conscience and your sense of propriety.

The most frequent fantasy for both heterosexual men and heterosexual women involves having sex with someone other than their current mate. This doesn't necessarily mean that the person having the fantasy is unhappy with his or her mate or that the marriage or relationship is about to break up. Fantasies are not reality, and they don't become fact unless you act them out, so there's no need to feel guilty. Instead, ask yourself the following questions:

• Are you playing a role in your fantasy that you don't or can't play in real life?
• Is there something occurring in your fantasies that you do not allow to happen in real life or wish would happen in real life but feel helpless to make come about?

For example, one woman who had been worried and disgusted by the rape fantasies that crept into her mind whenever she made love to her husband discovered, after some self-examination, that the most significant part of the fantasy and the part that aroused her the most was the rapist's total and passionate surrender to the experience—his being taken over by a force too great to control. She was able to then work out a new fantasy for herself in which she imagined her lover reaching orgasm and deliberately turned on this fantasy during lovemaking with her husband. It eventually took the place of the rape fantasy and was much more satisfying for her and produced no nasty aftertaste.

Fantasy as an Expression of Our Dark Side

Fantasies can be a way of bringing your dark side out in the open and thus robbing it of some of its power. It makes sense that we would be attracted to the forbidden because sex has always been forbidden. Whatever is forbidden is usually extremely sexually arousing. We need to look at our "forbidden" sexual attractions, see them for what they represent, and even feel the attraction completely— but that does not mean we have to act on our fantasies.

The more sexual repression we experience, the bigger our dark side becomes and, in turn, the more our tendency to act out our sexual fantasies. Good examples of how sexual repression only causes us to become more likely to act out sexually in unacceptable ways are the cases of Jim Bakker and Jimmy Swaggart.

Sharing Fantasies

Deciding whether or not to share your sexual fantasies with a lover depends, of course, on how secure your partner is. Sharing fantasies can foster intimacy and add spice to a relationship. It's important, however, that both partners realize that fantasy is different from infidelity.

Acting Out Sexual Fantasies

Most sexual fantasies should no more be acted out than we would act out a fantasy of killing someone we are angry with. Having fantasies about things we would never do is a marvelous way of letting off steam, of releasing pent-up feelings of anger, revenge, jealousy, and so forth. A good example of someone who seems to be open to acting out her sexual fantasies is Madonna. And yet she has been reported as saying that she never got over her ex-husband, Sean Penn. Here is a woman who has probably done everything under the sun sexually and seems to relish in shocking society with her outrageous sexual expressions, but who yearns for the closeness and excitement she once felt with one man.

Sex Games

One form of fantasy is fantasy sex games. The couple sets up a certain scenario that is particularly erotic to one or both and they play it out. Sex games in which the man pretends to be in the hospital and his lover pretends to be a nurse, or the man pretends to be a john while his partner pretends to be a prostitute, are especially common. These games can be very exciting and can bring new zest to a relationship. They can also help the couple to maintain monogamy since they may have less need to act out their fantasies with other partners.

For example, bondage practitioners will tell you that, practiced by mutual consent and with intelligent limits, bondage is an exciting game that can add a spark of variety to sex. They advocate that reluctant partners should join in the fantasy—it won't hurt and they might even like it a great deal. Unfortunately, there is a down side to these sex games. As far as heterosexual sex is concerned, most of these games are derogatory toward women since most men choose games where the woman plays such roles as a prostitute or is in a position of being dominated, such as a little girl or a rape victim.

Another problem is that any imbalance of power that already exists in the relationship can be exacerbated by such games, causing the less dominant one to actually feel further intimidated or even abused by his or her lover.

If the relationship is a healthy, strong one, with each partner feeling equal to the other, and if both parties have fairly high self-esteem, these games can be harmless. Unfortunately, as we discussed in a previous section, there is an imbalance of power in many relationships and these games can be harmful for those who continue to play out the same roles in their sex life as they do in their everyday relationship.

Extinguishing Fantasies

While books like Nancy Friday's *My Secret Garden* tell us that we need not feel guilty about our sexual fantasies, the problem is that just being told you shouldn't feel guilty doesn't necessarily make it so. If you continue to feel guilty about your sexual fantasies, no matter how many experts tell you that you "shouldn't," then perhaps you should focus more on trying to extinguish the fantasies—replacing them with others that are still stimulating but not so shame- or guilt-provoking—than on accepting them.

The way to extinguish a fantasy is to gradually "wean" yourself of it using the step-by-step method below:

- Go ahead and use your fantasy the way you normally would as a way of reaching orgasm, but this time, think of a more socially acceptable scenario (such as being in a loving relationship) immediately *after* you have reached orgasm.
- The next time you make love or masturbate, try using the more appropriate fantasy for a while. This fantasy will probably not cause you to become extremely sexually excited but use it nevertheless. You can once again use your old, less acceptable fantasy as a way of bringing yourself to orgasm, but as soon as you begin to orgasm switch to the more appropriate fantasy.
- Continue this process, making the time you use the inappropriate fantasy shorter and shorter in duration.

EXAMINING THE EFFECTS PORNOGRAPHY HAS ON YOU AND YOUR RELATIONSHIPS

Many people believe that in a free society adults should have a choice about what they read or watch, and therefore nothing should be done to restrict pornography in any form. Those who are opposed to restrictive and puritanical attitudes argue that a little bit of pornography "never hurt anyone." Some sex therapists even recommend pornography as a cure for certain types of sexual dysfunction.

Some people feel that pornography is useful because it directs uncontrolled sexual excitement to pictures so that the viewer is less likely to employ sexual violence against "real" people. But recent studies show that instead of being cathartic, pornography actually incites otherwise fairly nonaggressive men to attack women. In fact, even the kind of sex and violence shown on television may have this effect.

When pornography involves cruelty or exploitation of children, it becomes objectionable to most of us. But there is an undercurrent of violence even in "soft" porn and pin-up, as well. Pornography sets out to shut women up, to silence them. An advertisement for a life-size plastic doll describes it as "the bed partner that doesn't talk back, just obeys."

Many defenders of pornography say that women are free to consent or refuse to model sex scenes and that we should not limit their freedom to choose any kind of employment they like. But they do not realize that women and young children are often coerced into taking part in pornography. The pornography industry is closely linked with hard drugs and much of it is under the control of organized crime. Girls are sometimes sold by their parents to take part in pornographic films and pornographers may use their own children in this way. Many of those women who supposedly "choose" to participate in pornography were sexually abused as children and are reenacting the abuse by allowing themselves to be further victimized. In addition, horrific things are done to make pornographic pictures and films. Substances are sometimes introduced into women's vaginas for dogs to lick off; paint may be sprayed on a woman's body or boiling wax dripped on her breasts.

While there is certainly something to be said on both sides of the First Amendment debate, the important thing here is to ask yourself: How does pornography make me feel about myself? When I watch pornographic films or read pornographic material, do I end up feeling good about myself afterward? Does it raise my sexual self-esteem or does it lower it?

If you are a woman, does pornography make you feel humiliated and degraded? If you are a man, does pornography make you feel good about women or do you attain a sort of temporary feeling of superiority over them, or does it arouse violent instincts?

Those of you who say that you use pornography in order to arouse yourself or to rekindle the romance in your relationship also need to ask yourself: How does pornography affect my feelings about myself and my own body, and how does it affect my feelings toward my partner? While pornography can feel exciting at the time, many people suffer from a backlash of self-loathing or a feeling of distance or even dislike for their partner afterward. In addition, any "cure" for sexual dysfunction that makes men potent at the price of using women as impersonal sex objects should be questioned. Potency is less important than being able to relate to women as human beings.

A woman often feels that her lover's interest in pornography is an indication that he doesn't find her attractive or that he is not satisfied with their sex life. In addition, women often feel that their partners pressure them to watch videos and mimic what the actors do, or become immediately aroused regardless of what else is going on in their life.

Unless people feel extremely secure about their relationship and about their own sexual attractiveness, X-rated videos can cause them to feel insecure about themselves. These videos usually use actors who are unusually physically attractive and well-endowed, so that any comparison between the actors and average men or women can reinforce an insecure viewer's low opinion of her or his own body.

Not everyone is aroused by the same movies or scenes, so it is not possible to state that all women are aroused by one type of video while all men are aroused by another. But one study found that when men and women were given the choice between watching soft-core films (which the study defined as depicting sex within the context of a loving relationship) or hard-core films (sex only, no love or affection), women were more likely to prefer soft-core films.

The problem with hard-core pornography is that it too often equates sexual pleasure with dominance and cruelty. People in pornographic movies are treated not as objects of love but as objects to be abused, humiliated, and overpowered. Women, children, and animals are typically the victims, usually because they are smaller and least able to protect themselves effectively.

The message of this kind of material is not that sex is part of love. There is no tenderness, no mutual respect, no compassion or attempt to understand the feelings or needs of others. Sadism is not normally a part of healthy sex, and yet sadomasochistic acts are a part of most pornography. This is likely to send the message that women enjoy being abused, even raped. It desensitizes males to the crime of rape. It rarely promotes any understanding of women as sensitive human beings with intelligence and feelings.

Consider Substituting Erotica for Pornography

Erotica can be extremely stimulating without the aftereffects of shame, guilt, and self-loathing that generally follow an experience with pornography. The definition of erotica is "literary or artistic works having an erotic theme or quality." This is a very broad definition, but the major distinction between eroticism and pornography is that erotica does not portray women in degrading or subservient positions, and the inherent violence that is an integral part of pornography is absent.

As long as you continually involve yourself in sexual activities that make you feel guilty, ashamed, angry, fearful, or cause you physical or emotional pain you are not going to raise your sexual self-esteem no matter how much you focus on improving your sexual techniques or becoming a sexual gymnast.

Chapter Eleven

CHANGE THE WAY YOU INTERACT WITH YOUR PARTNER

LEARNING THAT PHYSICAL INTIMACY IS NO SHORTCUT TO EMOTIONAL INTIMACY

One of the most effective ways of raising your sexual self-esteem is to work on becoming a better lover. While doing so will not erase the effects of negative messages about sex or childhood trauma, or reverse past negative experiences with previous lovers, knowing that you are capable of pleasing your partner sexually can go a long way toward helping you to feel good about yourself sexually.

Becoming a better lover requires much more than learning sexual techniques. Since there are already numerous books written on the subject I will not repeat the efforts of other writers. In this section I will instead focus on ways *other* than learning sexual techniques to ensure that you are a good lover.

In order to become a better lover you will need to concentrate on the following:

- Learning that physical intimacy is no shortcut to emotional intimacy.
- Focusing more on your own physical pleasure.
- Learning the importance of touch.
- Learning to communicate openly about sex (including

communicating your needs clearly, without embarrassment and without guilt).

Sexuality can be the expression of many things. For some it is an escape from loneliness, since it may be the only time they connect with another human being on more than a superficial level. For some people, particularly men, it may be the only human touch they receive. For others sex is a form of stress reduction—they use sex as a way to relieve themselves of the tension brought on by work or other pressures. Still others use sex as a way of temporarily raising their self-esteem. With each new conquest they feel either more manly and macho or more feminine and desirable. And last but not least, some people use sex as an expression and symbol of power—a manipulation or way of taking control of others.

But intimate sex—sex that is meant as an expression of love or affection, as a way in which two people who care for one another connect in a meaningful way—involves much more than the physical act. It involves being willing and able to be open and vulnerable, to trust another person, to be desirous of pleasing another person, and at the same time to be willing to express one's own needs.

If you have had little experience with true intimacy your tendency may be to plunge into intimate sexual relationships prematurely or to remain disconnected emotionally even when you are sexually involved.

In and of itself sexual intercourse (or any other sexual activity, for that matter) does not remove loneliness and estrangement, yet countless people believe it will. Sexual contact is always more fulfilling when it comes in the context of openness, tenderness, and sensitivity to the needs of the other person. Love that has any depth means involvement. When sexual release comes in the context of trust, commitment, and safety, its pleasures take on heightened meaning.

Our sexuality is an integral part of our lives and as such it is both influenced by and affects every part of our lives. Nevertheless, sex should never be the focal point of our lives to the exclusion of other things. It should never become our purpose of living but rather its reward. By the same token sex should never become the most important aspect of a loving relationship nor the glue that holds the relationship together. Rather it should be the dessert—the celebration of a loving and tender bond.

Setting Emotional Boundaries

Many people need to learn to set emotional boundaries. In the past you may have allowed others to take over your life or otherwise control you, or you may have virtually "lost yourself" in others by becoming enmeshed in their lives. All of your energy and focus may have gone outward, toward others, so that you could anticipate and meet their needs.

While you may not have specific answers to the following questions, they will give you food for thought. By using these questions as a guide, you can begin to set emotional boundaries that are healthy for you.

• How much intimacy can I tolerate before I start to feel smothered?

• How much time can I spend with someone before I start to feel afraid or uncomfortable?

• How much can I share about myself before I feel I have shared too much?

CURBING YOUR URGE TO MERGE

Because they have difficulty being aware of their own boundaries, many people also have difficulty respecting or even perceiving the boundaries of others. They tend to "bare their souls" to others right away, very often in an attempt to capture the other person's attention. In addition, many women in particular operate on the assumption that the only way they can get a man to like them is to have sex with him. Learning to have nonsexual relationships or relationships that are more than just sexual is an important part of respecting and honoring your boundaries.

If you have a tendency to become "lost" in another person and become confused about the boundaries between yourself and others, try the following centering exercise after you have an intense exchange (whether it be a conversation, an intimate moment of touching and closeness, or a sexual experience).

- Sit alone quietly with your eyes closed.
- Start breathing deeply, imagining that with each inhalation you are coming back into yourself.

BUILDING BOUNDARIES, NOT BARRICADES

On the other hand, out of fear of losing yourself, you may have built barricades instead of boundaries. Intimacy may have come to mean intrusion to you and you may have become so fearful of giving yourself up in love or in passion that you have shut yourself off from any experience of emotional surrender, thus becoming alienated from others and isolated, disconnected, and alone.

If this is what has happened to you, you will need to learn to distinguish between autonomy and alienation, connectedness and dependency. For example, ask yourself "How far away can I go from another person and still feel connected?" and "How much am I willing to give up for love and security?" Everyone struggles with such questions from time to time, but some people are constantly dealing with these conflicts when they are in relationships.

Taking Risks

Learning to be intimate in a sexual relationship will take time and it will require that you be willing to take risks. Obviously, these risks should be taken slowly and carefully and even systematically—not haphazardly. This means taking a sexual or emotional risk when it is appropriate to how vulnerable it makes you feel at that stage of the relationship. Intimacy is often established one step at a time by taking a risk, then stepping back and giving yourself some time before you take another. Below is an example of the kind of continuum a healthy sexual relationship might follow:

1. Holding hands as you get to know one another by sharing your likes, dislikes, goals, and dreams.
2. Kissing as you begin to feel safe with one another and as you continue to get to know one another.
3. Deep kissing and petting as you begin to learn more about each other physically and to know each other's moods over time.

4. More and more intimate sexual sharing as your sense of safety with the other person grows along with your sexual attraction for one another.

5. Sexual intercourse (or a comparable act) is experienced following a discussion of one another's romantic and sexual histories, including the important issues of protection against AIDS and sexual fidelity.

6. Mutual exploration of one another's bodies as you continue to share one another's histories, including the sharing of sexual and other secrets.

7. More and more intimate forms of sexual sharing as a gradual deepening of the relationship occurs and time is given to getting to know one another's moods, needs, and personalities.

8. A commitment to one another that may include a promise of monogamy as each discovers that he or she does not wish to be with any other person and as each discovers that he or she can indeed trust the other with his or her body, history, secrets, and most important, emotions.

Begin with a small risk that doesn't have an enormous consequence if it doesn't work out. If it does work out, move on to a bigger risk. Continually reassess the relationship and what is happening to you all along the way. Keep asking yourself if you are being honest with yourself and with your partner, both sexually and emotionally.

If you begin to hide your feelings from your partner you can be sure that there is a problem in the relationship. It is essential to intimacy that you be able to express your feelings and that you be able to trust that your partner will honor those feelings. If you have begun to hide your feelings ask yourself whether the relationship still feels equal, mutual, and reciprocal (whether one has more power than the other in the relationship), and whether you and your partner are giving and receiving at similar levels. Ask yourself whether your level of trust is growing or whether you are distancing and withdrawing.

Not every sexual relationship has the capacity for intimacy. Ask yourself the following questions concerning your sexual partner to help you determine whether it is wise to take the risk of true intimacy:

• Do I truly respect this person and does he/she seem to respect me?

• Is this a person I can communicate openly with and does he/she seem to be able to communicate openly with me?

• Am I able to be honest with this person or am I lying, covering up, or putting up a facade?

• Do I believe this person is able to be honest with me?

• Do I feel safe enough to show my real feelings with this person?

• Are we able to compromise with one another?

• Do we work through conflicts well?

• Do we both take responsibility for the problems of the relationship or does one of us continually blame the other?

• Can I talk to this person about my childhood experiences, no matter how embarrassing they are?

• Can I talk to this person about my former relationships?

• Am I willing to talk about how I feel my past is affecting our relationship and is my partner willing to do the same?

• Is it possible for me to be myself in this relationship?

• Is there room for me to grow and change in this relationship?

If your relationship continues to deepen and to develop you can then take greater risks that require still more vulnerability. By carefully and systematically taking risks, one step at a time, and then sitting back to assess your level of trust and openness, you can create a healthy, conscious relationship instead of one driven by fear, compulsion, or unfulfilled childhood needs.

Fear of Intimacy

When you become intimate with someone you are letting yourself really be seen and known. That is why intimacy can be so frightening to most of us. The vulnerability and openness of an intimate relationship can feel deeply threatening because when we open ourselves up to another, that person has the ability to hurt us emotionally the way no one else can.

As you begin to establish intimacy with your partner you may feel unsafe and respond by withdrawing or building barriers between yourself and your sexual partner, or to sabotage the relationship as Jed did:

"Every time I get really close to my girlfriend I end up doing something to destroy our closeness. I pick a fight, or get critical of her, and then we break up for a while. We eventually get back together but I'm afraid that one day she won't come back to me. I don't know why I do this—it seems I can't help myself."

Even though you may consciously want to have a close, intimate relationship, something in your subconscious can set out to destroy it whenever you feel you are getting too close. We sometimes unconsciously arrange our lives so that we're on a kind of roller coaster getting close and then breaking up, so that we feel totally independent. Then we climb back on the roller coaster and begin all over again.

Another way of avoiding intimacy is to distance yourself sexually, thinking of sex as an activity rather than as a deep sharing of your innermost self. Men tend to do this more than women but both sexes are capable of it. Years ago, it used to be believed that males were less interested in and had less need for intimacy, but studies have shown this not to be true. Both men and women need and want intimacy; it is equally important for happiness to both sexes.

Still another way of dealing with a fear of intimacy is to allow yourself to share intimately while you're being sexual but avoid vulnerability in your day-to-day life with your partner.

Or you may find a certain level of intimacy comfortable in your sexual relationships but tend to panic when the relationship begins to deepen and grow. This happens most often when the intimacy of sexuality touches early childhood wounds.

In fact, as we have discussed previously, our fear of intimacy probably begins in our childhood. Anxiety about intimacy can usually be traced to a faulty relationship with parents or to childhood abuse.

FOCUSING MORE ON YOUR OWN PHYSICAL PLEASURE

Many people with low sexual self-esteem have spent their entire lives trying to figure out what their partners want and looking for ways to please them. They pay little if any attention to what would please themselves sexually and in asking that their own needs be met. Many people either deny they have sexual needs, fake orgasms, or are so involved in pleasing their partner and in performing that they are out of touch with themselves emotionally and physically.

Accepting physical and sexual pleasure can be a very difficult thing to do. Many people, and you may be one, are far more comfortable giving than receiving, and therefore consistently place the needs of others before their own.

If you remain riveted on your partner's needs, your partner may indeed become satisfied, but the chances are you will not. In fact, those who focus all their attention on pleasing their partner seldom experience very many physical sensations at all. They simply aren't paying enough attention to their own body and its responses to actually feel what is happening to them.

In order to truly be a good lover you will need to consider your own needs as much of a priority as those of your partner's. Those who put their partner's needs first actually do not make very good lovers because they are cut off emotionally and physically from a large portion of the sexual experience.

Most of us have been taught that if we are concerned with our own pleasure we are selfish. But being selfish about pleasing ourselves actually results in our being better able to give more to others. The happier and more fulfilled you are, the more energy you will have to give to others. If you are sexually satisfied your partner will only gain from your sexual experiences.

Working on Getting Rid of Performance Anxiety

In our society we tend to view sexuality as a performance. People become anxious in sexual encounters because they perceive that their partner has expectations of them—to have an erection, to lubricate, to have an orgasm, even to have multiple orgasms. This kind of anxiety in a sexual situation can be manifested by a combination of physical responses, such as rapid breathing, and mental concerns, such as "What's going to happen next?"

Those who suffer from low self-esteem feel they are unlovable, unattractive, and not sexy. Since they think so little of themselves, they may have a difficult time relaxing while they are having sex. They may instead be preoccupied with thinking about whether their partner finds them attractive or not, wondering whether he or she is being critical of what they see, and being self-conscious about the way they are responding. The way to remove performance anxiety is to take the focus off pleasing your partner and learn to concentrate on your own feelings of enjoyment and sexual arousal instead.

LEARNING THE IMPORTANCE OF TOUCH

Many of us have grown so accustomed to getting all our needs for intimacy met through sexual activity that we are unable to feel and express intimacy any other way. For many people, sex is the only way they really feel loved, yet there are many other ways of sharing intimacy, many ways of expressing love for one another other than being sexual: holding hands, caressing and massaging, taking a bath or Jacuzzi together, cuddling, scratching each other's backs, or just taking a walk together.

In addition, many people view foreplay strictly as a preliminary activity, a kind of appetizer, with intercourse being the main course. But it doesn't have to be that way. Many couples enjoy satisfying sexual activity (including orgasm) that consists only of "foreplay activities" such as stimulation of the genitals by hand, tongue, or mouth. This shouldn't be seen as any less "vital" than intercourse, and it can be just as satisfying for both partners.

We live in a highly sexual culture that is not very sensual (body contact that is pleasurable but not erotic). Our entire culture tends to focus on genital sex and almost disregards the pleasures of other kinds of physical contact. Even lovers don't seem to touch as much as they want. Although this is usually not true in the beginning of a relationship, it is almost inevitable that once a relationship becomes sexual, the nonsexual touching declines sharply.

Touching is important to us our entire lives—so much so, in fact, that the amount and quality of our nonsexual touching experiences are intimately related to how satisfied we are with our sexual activities. "Why is this?" you might ask. "Just what does touching have to do with the quality of my sexual behavior?" The answer is that for most people, sexual experiences are best, and the chances for avoiding sexual problems are highest, when they have sex only when it is sex that they want. When you use sex in an attempt to satisfy nonsexual needs—such as the need for comforting, the need for reassurance, or the need for physical contact— you run the risk of becoming disappointed. Sex that is motivated by other needs is often unsatisfying and can even lead to sexual problems since our bodies usually respond to what we *really want*. If all you really want is a hug, your body may refuse to respond sexually to even the most erotic touches.

When you share physical contact and affection only in the context of sexual activity, sex takes on an exaggerated importance. Sex becomes weighed down with all the needs that aren't being met elsewhere. Ask yourself what you really want when you think you want sex. Is it closeness to someone you care about, a feeling of connectedness? Is it understanding or support? Is it reassurance that the person you care about cares about you in return? Or is it intercourse or orgasm?

Once you have some idea of what you want at any given time, ask yourself what the best way of getting it might be. Do you really just need a hug or to be held? Or do you need to connect with your partner by having an intimate conversation, perhaps including the request for some verbal reassurance? How would giving or receiving a massage feel? If you begin to take the time to ask yourself these questions you will find that you will also begin to get your sexual needs and desires fulfilled in sex and satisfy needs for other kinds of contact and affection in more appropriate ways.

There will, of course, be times when sex is exactly what you want and need. But consider the following exercises for those times when sensual touch is more appropriate for your needs and desires.

Sensate Focus Exercises

The following exercises are called "sensate focus" exercises and originated with the work of sex therapists and researchers Masters and Johnson. In my practice, they have helped hundreds of couples suffering from a vast variety of sexual and intimacy problems. They are designed to help establish trust between the couple and to help them find alternative ways of touching and sharing intimacy. The term "sensate focus" refers to the fact that during the exercises you are to *focus* your attention as closely as you can on your *sensations*, how it *feels* to touch or be touched. For example, whether you are the one who is giving the touch or receiving it, make sure that you always focus all your attention on the point where your body comes into contact with your partner's skin. If your mind wanders off during the exercise, bring it back to the exact point between your skin and your partner's skin.

This way of touching, called caressing, has been proven to remove the pressure to perform, to allow each person to touch for his or her own pleasure, and to help one express tenderness, caring, and gentleness.

Caressing is different from massage or even what is commonly called "sensual massage" because instead of manipulating the large muscles of the body, you will be focused on the skin. Caressing is a slow, sensuous touch that is much lighter than massage and is done very, very slowly, using not just the tips of your fingers but your entire hand and even your forearm. You will caress your partner's skin with long, sweeping strokes using the flat of your hand and fingers, and your palm, wrist, and forearm.

Another difference between caressing and massaging is that massage is intended solely for the pleasure or therapeutic benefit of the person *receiving* the massage, while caressing is done for the pleasure of the person *giving* the caress as well. You may have noticed in the past that you became tired easily while giving a massage and may have even become anxious because you were so concerned as to whether you were doing it *right* and pleasing the person you were giving the massage to. The wonderful thing about caressing is that the person giving the caress enjoys it equally as much, and since you are not worried about how well you are performing, it will not feel like a task but a pleasure.

To understand exactly what I mean, try the following exercise:

Imagine that your right hand is the "giver" and your left hand is the "receiver." Touch your left hand using only the fingertips of your right hand. Which of your hands feels the pleasure of the touch? Most people will say that their left hand, the "receiver" feels the pleasure. But what about your right hand, does that hand feel any pleasure? Most people say no, they don't feel any pleasure by using their fingertips.

Now try "giving" to the left hand by using the flat of your fingers, and the palm and wrist of your right hand. Which hand feels the pleasure of the touch this time? Most people will say that *both* hands feel pleasure, both the "giver" and the "receiver." Indeed, it is hard to tell which hand is the "giver" and which is the "receiver" when you use the caress technique.

You and your partner may or may not choose to use a lotion or oil for the caressing. Some people do not like the feel of lotion or oil on their skin. If you both decide you'd like to use an oil or lotion make sure it is one that both of you like. Pay particular attention to the fragrance of the oil and make certain it does not elicit negative memories for either one of you.

Always do the exercises in a private, quiet environment. Take the phone off the hook, send the children to a baby-sitter, or wait until they are in bed at night. Some people prefer to have on some easy-listening music, but it is really best to do these exercises in silence. It is far too easy to become distracted when there is music; your intention is to focus on sensations only.

WHEN YOU ARE THE ACTIVE PARTNER

Always maintain contact with your partner as you are giving the caress to avoid surprising him or her with a sudden touch when you switch hands. If you use lotion or oil, warm it in your hand before you apply it, and maintain contact with your partner's body when you reapply the lotion.

You can use long, sweeping strokes of your forearm, your wrist, the palm of your hand, and the flat of your fingers, or you can alternate with shorter strokes, using only the flat of your fingers. Make sure that you do not use only your fingertips, however, because this can tickle your partner.

Make sure that you are going very, very slowly; the slower the better. If you think you are moving your hand slowly enough, cut your speed in half and see how this affects your ability to focus on the touch. Do not worry about whether your partner is enjoying the caress. It will be his or her responsibility to let you know if you are doing something uncomfortable. Since sensate focus exercises are intended to promote relaxation, both you and your partner will feel more relaxed if the exercises are done very slowly, with both of you closing your eyes.

While it is normal to become distracted now and then, try bringing your mind back to the place where your skin makes contact with your partner's skin if you find it wandering.

Do not speak while doing the exercise and do not ask for feedback during the exercise. Assume that the caress feels good or at least neutral.

While you will be focusing mostly on your own feelings while caressing your partner, you should be able to notice if he or she is anxious or tense. Obvious signs of anxiety include rapid or shallow breathing, a jumpy or quivering stomach, and muscle tension.

If you notice any of these signs in your partner, slow your touch down. If signs of anxiety do not go away, encourage your partner to take deep breaths. If your partner still seems tense, ask if you should stop the exercise for a while until he or she becomes more comfortable.

WHEN YOU ARE THE PASSIVE PARTNER

Close your eyes and try to relax any muscles that feel tense. Keep your attention on the place where your partner is touching your skin. Mentally follow your partner's hand as it caresses your body. Do not give your partner any feedback unless something is painful or uncomfortable. Do not moan or groan or wiggle around because this can be a subtle way of manipulating the active partner into continuing to touch a particular spot. Remaining completely passive will allow your body to experience pleasure more fully. If you become tense, try taking some deep breaths to relax yourself and focus only on the touch.

FEEDBACK

At the end of each exercise, you should talk openly and honestly with one another about your experience. The exercises will do no good if you lie about your feelings. For instance, please do not tell your partner you enjoyed the experience if you didn't or that you were able to concentrate if you weren't, just so that you appear to be doing things correctly.

Most people benefit greatly from giving and receiving feedback after the exercises. This kind of feedback can be the beginning of really honest communication between a couple, establishing trust and openness. They learn to communicate more openly and honestly about what feels good and what doesn't, and they learn what feels good to their partner.

Because it is so hard to remember instructions, here is a summary of things to remember while doing the sensate focus exercises:

1. Agree on the limits of the exercise beforehand and do not go beyond those limits.

2. Always focus on the point of contact where your skin touches your partner's skin.

3. When you are active, do the exercise for your own pleasure and do not worry whether your partner is enjoying it. Use a slow, light caressing technique.

4. Stay passive when in the passive role—no feedback.

5. Focus on sensual pleasure rather than sexual arousal.

6. If anxiety does not quickly decrease after the first few minutes of an exercise, stop the exercise immediately.

7. Don't work at it. Relax.

8. Provide honest feedback after the exercise.

The following exercises should bring you much closer together than you have ever been before and add to your repertoire of sensual ways of sharing. In addition, they will help build trust and provide each person with a feeling of being loved and wanted for reasons other than sexual ones.

THE FOOT CARESS

You may do this exercise one of two ways, either including a foot bath or not. If you leave out the bath, all you need is some oil or lotion and two towels. If you would like to include the foot bath, you will need two towels, a basin or tub large enough for a person's feet, liquid soap, lotion, and hot water.

The foot bath can be a loving, relaxing part of this exercise and should be included if at all possible. The foot bath also solves the problem of having to worry about whether or not your feet smell or are sweaty.

To start, the passive person sits in a chair with his or her feet on the floor. Since this exercise includes the ankles and part of the calves, you will need to wear shorts or have your pant legs rolled up. The active partner fills the basin with warm water and places the passive partner's feet in the water. If you do not have a basin large enough for both feet do one foot at a time. Add the liquid soap and slowly caress your partner's feet in the water. Remember to touch for your own pleasure, using a light touch, not a massage. Bathe one foot at a time, finding out how the different areas of the foot feel as you bathe them. Spend at least five minutes on each foot but you can take longer if you like.

When you are finished with both feet, lift them out of the water firmly but gently, dry them, and wrap them in separate towels. Put aside the basin. Now gently take one foot from the towel and caress it using the oil or lotion. Take as long as you like, staying longer on parts of the foot, ankle, and lower calf that you especially enjoy touching. Spend at least five to ten minutes on each foot.

As the passive person during the foot bath and caress all you need do is relax, enjoy, and allow yourself to be pampered. If your partner does something that bothers you, say something, but otherwise concentrate totally on the touch. Relax your feet and just let them hang from your legs. Your partner will lift them into the basin and move them—you don't need to help.

THE BACK CARESS

The back caress may be more threatening than the hand or foot caress since it can involve parts of the body that are often associated with sexual arousal, such as the buttocks and thighs. You both need to agree in advance that there will be no sexual touching and that you will confine your touching to areas of the body that are "in bounds." The back caress includes the entire back of the body from the neck to the feet, but you may want to confine yourselves to the upper back, above the waist only. This will be far less threatening for some people than including the buttocks and the backs of the legs.

This exercise can be done in the nude but for those who are uncomfortable with nudity I recommend instead that you both wear shorts, bathing suits, or underwear. Women may feel comfortable in a halter top or a bra.

As always you will need a quiet room where you will not be disturbed, with a bed or some other comfortable surface with plenty of room for both of you to stretch out. You may also want to use a large towel and some lotion or oil.

The passive partner should lie comfortably, facedown, with a towel underneath. He or she may keep arms at sides or underneath the head, whichever is most comfortable. The active person should lie or sit next to the passive partner without leaning on him or her.

The active person begins to caress the passive person's back, beginning at the neck. You can use either one hand or two, whichever is more comfortable. Slowly run your palm or your fingers over the shoulder blades and then down the spine. Remember, this is not a massage. The object is to use your hand to find areas that feel particularly good to you.

If you both have agreed, continue touching your partner, moving down the back to the buttocks and legs. Remember to stroke your partner slowly and try to keep your eyes closed when at all possible to enhance the pleasure and maximize your ability to focus on physical sensations. If you have difficulty focusing, slow your speed down and bring your mind back to the exact point of contact between your skin and your partner's skin.

Pay attention to how the various parts of your partner's body feel when you caress them with your palm, wrist, and forearm instead of just your fingertips. When you find that a particular part of the body feels especially good to you, savor the touch and linger there awhile. Pay attention to the various textures of the skin and the different temperatures in various parts of the body.

There should be no sexual touching with this exercise. Do not reach between your partner's legs and attempt to include the genitals. Do not place your hands inside the crevice of the buttocks. Your partner must be able to feel that you are not going to go beyond the limits of the exercise.

If you notice that your partner is tensing up, remind him or her to breathe and relax, and continue with the caress. If your partner still seems tense, is moving about, or is breathing rapidly after the exercise has been going on for a few minutes, stop the caress and talk quietly about this.

Each person should spend approximately twenty to thirty minutes doing the back caress. Complete the caress by making long, smooth strokes starting at your partner's shoulders and moving all the way down to the feet. You may want to indicate that you have stopped by firmly placing your hands on the bottoms of the feet.

When you are the passive partner, make yourself comfortable, breathe deeply, and relax your muscles. Keep your mind on the exact point of contact where your partner is touching you. Try not to move; just passively soak up the sensations. The only time you need to communicate with your partner is if he or she does something that hurts you or makes you uncomfortable.

If you become sexually aroused as either the giver or the receiver during the back caress, fine. Just enjoy the arousal and bring your mind back to the point of contact.

LEARNING TO COMMUNICATE OPENLY ABOUT SEX

You've heard this before—good communication between partners is as essential to sexual pleasure (and to good sex in general) as is any particular technique. No matter what a good lover you are, if you are not giving to your partner in the ways that make her or him feel good then both of you will suffer. Your sexual self-esteem will be lowered because deep inside you will sense that you are not pleasing your partner. Conversely, your partner's sexual self-esteem will also be affected since she or he may interpret your inability to please sexually as disinterest—or, worse yet, as a sign that you don't love her or him.

Unless you talk with your partner about her or his likes and dislikes you will not be able to discover how to please her or him. And your partner can't know what you like unless you tell or show her or him.

In a survey conducted by Philip and Lorna Sarrel, sex therapists at Yale University, it was found that among women who have told their partners exactly how they like to be touched, seven out of ten indicated they have orgasms "every time" or "almost every time" they make love. They concluded that the ability to share thoughts and feelings about sex with your partner is the single most important factor in a good sexual relationship. They also found that good communicators had intercourse more often and were more likely to be satisfied with its frequency.

There are two basic methods of communicating sexual information to your partner—nonverbally, through the use of body movements during lovemaking, or verbally, by talking with your lover either during lovemaking or at some other time. Both methods have good and bad points.

The primary drawback to nonverbal communication is that it

can be misunderstood. Often verbal communication is necessary to straighten out confusion created by nonverbal communication. This was the case with Van and Charmaine. It really turned Van on to have the woman be on top during intercourse. Instead of telling Charmaine this, he tried to communicate it to her nonverbally by maneuvering her body and placing her on top of him. Charmaine, on the other hand, was very uncomfortable being on top, so she would slide off as soon as she could. What would transpire would be a kind of wrestling match with Van struggling to get Charmaine on top and Charmaine struggling to get off. By the time they came to see me they were both angry over the situation. Van felt that Charmaine didn't love him enough to do what he wanted, while Charmaine felt that Van was domineering and lazy. She felt that Van wanted her to do all the work.

Once they began to discuss the problem in therapy, however, Van was able to understand that it wasn't that Charmaine didn't love him enough to try to please him but that she was uncomfortable being on top because she was self-conscious about her body. She was afraid that because Van could see her body so well from that vantage point he was going to be critical of her. Once Van heard this he was able to reassure Charmaine that he thought her body was beautiful and that, in fact, it was because he *could* see her body so well in that position that he preferred it.

Charmaine, hearing this, now understood that it wasn't that Van was lazy and wanted her to do all the work at all. Even though she was still uncomfortable at first, knowing that Van admired her body made it easier for her to be on top at times.

Many people have erroneously believed that the best way of communicating your desires to your partner is by doing to your partner what you would like your partner to do to you. Unfortunately, this method leaves just too much room for miscommunication.

On the other hand, sometimes nonverbal communication can be more specific than verbal communication. For example, many women need very specific clitoral stimulation in order to reach orgasm. Attempting to describe the type of stimulation needed can be difficult if not impossible. However, by directing her partner nonverbally, by actually taking his hand in hers and moving it in the desired manner, a woman can communicate her needs beautifully.

You may also find that trying to communicate during sex spoils the mood for you and you prefer to rely on body movements and sighs of pleasure. Or, conversely, you may find that talking about sex while you are making love enhances the experience for you. Some people find it extremely arousing to talk to their partner about what they want to do to her or him. What's important is that you develop some form of communication that is comfortable for you and your partner, whether it be verbal or nonverbal.

Your first attempts at communication, no matter what method you use, are likely to be somewhat awkward. There is probably no way to avoid the awkwardness of the first few minutes of the conversation, but you can make it easier if you open the conversation by reassuring your partner that you want to continue the relationship or by expressing your love. You may want to state that you don't believe you have adequately communicated your needs in the past, or reassure your partner that you are not blaming her or him. Then begin to discuss your concerns about your sexual relationship, which of your needs are not being met, and the changes you wish to occur in the relationship. Finally, encourage your partner to share his or her feelings and any suggestions that might make lovemaking more satisfying to both of you.

Many experts feel that the best time to talk about sexual matters is not when you're ready to have sex, or during sex, but at some other time. Then you and your partner will both be less likely to perceive suggestions and information as criticism.

Set aside a time to discuss your sexual relationship at a place and time that is conducive to such a discussion. You may want to begin the conversation at a favorite restaurant where you both feel comfortable or on a long walk or drive. Just make sure you won't be distracted or interrupted and that one or both of you is not preoccupied with something else.

You may want to use a book or television show to initiate the discussion. Or you might prefer to make a special appointment to talk. Make sure you don't bring up the subject during an argument or disagreement or after a particularly frustrating day. Picking a time when you and your partner are both relaxed and when you both feel close to one another will enhance the possibility of good communication.

If you are in an established relationship it is important that you tell your partner what you need in order to feel loved and it is also important that you listen to what your partner says she or he needs. If you can't do this by yourselves, a counselor can help you learn how to communicate about these crucial matters and negotiate a *mutually* satisfying arrangement.

It is equally important to open up the communication early on in a new relationship. Because of the lack of familiarity with each other it is even more important to share specific information early on. Also, letting your partner know what you like and don't like sexually early on in the relationship helps to prevent negative patterns from developing.

In new relationships people often make love to a new partner by doing the kinds of things they like, by doing what pleased a previous partner, or by doing what they have read women or men like. During the "honeymoon period" in a new relationship everything tends to feel good, but unmet needs tend to surface as time goes by. At that point, if you don't let your partner know what turns you on or off, you will only reinforce the belief that what is being done is okay, thus encouraging your partner to continue.

Asking for What You Want

Many people have the belief that their partners should be sensitive enough to their needs to know automatically what they want without their having to ask for it. How often have you heard someone say, "If I have to ask for it, I don't want it"? When you think about this it seems rather silly, doesn't it? Don't allow this kind of misguided thinking to get in the way of your receiving the kind of touches and stimulation that you really desire. Remember, no one is a mind reader, and no matter how well your partner knows you there is really no way he or she can know what you want sexually at any given time.

Some people are afraid to ask for what they want sexually for fear of being rejected. If they are able to ask at all they couch their requests in subtle language, hoping their wishes will be understood but protecting themselves in case they're not. Unfortunately, the fear of not getting their wishes can create a self-fulfilling prophecy. If you don't ask for what you want directly, your partner may never know what you want. And if you interpret not getting what you want as an indication that you were right not to ask because you wouldn't have gotten what you wanted anyway, then you won't make your needs known the next time, either. Although it is difficult, being vulnerable with your partner by openly communicating your sexual preferences is an excellent way of building trust in your partner.

People who love each other want to please each other, but they often do not know how. Men in particular report that they wish their partners would be more clear when they communicate their needs so they wouldn't have to fumble around trying to figure out their wishes. By not being specific enough with your partner about your sexual preferences, you are not only depriving yourself of sexual pleasure, you are depriving your partner of the pleasure of pleasing you.

A Great Sex Life Begins with One

You don't have to miss out on romance, sensuality, and exciting sexual feelings just because you are currently without a partner. Even single people can enjoy the excitement and fulfillment of a full sex life if they are willing to do the following: work on loving their own bodies; work on accepting themselves as they are; and work on treating themselves as they would a lover.

A woman I knew only briefly told me how she had decided to "take herself on as a lover" as a way of raising her sexual self-esteem. What she meant by this was that she actively behaved as if she were her own lover, treating herself in the way she would like a lover to treat her—setting the stage with satin sheets, candlelight, and music that she found to be very erotic.

Once a week, preferably when you are very relaxed and have plenty of time, make a date with yourself for a sexual encounter, just as you would if you had a date. Your date might begin with a sensuous candlelight dinner with soft music. Choose your food carefully, making elegant choices of either sensuous, erotic food (sushi, artichokes) or something light and healthy (salad, fish, vegetables). Eat slowly, savoring each bite, enjoying the texture and aroma of the food as much as you enjoy the taste.

Set the stage for your sexual encounter by making the room as erotic as possible. If you are a romantic, have candlelight, flowers, and scented sheets. If you are the rowdy type perhaps you would choose rock-and-roll or heavy-metal music, neon lights, and black satin sheets. Taking a long sensuous bath is some people's ideal way of relaxing and preparing for their sexual encounter, while others prefer a brisk shower.

You deserve to treat yourself as sensuously, as lavishly as you would treat a romantic partner. You deserve the same amount of time and detail in preparing yourself dinner as you would give a guest. And you deserve to make your house, and your bedroom especially, as sensuous and erotic as you would if you had company.

Chapter Twelve

GETTING HELP FOR YOUR PROBLEMS

It is a well-known fact that young men often suffer from premature ejaculation and young women often have difficulties having an orgasm when they first begin to have sex. But while we can initially chalk up our difficulties to inexperience and fear, if we continue to have problems during sex we understandably begin to worry. The fear of not being able to perform in the ways we would like to sexually can become a major problem in adulthood. Performance pressure is one of the deepest concerns for both women and men and it can cause us to avoid having sex as often as we'd like to or to avoid it altogether.

You have a sexual problem if your sexuality is causing you personal distress, such as anxiety, depression, or fear. If you feel you have a sexual problem, then you probably do have one, because worrying about your sexual functioning will undoubtedly interfere with your body's ability to function.

Sexual dysfunction is both a cause of low sexual self-esteem and a symptom of it. Having a sexual dysfunction can be absolutely devastating and can be one of the most significant factors in feeling sexually inadequate, as it was with Suki:

"Until I was twenty-five I was unable to reach orgasm or to really be able to relax and enjoy myself sexually. Sex was always a performance, mostly intended to please the man. I did not share my inability to orgasm with my partners but 'faked' orgasm so as not to give myself away. In fact, it wasn't until I had reached the age of twenty-five that I had my first orgasm with the help of a very understanding male partner.

"Once I was able to have an orgasm my sexual self-esteem increased considerably. I started focusing more on my own sexual pleasure and less on the man's, and I began to ask for the kind of stimulation I needed to bring me to orgasm."

On the other hand, sexual dysfunction, when not caused by physical problems, can be a metaphor for what is really going on with us—a measure of our self-esteem, an indication of how willing and capable we are of becoming truly intimate with another human being, a reflection of how we feel about sex and how we feel about our body.

Identifying and then resolving your sexual dysfunction will be one of the best things you can do for your sexual self-esteem. Since the first step to recovery will be for you to identify your problem and then look for its probable cause, I have included a section on each of the major sexual dysfunctions.

If you find that you are suffering from one or more of these dysfunctions you will need to spend some time examining your past as well as your present to find the probable cause. In addition, under each specific dysfunction we will discuss common causes and methods for treatment.

FEMALE SEXUAL DYSFUNCTIONS
Female Sexual Arousal Disorder

The most common dysfunction for women is "female sexual arousal disorder," the inability to become sexually aroused. This may involve the failure to lubricate or a lack of sexual excitement or pleasure. All women suffer from this problem from time to time because of boredom or relationship problems. It is only considered a *dysfunction* when the problem is chronic. This dysfunction can have many causes, including a fear of intercourse caused by negative parental messages regarding sex (such as: only "cheap" girls like sex, sex is unpleasant for women), a fear of pregnancy or disease, a poor body image, childhood sexual abuse, or rape as an adult.

When June was eighteen she finally gave in to her boyfriend,

Willie, after months of pressure from him. But the night they were to "go all the way" June could not become sexually aroused. No matter how hard he tried Willie couldn't get her to lubricate. This was not surprising given June's strict background. Both her parents had continuously warned her about the dangers of premarital sex. She was warned that not only was it a sin but that she was likely to get pregnant or get a venereal disease if she ever gave in. In addition, her mother told her that no boy would ever marry a girl who was not a virgin.

TREATMENT CHOICES

If you have felt sexual arousal in the past, you can feel it again. If you have never felt sexual arousal, you can begin to feel it. No matter what the cause, the immediate culprit is the anxiety that overwhelms you as you start sexual activity. It is important to know that anxiety is both physical and mental. Manifestations of anxiety include rapid heartbeat, perspiration, and muscle tension, as well as thoughts that cause worry or distress. Unfortunately, our bodies are created in such a way that we cannot be both anxious and aroused at the same time. To overcome sexual anxiety you must learn to recognize it and train your body to relax. The sensate focus exercises discussed previously can help you to learn to relax so that your body can feel the arousal it will naturally feel if you are not anxious.

Vaginismus

Vaginismus is an involuntary contracting or tightening of the vaginal muscles—particularly those around the opening of the vagina—that can make intercourse uncomfortable, painful, or even impossible. Sometimes it may also be accompanied by muscle tightness in the stomach, thighs, and buttocks. For women who were raped, either as children or as adults, and those who were molested by having fingers or instruments inserted into their vaginas, vaginismus is often a defense against pain. Although vaginismus is almost always caused by trauma such as child sexual abuse or rape as an adult, it can also be caused by negative parental messages and strong injunctions not to have sex prior to marriage.

There are different degrees of vaginismus. Some women experience it only in response to attempts at insertion of the penis, while others may not be able to insert anything into the vagina, not even a finger or a tampon. It is also possible that vaginismus can occur with one partner and not with others.

Many women have vaginismus without realizing it. Instead, a woman and her partner may think that the partner has an exceptionally large penis or that the woman is very small or very tight. Vaginismus is not related to the size of the woman's vagina. When properly lubricated and stimulated, the female vagina is designed to accept any size penis comfortably. It is rare for a vagina to be so small that it will not accommodate a penis, no matter how large.

Many survivors of sexual abuse will encounter this problem the first time they voluntarily choose to have sex but gradually get over it as they have more and more experience with sex that isn't abusive or violent. Others will periodically suffer from the problem whenever they are reminded of the rape or abuse from their childhood or adolescence. Still others will need to wait until they have completed more of their recovery before they will be relieved of this problem, since it is directly related to the sexual trauma they experienced and therefore requires that they gain some healing from the trauma first. Sally's husband, Kenneth, recalled:

"The first time I tried to penetrate my wife she was so closed up that I couldn't get inside her. I didn't know what was wrong, but I took it personally. I thought I must not be spending enough time with foreplay. But no matter how long I spent, she was never really ready. Finally we went to a doctor who told us what was wrong. That's when it came out that Sally had been raped by her stepfather and that's when she started therapy.

"It took her a long time before she was finally able to have intercourse with me. Fortunately, we learned to do a lot of other things instead. Even today I still have to be very gentle and move really slow or she will tense up. And sometimes, if she's been talking to her therapist about the rape and reexperiencing the feelings she had, she'll tighten up completely again and we won't be able to have intercourse for a while."

TREATMENT CHOICES

Whatever the cause, learning to relax is the most important factor in treating vaginismus. You can do this by doing any of the caressing or breathing exercises discussed in this book. When you are ready to work on this problem you can begin to do so by inserting your own fingers into your vagina. Then, when you feel enough safety and support from your partner, you can work on it together, first by inserting your partner's fingers into your vagina and then inserting his penis into your vagina. You should be the one who controls all insertion.

MALE SEXUAL DYSFUNCTIONS
Erectile Disorders

Many men suffer from problems with erections, referred to by professionals as "male erectile disorder," or an older term, "impotence." Some of these men have erections through masturbation but never with a partner, some have had erections in the past but are unable to now, and some have erections part of the time but are unable to consistently have them with their partners. Others are consistently able to achieve an erection but lose it during lovemaking and before ejaculation.

There are several different reasons why males suffer from erectile disorders. The most common reason is that their self-esteem and self-confidence were so damaged in childhood or by a lover that they literally feel impotent or powerless in life. Interestingly, common synonyms for the word *impotent* are "powerless," "ineffective," "helpless," "weak," and "disabled." This is, in fact, how males who were emotionally, physically, or sexually abused as children often feel as a consequence of the fear, shame, and humiliation associated with their upbringing.

Another common reason for male impotency is the fact that the erect male penis symbolizes power and aggressiveness, and many males do not want to be identified with these things. To many males, the erect penis also represents violence, intrusiveness, and pain. Seeing his own penis erect may remind a man of his own experience of being violated physically or sexually when he was a child.

TREATMENT CHOICES

In order for you to deal with your problem, you must learn to know your body well enough to determine at which stage of the sexual response cycle your response shuts down. You also need to determine whether your problem is to any degree physical.

Problems due to nerve damage or vascular damage are completely physiological. But other problems may be caused by a combination of physical and psychological factors. Because the mind can be responsible for changes in the body, many erectile problems have some psychological component.

A few simple questions can help you decide whether your problems are physical or psychological:

• Do you have erections when you masturbate? On a scale of one to ten, with one being no erection and ten being an extremely rigid erection, how hard are the erections you have with masturbation?

• Do you wake up with an erection in the morning? On a scale of one to ten, how hard is it?

If you can have a fairly strong erection with masturbation and upon awakening there is probably nothing physiologically wrong with your penis, and any difficulties you experience with a partner are likely to be psychological. The exercises in the book, most especially the sensate focus exercises, can probably help you overcome your erection problems.

On the other hand, if you do not have erections with masturbation or when you awake, there is a chance that your problem is physical. Aside from nerve damage caused by diabetes and other causes that can be permanent, most physical problems related to erections are temporary. For example, some drugs, such as those prescribed for the treatment of ulcers or high blood pressure, can cause temporary but emotionally devastating erection problems. Nonprescription drugs such as antihistamines can also temporarily interfere with erections, as can alcohol consumption.

Consult your physician if you suspect that your erectile problems may be physically caused. Otherwise, you probably need to focus on letting go of your performance orientation, paying attention to your own enjoyment rather than on pleasing your partner so much, and taking the pressure off yourself to have an erection and instead enjoying yourself and taking your time to savor the sensuous feelings in your body.

Premature Ejaculation

Another common sexual dysfunction experienced by men is premature or rapid ejaculation. This dysfunction is not defined by the amount of time or the number of thrusts before ejaculation but by the feeling the man has of not being in control over when he ejaculates. Men suffer from this disorder to various degrees, some ejaculating with little or no physical or sexual stimulation at all, some when they are rubbed up against, some as soon as they are touched by a hand or mouth, and some ejaculating immediately upon penetration or only a few seconds afterward.

A major cause of premature ejaculation is anxiety. Some men are not aware of how very anxious they are, while others may be acutely aware of feeling panicky at the very thought of a sexual encounter. Either way, their bodies have learned a response in which their tensed muscles, irregular breathing patterns, and distracting thoughts trigger ejaculation. By learning to recognize their level of anxiety, their level of arousal, and even more important, what the anxiety specifically relates to, they can learn to last as long as they want to.

Premature ejaculation often begins when the male's first sexual experience was highly charged with the fear of getting caught. This was Greg's experience:

"My girlfriend and I were always sneaking around having sex whenever her parents weren't home. Sex with us was always hurried and always tense since we feared having her parents come back anytime. We took incredible chances since I really think her father might have killed me if he'd caught us. Now when I have sex I just can't seem to relax no matter how hard I try and so I always end up coming too quickly."

Some men are extremely nervous about female sexuality, fearing that they are going to be sexually attacked by the woman or required to demonstrate their virility. This is often true of men whose mothers or other female authority figures were overly controlling, domineering, or seductive. We often assume that men are insatiably sexual and demanding since historically they are supposed to seek out conquests and be active and dominant, whereas women are passive, receptive, and compliant receivers. But, in fact, many men are far less confident than this; they may doubt their own sexual prowess or feel that women cannot really want them. A man may believe his penis is too small or his erection is not big enough, or he may think that a woman is bound to be put off by his body when she actually looks at him naked. Feeling that he has to prove himself, he then may get so excited at having achieved an erection and penetration that a bit of friction provokes immediate ejaculation.

Many men are premature ejaculators because for one reason or another, they literally want to get the sex act over with. Aaron was one of many of my male clients who expressed this sentiment: "I was always so tense and fearful during sex that I just wanted to ejaculate and get it all over with. Even though I sometimes felt guilty because I knew the woman wasn't satisfied, I mostly just felt relieved."

It turned out that Aaron felt a very strong sense of guilt about having sex since he was raised in a deeply religious family and was taught that sex was only for procreation. Although his body wanted to have sex, his head was telling him it was wrong.

Another reason for the unconscious desire to get sex over with quickly is a fear of intimacy, as Reed discovered during therapy: "I realize now that the reason I ejaculated so quickly was because I was uncomfortable being close to a woman. I wanted to have sex but I was afraid of becoming emotionally involved. My mother had been so possessive and smothering of me when I was a child that I assumed all women were the same."

TREATMENT CHOICES

Premature ejaculation can be one of the easiest of the sexual dysfunctions to treat. The prognosis for this problem has a lot to do with how both you and your partner react to each incidence of prematurity. If you each begin to blame the other for the problem not only are you not helping the situation but you will be harming your relationship. Men's reactions to prematurity vary widely. Some men apologize profusely, some imply that their partner is to blame, some carry on lovemaking as if nothing had happened, and some suddenly just lose interest in their partner. None of these reactions is conducive to working through the problem. The best reaction would be to neither ignore it nor make too big an issue of it. Women tend to prefer to communicate about problems, so mentioning it will make most women more comfortable and open the door to communication.

Many couples enjoy lovemaking even if the man ejaculates before the woman has an orgasm. It does not affect their capacity to experience delight in each other's bodies in other ways and he can still stimulate her to orgasm with his fingers or mouth.

Start/Stop Method

In some cases, especially those where the cause of the problem is simply the fact that the man has not yet learned to control his ejaculation, either because of inexperience or because of performance anxiety, this simple technique can change ejaculatory behavior in a relatively short amount of time. The essence of achieving control is for you (and your partner, if you have a steady one) to learn to recognize when a surge to orgasm begins and then to stop it before it reaches a crescendo. As soon as you begin to feel the *beginnings* of such stirrings stop all movement and wait a few minutes until control has been achieved. Then you can pick up the lovemaking where you left off. Most men will experience a softening of their erection, but as soon as movement commences the erection will likely return to full hardness. Observe closely and as soon as the next wave of excitement begins, stop once again and allow a pause before resuming stimulation.

PROBLEMS FOR BOTH SEXES
The Inability to Have an Orgasm

One of the most common sexual dysfunctions for both males and females is the inability to have an orgasm. In females this is called "inhibited female orgasm" (in the past it was referred to as "inorgasmia," "anorgasmia," "preorgasmia," or "frigidity"). In males the problem is called "inhibited ejaculation," "retarded ejaculation," or "ejaculatory incompetence."

Some people are unable to climax in any way, while others are able to climax while masturbating but not during intercourse or other types of lovemaking. Some can reach a climax only when they are in control of the sexual act, such as being on top, being the initiator, or being the one who is doing the moving.

The reasons for difficulty in achieving orgasms are varied, but the issue of control is almost always at the core of the problem. The act of sex is about losing control. Those who fear having an orgasm often fear others having control over them. This is often caused by having been overly controlled by parents or other caretakers, or from emotional, physical, or sexual abuse. When a child is sexually violated, for example, that child loses all sense of control over his or her body. Holding back from having an orgasm, even though it is an unconscious act, is one way of asserting control over one's body.

In addition, those who were abused as children as well as those who have felt betrayed by others as adults (an unfaithful lover, a friend who takes away your lover) will find it difficult to trust others. In order to have an orgasm with your partner, you must be able to feel comfortable, trusting, and vulnerable. Without trust, there is no true vulnerability. Feeling afraid of being betrayed, hurt, used, and then discarded, will keep you from relaxing enough to be truly vulnerable. You may be afraid of feeling pleasure for fear that someone will take advantage of you, as the person who abused or betrayed you did, or you may be afraid of loving someone for fear that you are just being used, as you were before.

TREATMENT CHOICES

The objective of the treatment of orgasm inhibition is to modify your tendency to obsessively observe your preorgasmic sensations and to allow yourself to abandon yourself to erotic feelings, which is a necessary condition of orgastic release. This can be achieved by structuring the situation so that you receive effective genital stimulation (either penile or clitoral) under the most tranquil of conditions.

While alone and relaxed, using lubricant, a vibrator, your favorite erotic fantasy, erotic literature, or erotic pictures, stimulate yourself in a very relaxed, unhurried way, breathing deeply. Do not worry about having an orgasm, do not rush, and do not allow your body to stiffen up.

Once orgasm has been reached through masturbation, the next step will be to learn to have an orgasm in the presence of a partner, first by self-stimulation and then by mutual genital stimulation by the partner. This process should occur with a gradual increase in intimacy. First your partner turns his or her back while you stimulate yourself. Then, perhaps at another time, your partner can hold you while you stimulate yourself. Eventually your partner will manually stimulate you to orgasm.

For Women Who Have Never Achieved Orgasm

In the absence of nerve damage or other physiological injury or defect, any woman can have an orgasm through masturbation. Many problems with orgasm are not caused by any deep-seated psychological conflict but by simply not knowing how the body works. Begin to explore your body in a relaxed atmosphere (there will be more help on how to do this in Part III). This kind of relaxed exploration, perhaps with the help of a vibrator at first, should help bring you to orgasm.

Once you have learned to bring yourself to orgasm through masturbation, you can teach your partner the types of touches and stimulation you need in order to orgasm.

For Men with Inhibited Ejaculation

Generally speaking, there seem to be two specific types of inhibited ejaculation. Some men, in their attempt to avoid premature ejaculation, have worked so hard to control their ejaculation that they overdid it. In other cases, the man developed an ejaculation problem as a result of anger against women or a specific woman. This anger destroys the intimacy in the relationship and causes the man's feelings to be dulled or "numbed out." If a man has ever been able to ejaculate during intercourse, he can probably learn to again. But if he has never been able to ejaculate in the vagina, he will probably need to enter psychotherapy in order to work on the psychological aspects of his problem.

An inability to ejaculate may also be caused by consumption of alcohol or some types of drugs. It can also be a sign of a medical problem such as an enlarged prostate, especially if the problem began rather suddenly. If this is the case, consult a urologist immediately.

Although sexual dysfunction can severely hamper your sexual relationships, there is hope. As was mentioned earlier, many dysfunctions are symptoms of childhood abuse and therefore subside or disappear entirely as you continue to work on your recovery. Others, with the help of a patient lover, can be reversed by learning and practicing the sensate focus exercises listed in Chapter 11 and by taking the pressure off of yourself to perform. Still others may need the help of a professional sex therapist but are nevertheless curable.

Lack of Sexual Desire—The Sexual Dysfunction of the '90s

Lack of sexual desire has become the number one sexual dysfunction in America. Stress, AIDS, herpes, and the overemphasis on physical perfection, all contribute to our having become a nation of people who are reluctant to express our sexuality with others. If we consider the pressure put on everyone, men and women alike, to be physically perfect, the pressure to be sexy and alluring, to have orgasms, please our partners, and still protect ourselves from venereal disease, it is a wonder we are able to have sexual relationships at all. More and more we are becoming isolated from others sexually, relying instead on masturbation, pornography, fantasies, and even phone sex. These practices in turn tend to make us feel ashamed, which leads to even more intense feelings of isolation, causing us to feel even less confident about expressing our sexuality with others.

CHRONIC LACK OF INTEREST

It is extremely rare to find someone who has never experienced sexual desire. The majority of people who now suffer from a lack of sexual desire have been turned on in the past and have either gradually or suddenly lost their interest in sex. A chronic and pervasive lack of sexual desire usually has very deep roots. Either sexual abuse or extremely repressive sexual conditioning is the likely cause, as was the situation with the following clients:

"I was the recipient of extremely negative parental and religious training about the evils of sex which thoroughly inhibited my sexual desire as an adult. I tried very hard to be a good child and to do what was expected of me. But because I was unable to express normal childhood or adolescent feelings of sexual arousal and interest, I felt sinful and bad. In an attempt to rectify this conflict and please my mother and father and to prove that I was pure enough to deserve God's love, I completely suppressed my sexual feelings."

"I repressed all of my sexual feelings in an attempt to forget the traumatic event of being incested as a child. I felt particularly special and loved by my father and at the same time guilty and worried about losing the love of my mother. This created tremendous anxiety in me. The way I coped with the situation was to cut off all sexual feelings."

"For some reason, every time I am in a long-term relationship, I end up losing my sexual desire. At the beginning of a relationship I feel extremely turned on but after about six months, I start losing interest in sex. I like doing a lot of holding and touching but I just don't get turned on very often. I used to think it was because I was losing interest in my partner but I have finally come to the conclusion that it is my problem because it happens in every relationship."

Sexuality is full of paradoxes, partly because of the fact that the mind and the body interact so closely. Learning these paradoxes and keeping them in mind will do much to help you with any sexual dysfunction or concern:

• The harder you try to make something happen sexually, the less will happen.
• The way to cure your sexual problem is to not try to cure it.
• The way to be able to have sexual activity whenever you want it is to learn to recognize when you do *not* want to have sex.
• The way to learn to relax is to learn to recognize when you are anxious.
• The way to learn to concentrate is to recognize when you are not concentrating.
• The way to be able to please your partner is to learn what feels good for *you*.

TAKING A TIME-OUT FROM SEX

Masters and Johnson, as part of their treatment for sexual dysfunction, put a ban on intercourse for a prescribed period of time (usually two weeks) during their treatment program.

The purpose of this ban is to take the pressure off so that the individual or couple can immerse themselves in the caress techniques and not worry about performing sexually. Ironically, most couples (even those who have been unable to have intercourse for years) break the rules and end the ban before the end of the two weeks.

A ban on intercourse works equally well for couples who are suffering from any difficulties with their sexual relationship, survivors of sexual abuse and their partners, and those who are sexually addicted and need a break from sex in order to return to it on different terms.

Benefits of a Time-out

One of the many benefits of experiencing a time-out from sex is that as a result of exploring alternative ways of expressing intimacy you may become far less compulsive and goal-oriented when it comes to sex. Too often we focus all our attention on our genitals when making love. There are other parts of the body that can be just as erotic and feel just as pleasurable when touched. Men in particular tend to focus all their attention on the penis and on ejaculation as opposed to intimacy and pleasure. A time-out will not only encourage you to find acceptable alternatives to your normal sexual activity but can also encourage you to work with your partner to develop mutually pleasurable, nonsexual touch experiences such as massage and cuddling.

In addition, if your partner feels that all you want is sex or that you are just using her or him in order to have sex, your partner will not be able to trust or believe in you. For this reason, taking a time-out from sex may be an excellent idea. Whether the time-out is for six days or six months, it can help your partner build trust in the relationship and realize that you really love her or him.

The Special Problem of Sexual Addiction

Joseph was referred to me by the county probation department after having been arrested for indecent exposure. Since he was not a voluntary client I expected him to be resistant. What I didn't expect was for him to be overtly seductive with me. From the moment he walked into my office there was an intense air of sexuality about him—from the way he looked me up and down to the fact that he sat inappropriately close to me. As he talked his eyes were intently focused on me in a way that made me uncomfortable.

He immediately started to explain why he was there. "I know you must think I'm some kind of pervert because that's the kind of guys who get arrested for this kind of thing. But I've got to tell you right away that I'm not some 'flasher' who is afraid to get it on with women. Believe me, I've got plenty of women who have sex with me all the time. I have a hard time keeping up with them all, if you know what I mean ... do you get it ... a 'hard time.'"

I didn't laugh at Joseph's joke but made a mental note to myself about how inappropriate it was for him to make a sexual innuendo to me—the therapist he had been referred to by the probation department because of an exposure charge.

As he continued talking he explained to me what really happened: "For several months now, I have been playing this game with this woman who works at the cleaners. I go in to take in some clothes around closing time and we flirt and joke around awhile—just long enough to get turned on. Then I go out and sit in my car and wait for her to close the store. As I see her closing up I pull out my penis and start to play with it so it's good and hard by the time she locks her door. Then she walks by my car and acts like she's shocked—like I'm some kind of pervert or something. Then she hurries to her car and drives away, acting all upset. I follow her to her house and by the time I'm inside we're both so hot we just go at it right on the living room floor. So, you see, it's all prearranged. The only problem is that this time a kid walked by and saw me—just my luck."

By the end of that first session I believed Joseph's story and didn't think he was a typical flasher. But I began to suspect that Joseph had an even bigger problem. I suspected he was a sex addict. As time went on, I became convinced of it.

Joseph's entire life centered around sex. Fortunately (or unfortunately), he owned his own business and could pretty much make his own hours, although even his business sometimes suffered because of his preoccupation with sex. Like a compulsive overeater who thinks about food constantly and is always planning the next meal or snack, Joseph was always planning his next sexual experience. In his own words: "I wake up in the morning thinking about sex, I think about it all day long, and I go to bed thinking about it."

Although Joseph had sex with as many as four or five sexual partners a day, he also felt compelled to masturbate at least twice a day. "I guess I need it pretty much all the time. The longest I've

gone is a day and that was when I was in the hospital with a broken leg" (which he got falling out of a window when a woman's
husband came back home unexpectedly). "By the second day in
the hospital, though, I had made friends with one of the nurses
and she helped me out, if you know what I mean."

Until his arrest and the subsequent therapy he was required to
have, Joseph didn't think of himself as having a problem. He just
thought he had an unusually strong sex drive and that because
women found him attractive he was just luckier than most men.
When he began therapy his attitude was, "Let's face it, if other
guys had the freedom and the luck I have with the ladies, they'd
be doing the same thing, believe me."

But Joseph was in a tremendous amount of denial about his
problem and how much trouble his obsession about sex caused
him. Although he had never been arrested before because of his
problem, as he continued in therapy he began to admit that his
preoccupation with sex had indeed caused him other problems.

Joseph had been married and divorced three times. Two of
his wives left him because they discovered him with other women.
His third and last wife left because she just couldn't take the pressure she felt to satisfy him sexually. "When she married me she
knew what I was like. She thought she could change me and make
me stay home if she gave me enough sex. But no matter how much
sex we had, I still couldn't pass up an opportunity. I just decided
that even though I want to be married, I'd better stay single because no woman is going to put up with my shenanigans."

And through the years Joseph had experienced his share of
mishaps connected to his sexual acting out. "I've been in lots of
fights with irate husbands and more than once I've had a jealous
husband try to kill me."

Once Joseph came out of his denial and took a good, hard
look at his life, it wasn't long before he was able to own up to his
problem. After several sessions I told Joseph that I thought he was
a sex addict and explained to him what that was. He agreed that,
indeed, the description I gave seemed to fit who he was.

What exactly is a sex addict? As you may have figured out, a
sex addict is addicted or dependent on sex in much the same way
an alchoholic, drug addict, or compulsive overeater is addicted to
his or her substance of choice. Sex addicts are, in essence, hostages
to their own preoccupation with sex. Every person they meet, ev-

eryone who walks by, and certainly every relationship they are in, has to pass through their obsessive filter. People become objects to be scrutinized. Sex addicts do more than notice sexually attractive people; they can't help but look even when they try, and there is a quality of desperation in the look. This element of desperation is what causes the sex addict to act in ways that interfere with work, more important relationships, relaxation, and even sleep.

There is almost always an element of secretiveness in a sex addict's life. Lying to cover up . . . clandestine meetings with people you shouldn't be with . . . pretending you really like and respect someone just so you can use them sexually . . . all these are part and parcel of a sex addict's life.

If you are like Joseph and need sex several times a day, if you are unable to feel sexually satisfied, even though you may have just had sex that day or even that hour, or if you find that you need to have sex in order to feel loved or feel good about yourself, you are probably a sex addict.

While you may insist that you desire sex with your partner because you love her or him so much or because your partner turns you on so much, the truth may be that your strong sexual drive has little or nothing to do with your feelings for your partner—or even with sex, for that matter. You may, in fact, use sex to push down feelings that are given no healthy outlet—such as anger, anxiety, and fear. Or you may have learned early on in childhood that sex can relieve tension and you may now use it as a stress reducer. You may have learned to masturbate when you felt upset, angry, or hurt, or you may have been introduced to sex very early on (perhaps by an adult). As an adult, a sex addict seeks sexual release whenever he or she is under pressure or is unhappy. Since having sex provides the addict with only a temporary physiological release and does not solve any problems, the demand for sex is continual.

Another sign of a sex addict, besides a compulsion for frequent sex, is a preoccupation with "kinky" sexual acts, such as bondage, flagellation, humiliation, or bestiality. Sex addicts may constantly look through porno magazines, watch X-rated movies, or become involved with alternative lifestyles, such as nudist colonies, swingers' clubs, S&M clubs, or bisexuality.

While your preoccupation with sex may not be as extreme as Joseph's, you may still be a sex addict. Like Joseph, you may be denying that you have a problem. Instead of viewing consequences such as lost jobs, broken relationships, arrests, venereal disease, or unwanted pregnancies as evidence that you indeed have a problem, you, like Joseph, may make excuses for your behavior, ignore it, blame others, minimize the damage, or rationalize your behavior.

You may have used any or all of these justifications or excuses for behavior that you know is extreme, compulsive, out of control, and even dangerous:

- I need sex in order to relax.
- I'm not hurting anyone.
- Men are dogs—we just can't help it.
- Just because I'm a woman doesn't mean I can't like sex as much as a man does.
- I guess I'm just oversexed.
- I wouldn't need to do this if I were getting enough at home.
- It wasn't my fault, she/he made me do it.
- I don't have any other vices.
- Other people are just a bunch of prudes.
- Everyone would do it if they could get away with it.

If you still doubt whether you are a sex addict or not, answer the following questions as honestly as possible:

1. Has a lover or mate ever left you because you were unfaithful?

2. Have you ever lost a job because you were involved in a sexual entanglement with a coworker, boss, or someone you supervised?

3. Have you ever been arrested for sexually inappropriate behavior?

4. Do you often get into relationships with people you don't even like just because you are sexually attracted to them?

5. Do you often get into sexual relationships that are intense, tumultuous, and ultimately destructive?

6. Has anyone ever found the pornography you keep hidden and become angry with you?

7. Have you ever had a car accident or come close to having one because you were exposing yourself or masturbating in the car?

8. Have you spent an enormous amount of money on prostitutes?

9. Have you run up outrageous phone bills by calling the 900 numbers?

10. Have you spent money on sex that your family needed in order to buy necessities?

11. Have you ever had sex with a stranger in a public rest room?

12. Do you make business travel plans on the basis of an affair you are having rather than in your company's interests?

13. Do you lie and say "I love you" just so someone will have sex with you?

14. Are you involved with two or more people at the same time while pretending to be monogomous with each one?

15. Do you have sex with your friends' lovers or spouses behind their backs?

WHAT CAUSES SEX ADDICTION?

At the core of a sexual addiction is a tremendous feeling of emptiness. This emptiness is often caused by being raised in a family where the child's needs for intimacy, closeness, and affection were not met. Hungry for love and nurturing, a sex addict tries to get it in the only way he or she knows how—through sex. Just as some people try to fill up their emptiness with food, sex addicts attempt to ease the pain of feeling empty with sexual gratification. But the emptiness is only eased for a short time and then the gnawings and cravings begin all over again.

Children who were deprived and neglected are at risk of becoming sex addicts for two reasons. First, children who are deprived of love and affection are more likely to begin to masturbate quite early on and to depend on masturbation as a way of feeling good.

Second, these children are at a higher risk of being sexually abused than children who are adequately cared for and supervised. A child molester generally has easy access to a neglected child who is desperate for love and affection. Once a child has been sexualized he or she learns that sex is a way of gaining acceptance and temporarily easing the pain of living. Children who have been sexually abused often become very active sexually, either passing on the abuse to other children or becoming compulsive masturbators.

Sex addicts have certain belief systems and delusional thought processes that contribute to how they perceive reality. Generally, sex addicts do not perceive themselves as worthwhile persons. They also don't believe other people would care for them or meet their needs if they knew the truth about them, including their addiction. They have made sex their most important need and truly perceive it to be so.

Many sex addicts use sex as a way to temporarily feel better about themselves or to feel powerful. The need to feel powerful may have come from having been sexually abused as a child, as it was in the following two cases:

"I thought I just had a strong sex drive. By the time I finally realized I had a problem, I was spending up to four hundred dollars a day on escort services and prostitutes. I felt powerful with prostitutes—it was my way of getting back at the women who had molested me. I lost my business because I put more time into satisfying my sexual needs than I did anything else."

"I got into pornography at age seven. I had been sexually molested and already had very bad feelings about myself. Pornography offered me an outlet for my pent-up feelings but it also made me feel even worse about myself. I stopped using the pornography when I got married but within a few months I started again. I started calling Dial-A-Porn, which crushed my wife when she found out. My marriage split up and I was arrested for stealing at my job to pay for my telephone bills before I realized I had a real problem."

Sex addicts will often blame their partners for not satisfying them sexually. They reason that if their partners would just have sex with them more often, or be willing to engage in the kinds of sexual activities that they want, they wouldn't have a need to frequent prostitutes, call the 900 numbers, or use pornography to masturbate to, as we see illustrated in the case of Jenna and her husband Toby.

Jenna: "My husband made me feel so inadequate. No matter how much sex I had with him it was never enough. He convinced me that I just wasn't sexy enough for him and that he had to seek other partners to satisfy his needs."

Toby: "I put a lot of guilt on my wife for not satisfying me sexually. I blamed her when it was my problem all along."

TREATMENT CHOICES

Sexual addiction, like all addictions, is part of the denial cycle. It escalates and progresses. What satisfied yesterday doesn't satisfy today. Therefore, many sex addicts have found that they must become abstinent from sex for a time in order to uncover the core of their problem.

Many sex addicts benefit from twelve-step programs like Sexaholics Anonymous or Sex Addicts Anonymous, while others prefer to work on their problem in therapy with those specifically trained to deal with this problem. In either case, you must seek outside help and not try to handle your problem alone. Much like an alcoholic, you need the support and guidance of others in order to break out of the addictive cycle.

When There Are Problems in Your Relationship

Problems in an intimate relationship can lower your sexual self-esteem tremendously. This is especially true when the problems you are having with your partner are either sexual in nature or have begun to affect the sexual side of the relationship. Whether you realize that your sexual relationship is suddenly not as good as it once was, your partner develops a sexual dysfunction, or your partner is no longer as interested in sex, a change in your sexual relationship can shake you to the core—making you doubt whether your partner loves you, whether you are still sexually attractive, and whether you can still perform adequately.

WHEN YOUR PARTNER NO LONGER DESIRES SEX

Most people experience an overwhelming feeling of rejection when a partner either suddenly or gradually seems to lose interest in sex. Normally we tend to blame ourselves, thinking that perhaps our partner no longer finds us sexually attractive—or even worse, that our partner no longer loves us. While these things can sometimes cause a partner's lack of interest in sex, the real reasons are usually much less painful and drastic.

For example, any kind of anxiety or frustration can destroy interest in making love. Fatigue is also a factor in diminished sexual interest, as is worry over one's health or the health of some member of the family.

To be good lovers, and this is true of either sex, self-esteem is needed. Concern over a promotion, an insulting remark made by a friend, or any kind of failure can erode self-esteem, and this is usually reflected in the bedroom.

Many women experience a lack of interest in sex after having a baby. A woman generally needs to take time for herself after having a baby, to regain her sense of self so she will feel like a woman again, not just a mother. Because new mothers give all their time to their new infants, sex may come to feel like another act of giving unless they regain their own sexual interest and arousal.

Conversely, men sometimes also experience a lessening of sexual drive following the birth of a child. Just as a new mother has to adjust to the newborn infant, her partner has to adjust to viewing his partner not only as a lover but as a mother. Some men have expressed difficulty after having seen the baby come out of their wife's vagina. One client shared with me: "I don't know, I always associated that area of my wife's body with sex and arousal. Suddenly I now have another association with it and it seems to be getting in the way of my becoming aroused."

In addition, when spouses are turned off to sex, or bored with the bedroom, there may be a great deal of resentment and unexpressed hostility between husband and wife. Disagreements and disappointment may have been swept under the table for too long, and in order for the marriage to be restored, these must be faced and explored.

Try to talk with your spouse. Ask if he or she knows what's wrong. Ask how he or she thinks your relationship could be better. If he or she doesn't know, or is unwilling to even discuss it, try to get him or her to professional counseling with you.

WHEN YOU AND YOUR PARTNER HAVE DIFFERENT LEVELS OF SEXUAL DESIRE OR INTEREST

If you are perfectly content with your level of sexual activity and interest, but your partner is not—or vice versa—this discrepancy can result in each person's feeling unwanted, rejected, and undesirable.

When Your Partner Is Unfaithful

Discovering that your partner has been unfaithful will make you doubt your masculinity or femininity, your sexual attractiveness, and your ability to sexually satisfy a mate. As a result of being with an unfaithful mate, some partners have suffered from sexual dysfunctions. In addition, knowing that your partner has been with someone else sexually will undoubtedly cause you to feel devastated and enraged.

Whether or not you and your partner will be able to remain together will depend on a number of things, mainly how much love exists between you and your partner and how well you can communicate the feelings you have.

It will be important to discover just why your partner was unfaithful, and you won't be able to find this out unless you're able to talk about it. You need to explore all the problem areas in your relationship in order for you to forgive your partner and try to heal the wounds left by this breach of commitment.

There are several reasons why people are unfaithful. Often the unfaithful party is trying to punish the other for some reason—perhaps because one feels that the other is not paying enough attention, has a domineering attitude, or is too critical. When one person in a relationship tries in vain to communicate dissatisfaction, pain, or concerns, and the other person does not listen, the unhappy party may resort to having an affair.

Sex researcher Morton Hunt suggests that there are four kinds of extramarital love affairs, at least as far as female participants are concerned:

• The casual kind, which might only be a fling.
• An act of rebellion, to get back at the spouse or to escape boredom or responsibilities at home.
• The kind where the woman develops a moderate commitment to another partner, but one that is definitely subordinate to the marriage.
• The kind that escalates into a heavy, full-time romance.

When Your Partner Is Promiscuous

If your partner is sexually promiscuous the damage to your self-esteem can be tremendous. All the understanding and rationalizing in the world will not help you whenever you discover that your mate has been unfaithful. Although you may understand intellectually and logically that your partner is acting out due to some sort of problem and that it has nothing to do with how she or he feels about you, emotionally you will not really believe it.

You will not be able to prevent your body from reacting, no matter how much your mind "understands" that the "other person" didn't mean anything to your partner. Summer, the wife of an extremely promiscuous man, told me:

"Each and every time my husband was with another woman I would become extremely nauseated and feel like throwing up. He would seem dirty to me, contaminated by the body of the woman he'd been with. It always took me a long time before I could let him touch me without feeling sick to my stomach, but finally I guess I let my need for him outweigh my body's reaction, and I'd be sexual with him again. Now, I realize that my body was telling me something. It was not healthy for me to continue having sex with him after these episodes, or to stay with him, for that matter. I was going against myself, against my own best interests. I'm in therapy now and having to repair the damage of being with him for so long."

In addition to the emotional damage it does to you, being with someone who is promiscuous can endanger you physically, exposing you to AIDS and venereal disease.

When Your Partner Has a Sexual Dysfunction

When your partner suffers from a sexual dysfunction, whether it be difficulty with orgasm, a lack of sexual desire, or another type of dysfunction, your sexual self-esteem will suffer right along with his or hers. Even though you may try to convince yourself that it is your partner's problem and has nothing to do with you, secretly you will blame yourself. In reality, while the particular sexual dysfunction that your partner suffers from is indeed his or her problem, the mere fact that you are in a relationship makes it a problem for you as well.

Your reaction to his or her problem will have a tremendous effect on his or her prognosis. If you are supportive and encouraging, the chances are much better for recovery than if you are critical, impatient, or take it personally. While it is extremely difficult to remain supportive when the problem goes on for a long time, and it may seem that becoming impatient is the natural thing to do, you do have more options than you realize. For example, not all women react in the same way when their partner ejaculates quickly. Some feel that he has done so deliberately and they resent it, some feel as if he has been using them merely as a sex object, and some judge him as being incompetent. Still others feel as if they have failed in some way because they were not sufficiently aroused to have an orgasm when their lover did. On the other hand, some women react entirely differently and feel rather pleased with themselves for being so exciting that their lover could not hold back.

If your partner has a sexual dysfunction of any kind, the resulting effect on your sexual self-esteem can only add to the problem. The last thing he or she needs from you is pressure. It is very important that you not pressure your partner to have sex or an orgasm. In fact, part of the difficulty may be that he or she is feeling pressured into having an orgasm, and is engaging in frenzied activity instead of slowly and sensuously enjoying the experience itself.

Neither men nor women enjoy being pressured to make love. When this happens, your partner is likely to lose confidence and begin to question whether something is wrong with him or her or with the relationship.

The following anecdote illustrates how a partner can contribute to a person's sexual problems:

Albert was married to a woman who constantly belittled him about ejaculating prematurely. After each sexual encounter she would let him know that he had failed to satisfy her, that she didn't think he ever tried, and that if he didn't start trying she was going to leave him. In desperation, he came into therapy, hoping that this would at least let her know that he was serious about changing. But this didn't stop her from pressuring him at all. In fact, she increased her comments, constantly asking him how long therapy would take, making him feel guilty that he was spending the little extra money they had on therapy.

Albert began to last shorter and shorter lengths of time until he was eventually ejaculating before he was able to penetrate. His wife became so impatient and frustrated that she finally refused to have intercourse with him at all and eventually filed for divorce.

Interestingly, after his wife divorced him, Albert began having a sexual relationship with another woman who did not put him down or pressure him, but was very understanding about his problem. Albert soon discovered that in no time he had absolutely no problem at all in lasting as long as he wanted.

While Albert's wife had not caused his problem, she certainly exploited his self-doubt and pressured him so much that he had little if any chance at all to work through his problem while he was married to her.

If you want a better lover, instead of demanding sex try to find out what is troubling your mate. Let your mate know that you care about his or her problems, that you love and appreciate him or her as a whole human being, not just as a sex machine. The more you can reassure your partner that you find her or him attractive and that you are not being critical or impatient, the more relaxed he or she will become and the more likely he or she will be to overcome the sexual dysfunction.

When Your Partner Is a Sex Addict

Savannah came to me as a last resort. She had been married to a sex addict for five years and she desperately wanted help in figuring out what she should do:

"My husband constantly makes remarks about women's bodies, about sex, and about male genitals. He flirts with almost every woman he meets and makes off-color comments to them about their clothes and their bodies. He embarrasses me all the time by telling dirty jokes to everyone who comes into the house—even when my parents visit. He masturbates compulsively and constantly watches pornographic movies. For a long time I thought I wasn't satisfying him, that I should have sex with him more often, or that I should do more to please him sexually. Then one day I realized that I was blaming myself for his problem."

If you are involved with a sex addict it is very important for you to know that you are not helping your partner by just putting up with his or her behavior. By doing so you are in fact enabling your partner to continue the behavior. The best way for you to help is to encourage your partner to seek professional help or to join Sexaholics Anonymous. If this does not work, you may need to leave the relationship for your good and for the good of your partner.

When Your Partner Was Sexually Abused

Being involved with a survivor of childhood sexual abuse can damage your sexual self-esteem unless you fully understand both how the sexual abuse affects sexuality and the process of recovery. While the sexual side of the relationship with a survivor of childhood sexual abuse often starts out to be good, often the survivor will begin to experience some sexual problems. Unfortunately, this will mean that the partner will encounter these problems right along with the survivor. Sex often becomes a burden for the survivor, a source of rejection for his or her partner, and a source of tension for both people in the relationship. While sex is ideally an expression of love that brings people closer together, sex between a survivor and her or his partner is an emotionally loaded experience.

Some survivors stop having orgasms entirely during parts of the recovery process, while others are able to have them only under certain specific circumstances.

Because of this, many partners of survivors begin to feel inadequate and wonder whether their way of making love is lacking. Male partners in particular may have difficulties because they may begin to doubt their masculinity. Some male partners begin to experience problems achieving and maintaining an erection or may experience problems with ejaculation—either ejaculating prematurely or having difficulties ejaculating at all.

Other partners become overwhelmed with loneliness and pain caused by the emotional distance they feel emanating from the survivor during sex, often without the survivor's even being aware of it. Problems such as lack of sexual desire and lack of sexual confidence may result and may become as troublesome for the relationship as the problems suffered by the survivor.

Many survivors have a distorted and negative view of sex based on memories of the abuse experience. If you approach your partner sexually there is always the chance that she or he will accuse you of only wanting sex. There is constantly the risk that the survivor will have a flashback and suddenly mistake you for the abuser. And there is the risk that something you say will trigger memories, or that you will accidentally touch a place on the survivor's body that is off-limits. You may try to be tender and gentle only to have your partner complain that the passion and fire isn't there any longer.

Your partner may have always had difficulty staying present when having sex, but this tendency may increase over time, especially if she or he is just beginning to have memories of the sexual abuse, or if therapy for the problem has recently started. This tendency may become very disconcerting to you as the partner as you become more and more aware of it, as was the case with Gus:

"My wife will seem to be really enjoying our lovemaking when all of a sudden she'll be gone. She grows silent and her body becomes stiff and I know then that she isn't with me anymore. Fortunately, I've learned to watch for these signals and I make sure we stop. I don't want to continue when I know she is no longer enjoying it, and even if I did I now understand that it would be damaging to her."

DO'S AND DON'TS

When you engage in sexual activity with a survivor, go slowly, stop temporarily whenever necessary, and be willing to shift from a sexual or intimate focus to a loving nonsexual one if the survivor needs to stop the sexual activity altogether. This will help the survivor begin to trust your intentions and your concern for her or him.

Because victims of sexual abuse were either physically forced or emotionally manipulated into having sex, you will find that if you ever become too forceful, aggressive, or controlling sexually, your lover will feel violated or revictimized. By the same token, if you coerce or manipulate a survivor into having sex when she or he really doesn't want it, you are reabusing a victim. Moreover, if you pressure, threaten, try to arouse guilt, or use any other type of manipulation to coerce a survivor into having sex in ways she or he doesn't like—she or he will also feel revictimized.

COMMUNICATE OPENLY

It is important for partners of survivors to be as open and honest as possible about their own feelings. Ask your partner questions to find out how she or he is feeling. You don't necessarily have to have an open dialogue during sex, although many survivors and their partners find that this is very helpful. But don't let too much time elapse between conversations, especially if you are confused or unclear about something. For example, if your partner went numb during sex, ask what happened. If your partner doesn't want to talk about it at the moment, wait until a good time to talk and gently ask again. Without pressuring with questions, find out if your partner was having a flashback or if you did something she or he didn't like. Tell your partner you want to know so that if it was something you did you can learn from it and not do it again. If she or he isn't ready to talk, give her or him some time. Often, people need time alone to understand what really did happen, or your partner may need to talk to a therapist or support group first.

If you start to get the feeling that your partner isn't relating to you anymore but rather to the abuser, stop whatever you are doing and check it out. A simple "Are you all right?" or "What's going on?" can sometimes bring a survivor back to the present. At other times you may need to be more specific by saying "Are you remembering something?" or "Are you having a flashback?" or "Honey, it's me." By talking and working together when negative feelings surface, you and your partner can overcome problems of dissociation and flashbacks.

LEARN WHAT THE TRIGGERS ARE

Survivors often are reminded of the sexual abuse by things that their partners do or say, and they frequently confuse their partners with their abusers. Certain of your gestures, ways of talking, or ways in which you show affection can remind your partner of the perpetrator and cause you to be seen as the abuser. This happens especially during lovemaking, when many survivors will temporarily feel that they are with the perpetrator instead of their current partner. Unless your partner feels free to tell you when you have done or said something that has triggered a memory you may never know what buttons you have inadvertantly pushed. Ask your partner to tell you the kinds of things the perpetrator said and did so that you will have a better idea of what to avoid.

You can't expect to totally avoid triggering bad memories for a survivor, of course, but if you at least know some of the things that might upset your partner ahead of time you have a better chance of avoiding some upsets. For example, even saying "I love you" may send a survivor into a tailspin, since the perpetrator may have said the same thing. Using degrading terms like "fuck," "bitch," "cunt," and "prick" will often remind survivors of the abuse and should probably be avoided.

Other things to avoid are: approaching a survivor from behind, making sudden moves such as grabbing your partner quickly, or touching his or her genitals in a teasing manner.

NO MORE GAMES

You will need to make sure that sex with a survivor is not a game on your part, a way for you to release your anger, or a way of making yourself feel powerful or in control. This is what the perpetrator did. Abusers use their victims to act out anger, to make themselves feel more powerful, or in an attempt to violate the innocence of someone else the way theirs was violated.

Sex with a survivor needs instead to be an honest, game-free expression of love, affection, caring, and sensuality or playfulness. If it is anything else—if it is a power trip, an ego builder, an anger release, a tension relaxer, an addiction, a way to avoid other problems—it will feel bad to the survivor and will be a repeat of the abuse he or she suffered as a child. You are asking for trouble when you bring in such things as fantasy rape, sadomasochism, fetishes, bestiality, urolagnia (urinating on your partner or having your partner urinate on you), and other such practices.

You cannot allow yourself to play the role of the authority figure, parent, or abuser, even if you both are aroused by this roleplaying. A survivor needs an equal relationship, with both people sharing their vulnerability and needs. You cannot allow yourselves to slip into the mistake of either one's being the controller. Even if the survivor wants to play these roles, even if she is the one who initiates it, you should not allow yourself to get caught up in it. It is a replay of the sexual abuse and it is unhealthy for both of you.

Kurt, the partner of Ted, a male survivor, shared with me how he and his lover became aware that they were reenacting Ted's abuse:

"Ted and I were pretty heavy into S&M. I was the dominant one and Ted was the submissive. But when I learned that Ted had been sexually abused by his older brother I began to feel squeamish about always being the dominant one. I started feeling like I was abusing Ted, even though he liked my dominance. It got so bad that I started having trouble getting erections.

"We went to therapy together and it turned out that Ted and

I were re-creating the abuse by his brother. I had actually been doing the same things to Ted that his brother had done. Even though this had always turned Ted on, we both realized that we had to stop doing these things. Otherwise, it was just too sick. It took us a while, but we were finally able to make some real significant changes in our lovemaking so that Ted wasn't constantly being reabused."

LETTING YOUR PARTNER BE IN CHARGE OF SEX

In order for a survivor to heal sexually she or he must stop doing anything she or he doesn't genuinely want to do. This will be a very difficult thing because a victim is used to having sex even when she or he doesn't feel like it. The sexual abuse, in addition to damaging a person in numerous ways, also taught the victim to be submissive, to be compliant, and to split off from the present when things become uncomfortable, unpleasant, or painful. A survivor will not only have difficulty saying no to sex, she or he will have difficulty saying no to sex that is repulsive to them or that causes great emotional or even physical pain. Instead of saying no or calling a halt to uncomfortable or painful sex, the survivor will "go away" in his or her mind, focus on something else, or find some other way of splitting off from how she or he is really feeling. All the while the victim's body is lying there engaged in an act that is traumatizing.

In order for the survivor to heal sexually she or he will need to make a conscious commitment to never have sex unless she or he wants it. To help the survivor, your responsibility will be to always ask whether or not she or he wants to be sexual at any given time, and whether she or he is sure about wanting to engage in any particular type of sexual activity. This will mean that you will both need to take a lot of time and focus a lot of attention on your sexual relationship. You'll need to reexamine every aspect of your sexual relationship, including how often you have sex, when you have sex (what time of day, whether it's okay to have sex when the children are at home, whether it's okay to have sex after therapy sessions), what kind of sex you have (fondling, intercourse, oral sex, anal sex), and even where you have sex.

This reevaluation will most certainly have a radical effect on your sexual relationship. The survivor may want sex only under very controlled circumstances. She or he may want only to engage in certain sexual activities. She or he may only want to be touched in certain places. Or she or he may want only to touch you and not have you touch her or him at all. A survivor may need a lot more foreplay than you had been previously led to believe, or she or he may not want any foreplay at all. A survivor may need to be massaged or caressed before or after sex, may want to be held afterward, or may only want sex if you have the time to talk before or after sex.

Many survivors only want to engage in sexual activities that were *not* a part of the sexual abuse. For example, if the perpetrator fondled the victim but did not engage in intercourse, the survivor may not want to engage in any kind of foreplay at all before intercourse. If the opposite was true, if the victim was penetrated without any foreplay, she or he may want only to be fondled, caressed, and brought to orgasm manually or orally. If the perpetrator did everything but intercourse, intercourse may be the only thing the survivor can do for now that is free of any association or memory and free of any trauma. If the perpetrator did everything but engage in oral sex, that may be the one expression of sexuality that is truly enjoyable to the survivor.

The same can hold true for which parts of the body a survivor wants to have touched and which part of your body she or he is willing to touch. If the perpetrator fondled a woman's nipples she may not want you touching them at all. If he touched her everywhere except her nipples it may be extremely pleasurable and erotic to her to have you touch or kiss them since they have no negative associations.

For many survivors it becomes important to be the initiator of sex, at least for a time, during recovery. This simple decision can change a lot about how the survivor feels about sex. No longer having to worry about responding to your overtures, she or he may be able to relax and feel sexual a lot more freely than ever before. This also provides the survivor with a sense of being in control—something she or he may never have had before regarding sex. This doesn't mean that you have to give up all control in all aspects of your relationship, or even in terms of your own sexuality, for that matter. It just means that you let your partner be the initiator, that you wait for her or him to make the first overture.

Many partners have actually welcomed this change, especially if they have always felt as if they were the ones who always had to make the first move toward sex.

At different times during their recovery, survivors may go through periods when they are afraid of sex, repulsed by it, or simply no longer interested. Although these "dry" periods will more than likely be difficult for their partners, they may be essential to the survivors. For many survivors, this time-out can be a healing in itself, providing them the time and space to free themselves of negative associations with sex and helping them to come back to sex with an entirely different outlook.

Many survivors despair at ever being able to get over their problems and many feel depressed and hopeless as more and more time goes by without change. But the situation is far from hopeless. As your partner progresses in recovery from the sexual abuse, the symptoms will tend to lessen and eventually disappear completely. As the survivor moves through the shame and continues to rebuild trust, as self-esteem increases, and as she or he is able to learn how to be intimate, your partner will gradually be able to enjoy healthy sexuality.

HOW TO HANDLE FEELINGS OF REJECTION

Even though you understand that your partner needs to be able to say no when he or she doesn't want to have sex, the rejection you will feel when he or she actually says it may be profound. This is especially true if you are used to your partner's almost always being receptive to you in the past.

Sometimes words of reassurance are all that you will need. If your partner can tell you that she or he loves you and wants to be with you, your hurt feelings may subside rather quickly. On the other hand, sometimes words alone won't do it. You may need to be *physically* reassured as well, as Eli did:

"I discovered that I could take my wife's 'no's' if she reassured me with a touch, or by holding me. She tried it and discovered that it helped her too because she was feeling so unlovable. It reassured her that I still loved her too even though she had said no. Now, if she isn't in the place to have sex, we spend lots of time cuddling, rubbing each other's backs, or just lying close together."

Some people have such a difficult time with rejection of any kind that when their partner begins to say no to sex they are completely devastated. They assume that if their partner doesn't want to have sex with them she or he no longer loves them. Or they may not consciously think anything at all but instead *feel* so absolutely devastated emotionally that they cannot think rationally. They become so overwhelmed with their feelings of rejection that they become withdrawn and hesitate to reach out to their partner again.

While it is normal for you to feel rejected when your partner does not want to have sex, often our feelings of rejection are not just about the current situation but instead trigger much deeper feelings of rejection from childhood. If you are unable to "bounce back" when you feel rejected, if you experience intense feelings of pain whenever you are rejected, you may need to work on your rejection issues in therapy.

It is vitally important that you understand that the survivor's difficulties with sex stem from the sexual abuse and are not a reflection of his or her feelings toward you. Keep in mind the reasons why a survivor has difficulty with sexuality and trust, and avoid trying to pressure your partner into sex with demands, guilt, or threats. If you continually push for gratification of your sexual needs, you will only set yourself up for rejection.

TAKE RESPONSIBILITY FOR YOUR OWN PROBLEMS

While your lover or mate has obvious problems, and these problems definitely do affect the relationship in a negative way, you may also have problems that affect the relationship. Whether it is acknowledging that you too have sexual problems, admitting that you too have problems with intimacy and trust, or facing the fact that you tend to be abusive, if you really want the relationship to work, you must be willing to look at and work on your part of the problems in the relationship.

In addition, in order to help build the trust and safety necessary for your partner to work through his or her sexual problems, and to begin to view sex in an entirely different way, continue to do the following:

1. Encourage your partner to say no at any time and to only have sex when she or he really wants to.
2. Discuss your sexual concerns openly and honestly and communicate your feelings without blaming your partner.

3. Don't pressure your partner for sex or try to manipulate your partner into doing things she or he doesn't want to do.

4. Find ways of sharing intimacy that are nonsexual, such as cuddling, massaging, and caressing.

5. Negotiate compromises with your partner that take into consideration your needs and your partner's needs.

6. Approach sexual activity in a patient, relaxed manner, emphasizing fun and intimacy instead of performance and goals.

7. Accept the fact that both you and your partner may experience different levels of sexual desire at different times.

Another way of taking the pressure off is to do the sensate focus exercises we discussed earlier. These were originally designed as a treatment for sexual dysfunction because they relieve both parties of having to perform and because they teach alternative ways of becoming intimate. There are many other such exercises, some of which were designed for specific sexual dysfunctions. These exercises can be found in any number of books, many of which I have referred to in the back of this book.

Through patience, commitment, good communication, and caring, you and your partner can weather your present difficulties and establish a fulfilling and healthy sexual relationship.

CONCLUSION TO PART II

You are not going to raise your sexual self-esteem by having lots and lots of sex, no matter how attractive your partners are, how much praise you get for your looks or your sexual prowess. And while exercise and a healthy diet can make you look and feel better and even raise your general self-esteem somewhat, they will not make you feel better about your sexuality if there are more deep-seated reasons for it's being low. If you have other issues you need to work on from your past these issues will continue to surface until they are dealt with. And even though it is now possible to alter and improve almost every part of the body from increasing or decreasing the size of your breasts to lengthening your penis (yes, it is possible), cosmetic surgery will not take care of how you feel about yourself inside. Virtually every significant change you need to make in yourself needs to come from the inside out.

PART III

ACCEPTING WHAT YOU CAN'T CHANGE

Introduction to Part III

"God grant me the serenity to accept those things I cannot change, the courage to change the things I can, and the wisdom to know the difference."

This prayer, called the Serenity Prayer, is used extensively by many people, including those in twelve-step programs. It states very succinctly and clearly what this book has been all about. As we have discussed, there are things you can and must change about yourself if you are going to raise your sexual self-esteem. But there are also things you must learn to accept about yourself. Determining the difference between those things you can or must change and those things you can't or shouldn't try to change will indeed require a great deal of wisdom on your part. For example, sometimes we push and push, trying to change things about ourselves that are simply not going to change. Or we focus on alleviating what turn out to be only symptoms of a far deeper problem.

And while many sexual problems or concerns can be eliminated or improved, many others cannot. For instance, feelings of sexual inadequacy can be relieved with proper information and positive experiences. And feelings of sexual shame can be lessened or even removed by discovering the origin of the shame. But you cannot stop the hands of time. While you can choose to stay active and in good physical condition, getting older is just one of the many things about yourself that you simply cannot change. Another example of something about yourself that you probably should not try to change is your sexual orientation. Whether you are heterosexual, homosexual, or bisexual, it is a very difficult thing to change and any changes that occur usually happen because of internal changes, not just by willing it to happen. If you are attracted to the same sex but because of societial or religious messages or pressure wish you were not, you will find that accepting your sexuality will raise your sexual self-esteem far more than trying to be what you are not.

Chapter Thirteen

ACCEPTING THE THINGS YOU CANNOT CHANGE

At this point, the most important thing you can do to raise your sexual self-esteem is to learn to accept yourself in spite of your imperfections and deficiencies. If you are constantly focusing on your faults and shortcomings—criticizing yourself for the way you are— you are not only not doing yourself any good but you are causing yourself harm. Those who constantly berate themselves are lowering their self-esteem in the process, making themselves feel worse than they did before. By beginning to accept yourself instead of criticizing yourself you will be doing the reverse—you will begin to feel better about yourself and thus your sexual self-esteem will become higher.

UNREASONABLE EXPECTATIONS

The best place to begin the self-acceptance process is to stop having unreasonable expectations of yourself. Many people suffer from low sexual self-esteem primarily because they have unreasonable expectations about such things as how many and what kind of orgasms they feel they are supposed to have, what size their penis or breasts should be, and how often they should want to have sex. Because of peer pressure and the media, many people are convinced that they are doing it too little or too much, that they are missing out on something, that others know some kind of secret about sex that they have missed out on.

There is entirely too much pressure put on all of us to perform sexually and not enough permission to explore and enjoy. But healthy sexuality does not mean flawless functioning. For example, it is completely normal for a man to ejaculate quickly once in awhile, or to have difficulties getting an erection at times. By the same token, it is normal for a woman to be unable to have an orgasm once in a while. And it is completely normal for both sexes to go through periods of time when they have very little desire for sex.

Healthy sexuality is not defined by the types of activities you do or how often you do them. Although most of us seem to need to compare ourselves with others, to find out whether we are having the same types of sexual activities as other people, or whether we are having sex as often as they are, comparisons are deceiving and fruitless. It is normal to prefer some sexual activities over others and even to dislike certain kinds of activities. It really doesn't matter what sexual activities your friends like—the important thing is what makes you happy. If you spend too much time and energy comparing yourself with others sexually, you will develop a performance-oriented attitude that will interfere with the arousal and intimacy you could be experiencing.

Healthy sexuality has much more to do with a healthy attitude about sex than anything else. This includes having reasonable expectations of yourself and your partners instead of expecting yourselves to be sexual gymnasts, perfect physical specimens, or experts in sexuality.

Another aspect of accepting yourself is to accept the fact that you may never attract or get involved with a movie star, a model, a millionaire, or a star athlete. While it is fine to have sexual fantasies about having sex with a movie or rock star, to get turned on when you see a gorgeous woman or a magnificent specimen of a man, the difficulty arises when you begin to believe that you can indeed *have* a relationship with a star, beauty queen, or model. If you are like most of us ordinary people, the likelihood of your even meeting one of these people is remote, much less the possibility of actually having a relationship with them.

ACCEPTING YOUR BODY

Self-acceptance at any level depends in part on accepting your body as it is. This requires that you learn to admire your body and revel in what it can do rather than focusing on its imperfections or perceived flaws.

You will need to begin to accept every part of yourself. Our bodies are vehicles that carry us where we want to go, that provide for us a great deal of physical and sensory pleasure, that house our brains and vital organs and provide for the very breath of life. Instead of focusing on the imperfect parts of your body you must begin to accept your body as an inextricable part of yourself.

Your body image has a tremendous impact on the quality of your sexuality. If you feel flawed on the outside you will very likely feel undesirable sexually. If you view yourself as unshapely and unattractive, you will be much more likely to want to have sex late at night, in the dark, and under the covers. And deep down inside you will suspect your lover of cataloging your body faults even as you are making love.

In fact, for many people, their view of themselves has as much impact on their ability to form intimate, loving relationships as does their actual physical condition—in some cases, more. The feeling of being undesirable can gradually change as we learn to change the messages we give to ourselves and begin to believe we are all desirable in our unique ways.

Our bodies come in all shapes and sizes, no two being alike. Yet in spite of this most of us carry an ideal image in our heads of what we *should* look like. Unfortunately, this image—the image indelibly etched in our minds by the media—is usually one that we can never reach: the perfectly shaped Adonis or beauty queen. We are never satisfied with how we look. If we are tall we wish we were shorter; if we are short we want to be taller. We become convinced that if our breasts were just larger, or our penis was just longer, our sexual insecurities would be over. We focus on our "bad" points instead of on our good ones, and because of this we assume everyone else does the same thing when they look at us.

Although we can appreciate others' beauty even when they aren't "perfect" and can understand at least intellectually that everyone has different ideas of what beauty is, if we are critical of a certain part of our body, we assume everyone else is as well. Even when someone else disagrees with our assessment of our body we argue with them, assuming they are being polite or that they just haven't looked closely enough.

All too often we are far more critical of ourselves than our partner is. In fact, the parts of our bodies that embarrass us—a scar, small breasts, a large butt—are frequently considered special to our partners. Instead of making our partners feel critical, our flaws are often endearing to our partners, making us uniquely ourselves.

Male Concerns

ACCEPTING THE SIZE OF YOUR PENIS

More men than women worry about whether their genitals look normal. Questions about penis size, appearance, and shape are, in fact, the second most frequently asked questions by men who contact sex research institutes like the Kinsey Institute. Most of the inquiries are about the fact that a man believes his penis is too small.

In spite of the fact that so many men worry, the vast majority of men measure within the average genital size range and have a penis that is approximately five to seven inches long when erect, a length that is more than adequate for sexual functioning. Actual difficulties with sexual functioning or reproduction, in fact, rarely occur unless the erect penis is less than two inches long. The size of a penis when it is flaccid does not predict what its size will be when it is erect. In fact, at erection smaller flaccid penises lengthen by a greater percentage than do larger flaccid penises.

Since most men fall within the normal range, why do so many men worry about the size of their penises? It may be that some judge themselves against the genitals depicted in erotic films and magazines, where men are usually hired precisely because they have larger-than-average penises.

The perception that one has a small penis may have begun while in adolescence, possibly before the penis was fully developed. Since not all boys' genitals begin to grow at the same age or at the same rate, many young men made unfavorable comparisons before they reached full maturity, and the thought that they are small stays with them even after they have reached a fully mature average size.

Many men assume—just as women do about breasts—that the opposite sex prefers a large penis. In one study, when men were asked to list what they thought women find sexually attractive, they gave very high priority to large penises. But the women surveyed said they preferred firm muscle tone, well-groomed hair, a clear complexion, and white teeth.

Although some men worry that penis size is essential to being a good lover, the female genital organ most important to sexual arousal and orgasm is the clitoris, not the vagina, and it is more easily stimulated by the touch of a hand than by the thrust of a penis.

As for intercourse, there is no scientific research suggesting that women generally prefer large penises. Ironically, though, there is research showing that most women do not care about their sexual partner's penis size. A woman's vagina expands as the penis is inserted and just enough to accommodate the penis. She doesn't need a large penis because the vagina can really only feel stimulation in the two inches or so nearest the vaginal opening. Physiologically, a penis that reaches this area is adequate for vaginal stimulation.

Nothing—no creams, pumps, vitamins, injections, pills, or any other of the hundreds of products or services advertised—will increase the size of the adult penis. Some of these products may, in fact, have a harmful effect. Pump devices, for example, have been known to damage fragile erectile tissue. (Although there is a new plastic surgery method for lengthening the penis that has been used on a few men in the last few years, it is so new that there has been no time to test the long-term effects of the procedure.)

The only time a man should be concerned would be if his penis is two inches or less when erect. He should then have an evaluation by a urologist to see if there is a correctable problem involved.

If you continue to feel self-conscious, embarrassed, humiliated, or depressed because you think your penis is too short—whatever the size actually is—you should probably talk to a psychotherapist. Therapy can help to boost your self-esteem and help you to further understand that your body is fine the way it is.

A few men, of course, worry about the opposite problem—

having too large a penis. But before you assume your penis is too large, consider some other possibilities. Perhaps your partners aren't fully aroused before you attempt penetration. When a woman is sexually excited her vagina becomes lubricated and it expands, usually enough to accommodate any size penis. Try taking a longer time with foreplay, making certain that the woman is adequately lubricated and aroused, thus making intercourse more comfortable and insertion and thrusting less painful.

You may also want to try positions in which the woman can control the depth of penetration and her own movements, such as the woman on top or side-by-side positions. Let your partner control insertion so she can use an angle that's comfortable for her. If your partner feels discomfort or pain, stop deep or hard thrusting. Many women find shallow and gentle thrusting more pleasurable. If her pain persists, withdraw and continue with techniques that don't include intercourse. If trying different techniques doesn't work, consult a counselor who can offer suggestions that are specific to you and your partner.

CONCERNS OTHER THAN SIZE

Brian, a client of mine who had been unable to have sex with women, finally told me about one of the reasons he felt so insecure sexually. "My penis curves up so much that I feel like a freak. I am embarrassed for a woman to see it and intercourse is extremely difficult unless the woman positions herself in just the right way, and even then it's painful."

Many normal, healthy men have slight penile curves up, down, or to one side during erection, and some suffer from more severe curves that are often painful—like the one my client Brian suffered from. This more severe condition is called "chordee." Chordee occurs when the urethra (the tube in the center of the penis, which carries urine from the bladder to the outside) is shorter than the penis. This makes the penis bend, especially when erect. Severe chordee is often diagnosed at birth or during childhood but when the condition is less severe (when the urethra is almost, but not quite, as long as the penis), the condition is not obvious until a young man's penis grows during puberty. Knowing that chordee can usually be surgically corrected, I recommended that Brian see a urologist who specializes in treating male sexual dysfunctions. The doctor evaluated his physical condition and arranged for surgery. After the surgery, Brian's self-esteem was improved greatly.

Female Concerns

Since female genitalia are not as accessible to the eye, women don't focus on the way they look as much as men. Instead, women tend to worry more about what their genitals *smell* like. The messages women hear from advertisers is that their genitals are dirty and smelly and that they need to douche, use feminine deodorant spray, and use panty liners to keep themselves "fresh." Smelling "fresh" has become an obsession to women who worry about turning men off with the natural smell of their genitals. Such a terrible message is bound to affect a woman's body image.

Although it is unusual, some women *do* worry about what their genitalia look like. This was the case with Katarina, who thought her labia minora (the inner genital lips) were extremely large and purplish in color. This is what she shared with me:

"I feel so ugly that I insist on making love only in the dark. I don't want my boyfriend to see me because I'm afraid it will turn him off."

But after Katarina described the appearance of her genitals I assured her that they sounded quite normal and that it is not unusual for the inner folds to protrude beyond the outer folds. Since most women do not have the opportunity to see the wide variation in other women's external genitalia they often believe that their own are unusual. I also explained to her that women's external genitalia vary greatly in size, shape, and color (from pale pink to purplish black). The appearance changes during puberty, especially with the normal growth of the labia minora. There are also changes in shape and color during sexual arousal.

ACCEPTING YOUR BREASTS NO MATTER WHAT SIZE THEY ARE

If men worry about genitals, women worry about breast size. Like men who pine away for larger penises because of their belief that all women desire this in a partner, many women believe bigger breasts are very important to the opposite sex. But research on what men find desirable about women's bodies has shown that only fifty percent mentioned breasts at all, and that half of these said that small breasts were most desirable.

The "ideal" breast size has varied throughout American history. During the 1920s the idealized shape of a "flapper" included a small bosom, and many women bound their breasts tightly to achieve that fashionable look. In the late 1940s a fuller silhouette was popular, so for the next decade or so women wore bras that were constructed to push the breasts up and out. Then effective surgical techniques became more available and some women chose to increase their breast size by this permanent method. In the 1980s the fashionable shape seemed to be going toward having smaller proportioned breasts on a lean, athletic body, and now, in the 1990s, fuller breasts are once again popular (although as of this writing a new trend toward "Twiggydom" is rearing its ugly head once again).

No creams or lotions, with or without hormones, have been proven effective for increasing the size of women's breasts. No exercise will increase the amount of breast tissue, so it is not possible to increase actual breast size with special exercises or exercise equipment. The only things that can be changed are the muscles under the breasts; exercises designed to strengthen and firm the pectoral (chest) muscles may slightly increase the measurement around the bust, but the breasts themselves, made up primarily of fatty tissue, cannot be enlarged through exercise. Improved posture (back straight and shoulders held down and back) may also help give the illusion of larger breasts. Cosmetic surgery (called "augmentation mammoplasty") to insert forms filled with silicone gel—or, more recently, a saline solution—remain the only effective way of increasing breast size.

Over twenty-two million women have had breast implants in this country. It is interesting to note that in the past twenty-five years the number of plastic surgeons has quadrupled: In 1965 there were 1,133 plastic surgeons compared to 4,492 in 1990. These figures say several things: First of all, there are tremendous numbers of women *and* men who feel so dissatisfied with the way they look that they would go to the exteme of having plastic surgery; and second, that with all those plastic surgeons needing patients, there is a tremendous amount of pressure being put on us to use their services.

It is becoming more and more clear that learning to accept one's body as it is will always be the safest option. With the current information about the danger of silicone breast implants it has become crucial for women to begin to accept their breast size and their bodies in general *as they are* and not continue to strive for an image of perfection that is impossible.

Too many women have had breast implants for all the wrong reasons—to please someone else or because they believe that bigger breasts will change their lives, pull them out of depression, attract men, land them better jobs, save their marriages, or turn them into beauty queens. When women think like this, when they have these kinds of unreasonable expectations, they probably need to consider seeing a psychotherapist rather than a cosmetic surgeon, because they are dealing with the wrong problem.

Sonya, like so many women, felt inadequate because she had small breasts. After her breast augmentation surgery she said to herself, Finally, I am a woman. How sad, of course, that she needed to have the surgery in order to feel like a woman.

Why is it difficult for women to accept what nature provided? Often the reason lies in the overemphasis placed on outer beauty and our drive to expect perfection.

The pressure women feel to fit a certain picture of perfection is so extreme that not long ago plastic surgeons called small breasts "deformities." While women with very small breasts may *feel* that they are abnormal, they are not.

Like the fifteen to twenty percent of the estimated one million women in the United States who have implants, Sonya ended up with lasting side effects. Her implants hardened, and vainly hoping to end her discomfort, she had them surgically replaced five times. "My body just rejects implants," says Sonya, who is angry, bitter, and still confused about what medical steps to take next. "I am scared to death because I have silicone in my body, but there seems to be no way to undo it.

"I hate my body a thousand times more now than I ever did before. I would sell everything I own to be able to have the body back that I gave up."

Sonya's story is just one of many. This is what many of my clients who have had breast augmentation have said:

"I had twelve surgeries because of silicone and problems associated with silicone. I thought I was properly informed—I was told that they could get hard—but I was not told that they could possibly rupture and send silicone throughout my body."

"I had a fever for two years and large red blotches all over my face."

"I suffered from scar tissue and red splotches. I've had five dif-ferent implants in a period of eight years, the last to remove the final set of implants and scar tissue. I am going to raise my daugh-ters in such a way as to encourage them to like themselves from the inside out and to have enough self-esteem so they don't feel they have to buy into society's cockeyed view of what beauty in a woman is supposed to be."

BREASTS THAT ARE TOO LARGE AND OTHER CONCERNS ABOUT BREASTS

Not all women are displeased with their breasts because they are too small. Some women are concerned because their breasts are too large, causing back, neck, and shoulder problems. Because breasts that are too heavy can indeed cause medical problems, breast reduction is not usually just a cosmetic consideration. While breast reduction surgery (removal of some of the fatty glan-dular tissue) is more complicated than surgery to enlarge the breasts and may leave some scars, this is usually considered a small price to pay by those women whose heavy breasts cause them pain and embarrassment, and interfere with athletic activities.

But aside from the medical problems caused by breasts that are too large, women seem to be entirely too self-conscious and critical about the way their breasts look. They are unhappy with the way their nipples look, with the fact that they have stretch marks, or because their breasts hang too much. One client complained that her nipples were too large, another complained that they were too dark, and still another complained because her nipples were in-verted. This last client even considered plastic surgery for her in-verted nipples until she learned that none of the surgical procedures proposed to correct this condition appeared to be widely effective. She learned that in some cases the nipples have inverted again after surgery, in others, surgery severed the milk ducts, preventing breast-feeding.

Patti had asymmetrical breasts (one of her breasts was larger than the other one), and this made her feel awkward and embar-rassed. After consulting a plastic surgeon Patti was told that she had four options: breast augmentation surgery to increase the size of the smaller breast; reduction mammoplasty to reduce the size of the larger breast; camouflage the size difference with clothing and by padding one bra cup; or having counseling to learn to accept her body as it was.

She was afraid of breast augmentation because of the fact that so many of her friends were suffering from problems due to silicone hardening and other problems, and she wasn't convinced that the new saline breasts would be any safer. She also didn't want breast reduction because she was told that it was more complicated than surgery to enlarge the breasts. While she continued to try to camouflage the size difference, she knew that hadn't worked entirely in the past and would probably not really solve the problem. So Patti decided to seek therapy because she began to suspect that perhaps the size difference between her breasts was not as noticeable as she imagined and perhaps her problem was more emotional than physical.

After seeing Patti for a few sessions I began to realize that she was extremely critical of the way she looked. In spite of the fact that she was constantly on a diet and was quite thin she complained about how large her hips and thighs were. She was forever changing the style or color of her hair and was never satisfied with how it looked. Her obsession about the difference between her breasts turned out to be just another of her preoccupations about her looks.

When I asked her why she was so critical of her looks, Patti answered:

"I don't know, I guess it's because everyone I know makes such a big deal out of looking great. It's all my friends talk about, it's all you see on TV or read about in the magazines. And no matter what men say, it really is what they look for in a woman. Women who look great get all the looks and all the men—there's no two ways about it. I'm critical of my body because it makes me continue to work at making it better."

LEARNING TO LOVE YOUR BODY

Unfortunately, Patti is not alone in her thinking. Many women constantly work at improving their looks, no matter how painful or even how dangerous it may be. Aside from the dangers of breast augmentation, women endanger their lives every day with crash diets, starvation, binging and purging, and obsessive exercising.

As was stated earlier, women in particular are chronically dissatisfied with their bodies, although men are becoming more and more preoccupied with their physical appearance as well. It has been said that it is likely that all women in America dislike some part of their bodies. This is largely due to the fact that America's ideal is the slim, smooth, hairless, flawless, airbrushed centerfold, with generous curves permitted only in a few key places.

Many women in this country give up large portions of their lives and sanity in search of the ultimate in unattainable perfection—as defined by American advertising, which convinces women that their worth as human beings is defined by their dress size.

If women felt beautiful and worthy as they are, the cosmetic surgery industry would undoubtedly not be as big as it is. In addition, advertising would not be contributing to the eating disorders of American teenagers or to the incredibly low self-image so many American women have of themselves.

Some people are obsessed with keeping their bodies "perfect" in order to hide their insecurities or other problems or addictions. Those who are codependent or who tend to gain their sense of self-identity primarily through the admiration of others focus on their bodies and keep them looking good, not from a sense of loving their bodies or caring about themselves, but in order to attract partners.

In addition to endangering your health, being preoccupied with your looks also continuously lowers your self-esteem. It is difficult to dislike your body or a specific part of your body and still like yourself, as my client Trina discovered:

"I have recently become aware of just how much my hatred of my breasts affects every area of my life—possibly even my health. My breasts have always been a source of great shame and embarrassment for me. By the time I was thirteen years old I had to wear a size thirty-six double-D bra. The boys at my school teased me mercilessly about the size of my breasts and for some reason thought that because I had large breasts I must be a tramp or a bimbo. They would yell out to me, 'Hey, Trina, how about letting me feel those knockers?' and they would try to grab my breasts whenever they got the chance. All through school I tried in vain to cover up my breasts with baggy sweaters and coats. I even wore sweaters in the hot summer. I also tried to hide them by slouching my shoulders forward and crossing my arms over them. To this day I have terrible posture. I just can't get myself to stand up straight and pull my shoulders back. My breasts are such a terrible source of shame for me that I am afraid I am going to get breast cancer or something."

Many women in particular suffer from serious perceptual problems when it comes to judging their size. Many are hopelessly at sea when it comes to evaluating how they look. And most women are also adrift when they try to guess what others find attractive.

Recently, two Florida psychologists devised a study that examined male and female ideals about body image, using breast size for women and chest size for men. The results, published in the *Journal of Social Behavior and Personality*, show that neither sex has a correct perception on the other's ideal. Women believe that men prefer larger breasts than men actually prefer. And men believe women prefer larger pectorals than women actually prefer.

The researchers of this study, J. Kevin Thompson and Stacey Tantleff, recommend that those contemplating plastic surgery (experts suggest that half of such patients may soon be men) should reconsider if they are driven by what they think the opposite sex will prefer.

You don't have to lose weight, gain weight, develop more muscle tone, or have plastic surgery in order to feel good about your body. You don't have to change your body in order to love it. Instead you can decide to accept, love, and feel gratitude toward your body just the way it is.

Loving our bodies is a difficult task for many people and it will take time to learn to do so. Eventually, with practice, you can begin to appreciate and enjoy your body's uniqueness.

The First Step Toward Loving Your Body—Getting to Know It

Getting to know your body is the key to unlocking your sexuality. Sex has a great deal to do with the way we express ourselves through our bodies. From physical well-being springs sexual energy.

Many of us have spent years being emotionally disconnected from our bodies. This estrangement is inevitable considering that we have been taught to regard the mind as separate from the body and to think of ourselves not as bodies but as intellects who own or have bodies.

The extent to which we experience this alienation from our bodies is made most apparent when we are ill or when our body does not perform the way we want it to. Instead of seeing our body and mind in partnership, we see our body as the enemy—as betraying us or "spoiling" our good times or getting in the way of our career, relationship, or whatever else has been disrupted by the illness.

The following exercises have proven to be excellent methods of helping people to connect with their bodies and of creating a more positive body image.

THE MIRROR EXERCISE

Set up a full-length mirror in a place where you can be private. Undress in front of the mirror, making sure the room is warm enough for you to be comfortable in the nude. Now begin to examine your body carefully, with a neutral, curious eye, not a critical one. It might help to maintain a neutral stance if you talk out loud, describing what you see, starting from your head and going all the way down to your toes. For example: "My hair is brown and curly. My forehead is high. My eyes are hazel. My lips are full and sensual. . . ."

If you find that looking at yourself naked is a bit frightening and uncomfortable, you're not alone. Most people, especially women, find it difficult to look at their naked bodies. If you find this is true for you, keep trying, even if it means discontinuing the exercise and trying at another time.

Look at your body from all angles and in various positions— sitting, bending over, kneeling. Use a hand mirror or a second full-length mirror to see your back. Continue to look at yourself for at least fifteen minutes, even though you may feel embarrassed and inhibited.

Once you have some idea of how you look, work on letting go of your need to chastise yourself for your real or imagined imperfections. Try looking at yourself in an objective, nonjudgmental way—perhaps the way you might look at a friend. Say out loud to your reflection in the mirror, "You're okay, your body's fine. I like what I see."

Repeat this exercise a few days later. If you are like most people you may need to complete the exercise at least two to three times before you notice any change in your attitude toward your body. Once you are able to look at yourself naked in the mirror without criticism or disappointment, you will gradually begin to feel a sense of familiarity and acceptance.

THE SELF-LOVE EXERCISE

Looking at each part of your body, verbally express love to every part as you would to the body of a beloved child. Thank your body for all that it does for you. For each part of your body, think of all the ways it helps you and all the ways it brings pleasure into your life. For example, thank your feet for carrying you around, for helping you walk and run and dance, for providing balance. Thank your stomach for storing and processing your food, for protecting your inner organs; thank your spine for holding up your frame and for allowing you to bend over.

GENITAL EXPLORATION

Many people feel repulsed by their genitals, thinking of them as dirty, smelly, and ugly. At the very least we feel a strange disconnection with them. We have difficulty talking about them and the very thought of them may make us feel uncomfortable. It is not surprising, therefore, that we have a difficult time enjoying the feelings they give us.

Most of us, especially women, don't even know what our genitals look like. Unless we become comfortable looking at our own genitals we will continue to be uncomfortable when our lovers look at them.

Males, perhaps because their genitals are so accessible and are touched frequently in order to urinate, have much more knowledge of their genitals than do women, who seldom, if ever, look at their genitals.

Because so few women have ever seen another woman's genitals many falsely assume that theirs are abnormal if they don't look exactly like the textbook drawings they have seen. *Sex for One: The Joy of Selfloving*, by Betty Dodson, is an excellent book showing the many variations of female genitalia.

Genital Exploration Exercise for Women

This exercise will help you discover exactly what your genitals look like and what happens when you touch various parts of yourself. Choose a time when you are relaxed.

• Using a hand mirror and a flashlight, sit propped up on your bed with pillows behind your back and your knees bent and open.

• Begin looking at your genital area when you are not excited. Pay attention to just how many different parts you can see and which parts you know the names and functions of.

• Now begin to explore each part with your fingers, touching your outer lips, your inner lips, your clitoris, and the vaginal opening. You may feel guilt and shame at first, but remind yourself that this is an important part of your body and that there is nothing wrong with exploring it.

• Try to notice how each part feels as you touch it. Is it slippery, bumpy, or smooth? Notice how the rest of your body feels as you touch each part.

If you find that you are just too inhibited, feel too repulsed, or suffer from too much guilt and shame to do the above exercises, you are not alone. The following books may help you work past your stuck places: *Sex for One: The Joy of Selfloving*, by Betty Dodson; *For Yourself: The Fulfillment of Female Sexuality*, by Lonnie Barbach; and *Becoming Orgasmic: A Sexual Growth Program for Women*, by Julia Heiman, Leslie LoPiccolo, and Joseph LoPiccolo.

Self-Stimulation

Some people fear that if they masturbate they won't want to have sex with a partner. This, of course, is not true since most people have enough sexual energy for both masturbation and sex with a partner.

In fact, masturbation is likely to improve your sexual relationships with others since the more you know about how your body responds, the more you know what you like. This can help you communicate to your partner exactly what gives you pleasure.

When you know what excites you and what brings you to orgasm, you can begin to communicate this to your partner. When your partner no longer has to guess at what kind of touch you like, what you are in the mood for at any particular time, he or she will feel free to be more experimental and more responsive.

In addition, masturbation is a good way to express love for yourself. No one knows your body as well as you do, and no one but you can know what you are feeling from moment to moment. There is no one else's pleasure to think about but your own and no one else's needs to distract you. If you don't like what you are feeling, you can stop or change the way you are touching yourself immediately—you can soften your touch, press harder, go more slowly or more quickly.

Loving Yourself Even If You're Fat

In this "thin-is-in, fat-is-out" culture, fat people are treated as the scum of the earth. Anyone who is overweight is silently and sometimes not so silently criticized for being lazy and gluttonous.

Ever since the fitness craze began and the "quick-weight-loss programs" have blossomed into a multimillion-dollar business we have seen one celebrity after another attest to the ease with which they were able to lose "all the weight they wanted." Week after week we have heard how everyone from Tommy Lasorda to Lynn Redgrave took off excess weight "easily and effortlessly."

In a society where we are told to "just do it," there is little understanding of just how difficult and even dangerous it is for overweight people to try to lose their excess weight. When someone is terribly overweight it is not as simple as putting on a pair of Nikes and going off for a brisk walk or run. And even those who are physically able to exercise have to endure the constant harassment of others.

Lana shared with me: "I remember vividly one of the first times I mustered up enough courage to venture out on a walk. Wearing walking shorts, Reeboks, and a T-shirt, I rounded a corner only to walk right into the middle of some teenagers who found it necessary to comment on the way I looked. Humiliated, I cut my walk short so as not to risk any further attention to myself. Needless to say, I didn't venture out again for a long time. Many months later I decided to get a bicycle so at least I could make a quick exit the next time some insensitive oaf made a disparaging comment. Even then I had to really talk myself into it every time I left my house—and to try to erase from my brain the image of what I must look like on that bicycle."

The irony of it all was that Lana had to have high enough self-esteem before she could even go out of the house on that bicycle. She had to feel good enough about herself in other ways in order to risk having her ego temporarily flattened.

This is the situation with many people who are overweight. In order to gain the motivation necessary to go on a diet, restrict their intake, or begin an exercise program, they first must feel good enough about themselves to do it. Often overweight people don't care enough about themselves to eat in a healthy way or to begin exercising. If you hate yourself, hate your body, what could possibly motivate you to take care of it?

And then there are those who have been on every diet and been involved with every weight-control program but have been unable to keep the weight off once they have lost it. There are those who were so obsessed that they starved themselves for months, either going on a liquid diet or some other extreme form of diet where their intake was severely restricted.

STOP DIETING AND START LIVING!

As more and more people gain back all the weight they lost on Optifast, Slimfast, Jenny Craig, or Diet Center; as more and more research now proves that diets don't work and more and more doctors warn against the health dangers of gaining and losing weight, more people are coming to the conclusion that it is far healthier to remain overweight than to continually go up and down in weight. Many are realizing that the seesaw ride of up and down weight is taking its toll emotionally and physically on their lives.

EXPLORING THE REAL REASONS YOU ARE FAT

Being overweight, especially at this time in history, is considered to be the biggest sin against one's body. Fat people are looked at with either disgust or amazement—almost as if people are saying "Don't you know how disgusting you look?" A fat person, particularly a fat woman, is seen as the antithesis of sexy and is often either ignored or criticized by the opposite sex. With this kind of treatment by others it is extremely difficult for an overweight person to feel good about himself or herself, particularly sexually. For this reason it is especially important that you begin to have compassion for yourself and begin to come to an understanding of the reasons why you are overweight.

In working with overweight women, Susie Orbach, a feminist therapist, encourages her clients to understand that the extra weight served some purpose in their lives:

"The fat was an attempt to take care of herself under a difficult set of circumstances. As she moves towards a conscious acceptance of this aspect of the fat, she can utilize the self-protective impulse in a different way. As she is able to understand that she became fat as a response—to mother, to society, to various situations—she can begin to remove the judgment that it was good or bad. *It just was.* . . . An understanding of the dynamics behind getting fat can help remove the judgment. When the judgment is given up and you can accept that the fat just was, you can go on to the question of, 'Is it serving me well now?' " (*Fat Is a Feminist Issue* by Suzie Orbach, Berkeley Medallion).

The truth is, those who suffer from being overweight are fat for a reason. Not because they overeat, not because they don't exercise. These are merely symptoms of far deeper problems. These problems almost always stem from either sexual, physical, or emotional abuse. Unless the overweight person acknowledges the abuse he or she suffered as a child, adolescent, or adult, and then works on healing the inevitable wounds caused by such abuse, he or she will not lose weight and keep it off. The extra weight serves as padding against the physical and emotional pain already suffered and that which is anticipated.

Numerous studies have found a strong correlation between child abuse, particularly sexual abuse, and being overweight. In addition, it has been estimated that one in four American children are overweight. This is an interesting figure since it corresponds directly with the figures for how many American children are sexually abused—again, one in four.

While there can be other factors contributing to being overweight, such as genetics and family customs, we need not look any further than our televisions for proof of the connection between sexual abuse and being overweight. Most of our most popular overweight stars have acknowledged that they were abused as children. Oprah Winfrey, Roseanne Arnold, and Delta Burke were all sexually abused as children and all battle with their weight. Recently, Oprah and Roseanne have both acknowledged that they needed to deal with their childhood abuse before they could lose weight. Louis Anderson has also spoken publically about his recovery from growing up with an alcoholic father and that this has helped him to begin to lose weight.

Exercise—Why Are You Fat?

Make a list of all the reasons you are overweight. Take as much time as you need to make your list but do not get your answers from others or from books or other sources. Try to come up with your own reasons, based on your own understanding of yourself.

MYTHS ABOUT FAT PEOPLE

In addition to being critical of those who are overweight, many people have a number of misconceptions about those who are fat. Among the most common myths about overweight people are:

- They are unhealthy.
- They are unhappy.
- They are selfish and greedy.
- They aren't attractive.
- They aren't sexy.

The fact is that none of these myths is necessarily true. Many overweight people are healthy, especially if they have not gotten caught up in yo-yo dieting. Overweight people who are active physically and who eat healthy food can live as long as thin people. Nor are overweight people necessarily unhappy, especially those who have learned to accept themselves the way they are and not focus all their attention on their weight. The "fat-acceptance" movement has done much to help overweight people learn to live happy, productive lives. While the underlying causes of being overweight can cause you to be unhappy, if you are working on these issues in therapy, knowing that you are doing something about the problem will help you to stop being critical of your weight—the prime cause of whatever unhappiness a fat person usually feels.

Overweight people are neither selfish nor greedy, in spite of the old stereotype of the gluttonous fat person. In fact, overweight people tend to be overly giving, either as a compensation for being overweight or because they have such low self-esteem that they feel they must be overly generous in order for people to like them.

Being overweight does not mean that you are unattractive. Magazines like *Big, Beautiful Woman* have exploded the myth that overweight women cannot be beautiful by featuring large models who are simply gorgeous. Women like Delta Burke, Liz Taylor, and Carnie Wilson are certainly beautiful, no matter what size they are. And what about Orson Welles, Luther Vandross, and Kenny Rogers—gorgeous men no matter how big they got.

And last but not least—the myth that overweight people are not sexy is perhaps the most false of the misconceptions. For many, many men, there is absolutely nothing more sexual than a voluptuous woman. And many, many women find large men extremely sexy. In fact, there are men and women who *prefer* to date overweight people. Organizations like NAFA (the National Organization for Fat Acceptance) hold conferences and meetings where normal-size people come to meet "people of size" for the purpose of dating.

If you don't think an overweight person can be sexy, think of Mae West. By today's standards she was overweight, and yet she is still considered one of the greatest sex symbols of all time.

BELIEVE IT OR NOT, FAT PEOPLE CAN HAVE GOOD SEX

It only makes sense that overweight people enjoy sex and can make wonderful lovers. They are typically very sensual people who enjoy not only the taste, texture, and smell of food but the taste of coffee-flavored kisses, the luxurious feel of skin, and the smell of perfume-scented sheets. Overweight people tend to get lost in all of their senses and to throw themselves wholeheartedly into whatever they are doing. What could be sexier than that?

HAVING COMPASSION FOR YOURSELF AND YOUR BODY

Your body is what it is for a variety of reasons—heredity, environment, diet, exercise, your emotional state, age, illness, and so forth. Many people, instead of having compassion for themselves and what they and their bodies have had to go through in life, are critical of their bodies, feeling that somehow their bodies betrayed them. But our bodies do not betray us. They are instead a direct reflection of who we are, based on where we have come from and what we have had to endure. Betsy, a client of mine for several years, shared the following with me regarding her gradual ability to appreciate her body for what it had been through and to accept herself for who she is:

"With a lot of difficulty, I have come to accept myself the way I am now and to have compassion for myself. I am fat because of the sexual and emotional abuse I suffered as a child. I learned early on that men would leave me alone if I was fat so I became fat in order to feel safe. I didn't do this consciously, but subconsciously I did make the decision to be fat rather than have to endure the kind of constant sexual harassment I experienced as a young girl."

Betsy was a very pretty young girl and she got a lot of positive attention for her looks. But as soon as she entered puberty, she started getting the wrong kind of attention from the males in her family. Both her father and her two brothers started making sexual comments to her about how well her body was developing and how sexy she looked. She couldn't walk through the house without one of them making some kind of remark about her "sexy" body. She felt so embarrassed and humiliated that she wanted to disappear. Betsy began to eat out of despair and within a month she had gained about thirty pounds.

Betsy continued: "Now, whenever I start to lose weight I always feel afraid of the kind of attention I am going to get from men. I want to be noticed, of course, just like every woman does, but being noticed has such painful memories attached to it for me. I didn't feel safe in my own house and that caused me to feel unsafe in the world. Whenever a man looks at me sexually I become extremely frightened.

"With all I have been through I am not about to become critical of myself for being overweight. If I need to have some extra weight on me in order to feel safe then that is just the way it has to be for now. I hope I will be able to lose the weight someday but even if I don't I'm still going to love myself and love my body."

LOVING YOUR BODY AS IT CHANGES

Our body image can change as our bodies change. Aging, pregnancy, illness, disability, surgery, and any other event that affects the body can influence the way we feel about it.

Sexuality and Aging

There is no such thing as being "over the hill" sexually and no reason why older people cannot continue to enjoy sex and remain sexually active. Older people do, however, experience specific changes in sexual response as they age. When, or even *if*, these changes occur varies widely. Many changes that do occur may be due more to medication, chronic illness, or the psychological expectation that older people should not have sex than to the aging process itself.

Older women may notice the following changes during the arousal phase: less muscle tension, less vaginal lubrication, and reduced elasticity of the vaginal walls. The intensity of muscle spasms at orgasm may also decrease.

Changes in male arousal may include: needing more time and more direct stimulation of the penis in order to get an erection and reach orgasm, erections that may be less firm, and testicles that may not elevate as high in the scrotum during arousal. At ejaculation, there may be less semen, and orgasmic muscle spasms may be less intense. It is also common for men to feel less of a need to ejaculate during each sex act, and the refractory period (the time between one ejaculation and the next time a man can ejaculate) may increase.

Those who don't realize that these changes are normal and that they don't have to decrease sexual pleasure often panic at the first sign of change. They may begin to believe that their sex lives are over, stop having sex altogether, or cease being physically affectionate with their partners.

Those who understand that these changes are normal may, in fact, welcome them and view this new stage in their lives as a chance to be more leisurely in their sexual encounters and less pressured by performance standards and the urgency for release. In fact, some couples enjoy these changes and use them to improve their sex lives. For example, men who had problems with premature ejaculation in their youth may find that the decreased urgency to ejaculate permits them to have intercourse for longer periods of time.

Many couples who are not able to have intercourse continue to express affection and physical intimacy in ways other than intercourse, such as mutual touching or oral-genital activities. As was mentioned earlier, healthy and satisfying sexuality can include many different ways of physically expressing love and caring.

But none of these changes, for either women or men, signals the end of pleasurable sexuality. Instead what is required is more patience and fewer expectations of both yourself and your partner. Expecting yourself to function as you did as a young person will merely set you up for disappointment and will lower your sexual self-esteem. Self-acceptance, as we have been saying all along, will do much to help you continue to function sexually for many, many years.

Illness, Surgery, and Medication

There are sexual side effects from disease, surgery, and drugs. But there is no reason to surrender sexuality to illness, medication, or surgery, even in the face of advancing age.

Unfortunately, many doctors do not prepare their patients, or their patients' partners, for the possible impact on sexual functioning of illness, surgery, or medication. Patients need to be informed about a potential change in sexual response, whether it is lack of erection, difficulty in achieving orgasm, or diminished sex drive, so they can know what to expect and can begin to adjust to these changes.

Conversely, sometimes, as with surgery for noncancerous enlargement of the prostate, patients *believe* there should be a negative effect on erections even though most surgical techniques do not affect the ability to have erections. Ironically, this belief itself can cause erectile problems. Or these men will often misinterpret one change in sexual functioning (such as the absence of ejaculation at orgasm) to mean that *all* other functions, such as getting erections, are also lost. Again, this is often not true. This is why receiving accurate information on sexual functioning is essential whenever a physician diagnoses a disease, suggests surgery, or prescribes medication.

Many older patients complain of doctors who tell them that striving for sexual functioning, at their age, is a fruitless or silly pursuit. Other doctors just seem to be embarrassed about discussing sex or refuse to discuss it at all. For these reasons, you may have to insist on a thorough explanation of how your sex life may be affected, and change physicians if you don't get answers to your questions.

Most important, do not accept anyone's opinion that you are too old or too sick to be concerned about sex. Our increasing understanding of the immune system indicates that showing love and caring through touching and physical closeness is an important component of physical health and recovery from illness or surgery. While the road to sexual recovery isn't always smooth, those with the patience and perseverance to explore treatment options will have success in regaining sexual enjoyment.

SURGICAL SCARS

Many people, especially women, are embarrassed by surgical scars. In fact, some people are so embarrassed that it interferes with their sexuality, as was the case with Florence. Florence was very interested in a man she had recently been dating but she was hesitant to get any more involved with him. She finally confessed to me that she thought he might be turned off by the scars she carried after her mastectomy. I encouraged Florence to talk to him about her concerns.

Ironically, the man told Florence that he had a few scars of his own across his chest from a wound he received in the Vietnam War. He confessed to her that he had been worried that his scars would turn women off. Happily, they were both able to accept each other for who they were—not how they looked.

As I suggested to Florence, tell the truth to any person you are seriously interested in. Hours, days, or even weeks before any intimacy, tell her or him about the surgery you survived, and if he or she is the right kind of person, it won't make any difference. Any person who would reject you because of your scars or an absent breast is a person from whom you should flee as fast as you can.

Another client of mine also had a story with a happy ending. Mandy had had two major surgeries. One left a very unattractive jagged scar across her belly. As I suggested, she talked with her potential lover about her concerns before they became sexually intimate. The first night they were intimate, he kissed her scar tenderly and lovingly. Mandy was so touched by this that all her fears went out the window. She never undressed in the dark again.

Physical attraction is mental and emotional. If someone loves you with his or her whole heart, mind, and body, it will not matter that you are missing a breast, an arm, a leg, or any other part.

If You Think You Are Attractive to Others—You Probably Are

Self-confidence is an important part of sex appeal. Most people find those who are independent and self-confident to be very sexy.

A person might be very attractive and still think of herself or himself as being unattractive. For example, it's not unusual for attractive females to not fully appreciate their beauty. As mentioned earlier, a female is likely to think she is too fat, too thin, too short, too tall, or that her breasts are too large or too small.

While it is possible to appear sexy to someone else even though you don't see yourself that way, it's difficult for you to be able to enjoy sex if you have a negative view. Self-esteem is closely related to sexuality in the sense of enjoyment. The person who thinks of herself or himself as ugly is much more likely to have sexual hang-ups and inhibitions.

Body Image Inventory

Answering the following questions will help you to get a clearer picture of how well you know your body as well as how you perceive it.

- What part of your body do you like the most? Why?
- What part do you like the least? Why?
- What part of your body brings you the most pleasure?
- What part brings you the most embarrassment?

There are a lot more things than how we actually *look* that influence whether we have a good body image or a poor one. How you feel about yourself inside, the amount of shame you feel about your body in general and your genitals in particular, how much you have been influenced by peer pressure and the media to expect perfection from yourself—all these things affect your view of yourself. How you feel about yourself *inside* has a lot more to do with your body image than how you actually look.

Chapter Fourteen

DISCOVERING AND ACCEPTING YOUR OWN UNIQUE SEXUAL PERSONALITY

Our sexuality is an important aspect of our identity. In fact, it has been said that sexuality is the most personal component of self. We cannot separate our sexuality from our identity—any more than we can separate our intellect or emotions from our identity. It is one of the many ways we have of expressing our individuality, our individual energy, our life force.

No matter how well you may think you know yourself, you cannot fully grasp the source and meaning of all of your sexual feelings, impulses, fantasies. It would be too overwhelming for you to see and completely understand these aspects of yourself except over time and in bits and pieces. Nevertheless, it is important that as much as possible you come to know yourself sexually, to understand your private sexual interests, behaviors, and capacities and their sources—in other words, that you discover your sexual personality.

You have already done most of the groundwork toward discovering and accepting your sexual personality by exploring how your sexual personality was formed—by discovering what influenced and affected your sexuality. With this better understanding of why you are the way you are, you are probably already more accepting of yourself.

Each individual's sexuality is unique because his or her character is unique. Character organizes the personality and creates a specific style for each woman and man. Even though this style continues to develop throughout a person's life, its essential features are permanent. Character consists of what is usually true about a person, not what is true under special circumstances.

The same is true of your sexual personality. While some things about you may change, your basic sexual style remains the same and cannot be easily changed. Therefore, it is important that you learn what your basic sexual style is and that you learn to accept it if at all possible.

While it is vitally important that you do not continue esteem-robbing sexual behavior, as we discussed in Part II, it is equally important that you discover what your sexual personality is and that you are true to it. As long as your sexual behavior does not hurt you or someone else, accepting your sexual preferences as part of your overall personality will be a major step toward accepting yourself the way you are.

Although some aspects of your sexual personality can change throughout your life (such as your level of sexual desire), most aspects remain pretty much the same. Many facets of the sexual personality are formed in childhood and adolescence. In fact, our first sexual experiences profoundly affect our sexual preferences.

Discovering your sexual personality can provide you with valuable self-knowledge that will enable you to know what you prefer sexually. This, in turn, will enable you to begin to ask for what you want from your partner or partners. Armed with this newfound information you can begin to seek out those people and those activities that will be most pleasing and fulfilling to you.

All too often we tend to take what we can get sexually, or to become involved with those who are sexually available instead of holding out for the kinds of sexual partners and activities that will be most satisfying to us. When this happens we find that we require more and more sex to satisfy the needs that are not getting met. This phenomenon can be compared to the experience of being hungry for a particular type of food but settling for whatever is in the refrigerator. While your physical hunger may have been satisfied, your *appetite*, your desire, has not. You may find that throughout the night you make several return visits to the refrigerator, snacking on its contents and still craving something else. Had you eaten what you originally craved you not only would have been far more satisfied but would have probably eaten less.

Just as a desire for love cannot be satisfied by numerous sexual affairs, and just as we cannot fill our emptiness caused by childhood neglect or abuse by promiscuous sex, we cannot satisfy our sexual appetites and desires with substitutes. As much as possible we need to give ourselves the real thing.

One of the most profound examples of someone's trying to substitute other things for what was really desired was the case of Clay. Clay secretly desired fat women. He thought they were the most beautiful and sensual creatures on earth and he fantasized constantly about being with one sexually. But Clay, like most Americans, had been raised to believe that thin was beautiful and fat was not. All during high school, while quietly dreaming of being with Chelsea—the fat girl in his class with the beautiful angelic face—Clay succumbed to peer pressure by dating the more popular thin girls. "I'll always remember my disappointment whenever I'd start to make out with one of those popular girls. They seemed so bony to me, so hard-edged. I longed to hold someone I could melt into like a pillow."

While Clay had many sexual encounters throughout high school and college, he was never really satisfied. By the time he was out of school, away from the watchful eyes of his fraternity buddies, and no longer had to uphold the position of being "big man on campus," Clay began to date the women he had longed to date. "At first I was uncomfortable with the looks I'd get from other people when I was out with a big woman. But all that disappeared the first time I held and kissed one. It felt so wonderful to hold someone who was soft and sensual instead of bony. And the first time I made love to a big woman I felt like I was in heaven. For me, it was what lovemaking was meant to be. I couldn't believe I'd deprived myself of this ecstasy for so long."

It is about as easy to change our sexual personality as it is to change our emotional personality. Because of this it is vitally important that we learn to understand it and, ultimately, accept it. Accepting your sexual personality can mean the difference between a fulfilling sexual life and one that is sterile and meaningless. It can mean that, like Clay, you can be with partners you are sexually attracted to instead of placing so much importance on what others think. This includes being attracted to the same sex, to other races, and to those who are much older or younger than you.

It doesn't mean, of course, that you give yourself total permission to engage in any sexual act you would like to, even if the act is illegal or outside your own value system. It does mean, however, that you nurture an attitude of personal tolerance and personal forgiveness for aspects of your sexual personality that have, at least in the past, been beyond your control and beyond your understanding. Coming from this less judgmental mind-set, you can investigate your sexual personality from a curious, rather than a critical, point of view to discover the origins of your personal quirks and idiosyncrasies and to decide whether they are something you can actually act out or not. Ironically, discovering the sources of our sexual attractions and desires and admitting them to ourselves without judgment are often the very ways to change them if we choose to do so.

Our sexual personality is made up of our gender identity, our sexual orientation, our sexual intention (what we want from sex), sexual desire, arousal, and orgasm. These factors are usually beyond our control and therefore probably need to be accepted rather than making futile attempts at changing them.

GENDER IDENTITY

Gender identity—the sense of oneself as male and masculine or female and feminine—is obviously a basic and very important aspect of the sexual personality. While people believe that human beings are divided into males and females from the beginning of life to the end, that males always have a penis and scrotum and females always have a clitoris and labia, sexuality is far more complicated than that. There are so many levels of basic maleness and femaleness that scientists have found it necessary to formulate a set of categories to describe human sex, gender, and reproductive capacity fully and accurately. These are the stages by which sexuality develops from conception to adulthood. Each stage provides the foundation for the next in male and female development.

• Chromosomal sex. (Do a person's cells have the XX-female or XY-male chromosome pattern?)
   • Gonadal sex. (Does the person have testicles or ovaries?)
   • Horomonal sex. (Does the person have more of the so-called

male or androgenic hormones, or more estrogens and progestins, the so-called female hormones?)

• Sex of internal organs. (Does the person have a prostate gland, or is there a uterus and ovaries?)

• Sex of external organs. (Is there a penis or a clitoris, a scrotum or labia?)

• Brain sex. (Does the brain have male or female structures and levels of chemicals?)

• Sex assigned at birth. (What was said when the doctor looked at the newborn: "It's a boy" or "It's a girl"?)

• Gender identity/role. (Does the person think "I'm a girl" or "I'm a boy," and what does the person say or do to make others think "That's a girl" or "That's a boy"?)

• Sexual orientation identity. (Is the person attracted to and does he or she fall in love with the same-sex or opposite-sex partners?)

During the nine months prior to birth, an extremely complex and fragile biological process involving chromosomes, hormones, tissue structure, and growth occurs. Many steps in this process (called sexual differentiation) are subject to difficulties. One possible result is that a baby's external genitals may not "match" its internal sex organs. Or all the aspects of sex may in fact appear to "match" at birth but at puberty an apparently normal boy develops breasts and his penis does not grow.

It is actually quite miraculous that for the vast majority of pregnancies this complicated, interlocking series of biological events culminates in the birth of a perfectly formed (inside and out, top to bottom) healthy baby boy or baby girl. It is at this point that psychological and social factors, culture, upbringing, and other environmental influences begin to play the major roles in a person's sexual development.

While biology is certainly influential, it alone does not dictate gender identity. As we discussed in Part I, the way parents react to the sex of their infant is a vital cause of the toddler's early gender sense. Based usually on only a quick look at the baby's genitals the doctor announces "It's a girl!" or "It's a boy!" This seemingly simple statement will have a profound effect on the baby's life. In fact, the answer to the question "Is it a boy or girl?" helps determine how we respond to a baby: the way we handle it, the way we play with it, even the way we talk to it. For example, many people who might toss a baby boy into the air would refrain from doing so with a baby girl.

Several rare yet dramatic examples have made the scientific world realize just how strong an influence family behaviors and beliefs may have and how the interaction between infant and family can override biological influences. One key factor seems to be the family's belief about the child's true sex. This causes the child to label itself a girl or a boy and encourages her or him to behave in ways that others will recognize as specifically feminine or masculine. One such case was that of a male infant who, thought to be a girl at birth because of genital abnormality, grew up to have a female gender identity and then was discovered to have male chromosomes.

While an individual's gender identity ("I am a boy" or "I am a girl") becomes established at between eighteen months and three years of age, this doesn't mean that children fully understand what it means to be female or male. For gender identity that matches the anatomy to develop, the toddler must accept the label "girl" or "boy."

In order to accept the label "boy," the child has to accept being different from Mother and accept the fact that his future is tied to maleness. A mother can promote male gender role behavior in her son by subtly encouraging him to be different from her. But when the mother has a need to prolong the infantile closeness with her son, she may cause the toddler to be afraid of trying new things, taking part in rough-and-tumble play, and being a boy. Fathers usually play a subtle, supportive role in this process if they are loving models for sons to identify with and if they take an active role in their upbringing.

For a girl to accept the label "girl," she has to take some pleasure in being like her mother. If she feels secure in her attachment to her mother, she can accept the fact that her future is tied to femaleness. Typically she does not have to undergo the disruption that boys do in order to achieve an identity separate from that of the caregiver. For this reason, serious gender problems are less common in girls than in boys. When girls do have such problems it is generally because they could not form a trusting bond with their mothers early in life and their fathers, if present, did not seem to be delighted in their femaleness.

Once the core identity is established, the child will likely never lose his or her sense of maleness or femaleness. But gender identity, like other aspects of personality, continuously evolves. Each developmental step the child takes is an opportunity to create more layers of his or her sense of self along the gender dimension.

Genetic makeup, hormones, brain development, anatomy, social and family influences—all these factors comprise the elements that mold each person into an adult woman or man; we then carry these influences with us into our relationships with others, particularly sexual relationships.

Errors of the Body

The process of establishing a clear chromosomal, gonadal, or hormonal human sex pattern is sometimes not completed. External genitals may not look either completely male or female, and what is inside the body may not match what is outside. Some of these problems of biological development are obvious at birth; others are not noticeable until puberty or even later (as when an individual tries to become a parent but cannot).

There are other completely different types of mismatches, biological and psychological. Sometimes a person is completely male or female in all biological and physical respects but psychologically *feels* that he or she is of the other sex. Among the most common types of unfinished biological development are problems with genitals. Especially in males, the complex process that causes the testicles to move down from the abdomen into the scrotum and the penis shaft to fuse around the urethra may not be finished at birth. Similar processes that develop the male and female internal reproductive organs can also go wrong, leading to either missing or duplicated tubes, ducts, and organs.

Transsexualism

For most people the psychological concept of being either a male or female is permanently fixed by the age of twelve to eighteen months. The person's gender identity—and, as he or she matures, the masculine or feminine gender role and behavior—matches the biological sex. For some, however, the sex they identify with psychologically (*feel* that they are) does not match their chromosome pattern, gonads, hormone levels, internal sex organs, or genitals— even when all of these biological characteristics are perfectly matched.

THE DIFFERENCE BETWEEN TRANSSEXUALISM AND TRANSVESTISM

A *transvestite* is someone who wears the clothes of the opposite sex (called cross-dressing) and who clearly understands that he (most are male) is a man and likes having a penis to use for sexual activities. The sexual partners of a transvestite also clearly view the individual as male and think of their sexual interaction as either heterosexual (in the case of a woman whose male partner needs to wear female clothing to have an erection) or homosexual (when a man has sex with another man who wears women's clothing).

Most transvestites who are involved with women sexually are completely heterosexual behaviorally (meaning they want to have sex only with women). The only difference between them and other heterosexual men is that they just happen to feel more sexually aroused if they wear (or imagine wearing) ladies' garments.

One survey of men who subscribed to a magazine for transvestites found that the majority were above average in intelligence and career attainment, and that more than seventy-five percent had been married and were parents. The vast majority were sexually attracted to women, not to men.

Although nearly half of transvestites surveyed did not wear opposite sex clothing outside the house, some did. Many women have quite happy marital and family lives with transvestite men; some even help their partners by buying the female undergarments they need and cooperating in keeping this secret from family and friends. Other women find the behavior distressing and say that it hinders their ability to become sexually aroused.

True *transsexuals*, on the other hand, honestly feel that they are trapped in a wrong sex body, so when they wear clothing or hairstyles of the opposite sex it is an expression of what they feel is their true gender. Unlike the majority of transvestites, male transsexuals are usually no more aroused by wearing feminine clothing than are biological females who wear a dress or biological males who put on suits and ties.

Another difference between transsexuals and transvestites is that transsexuals are literally offended by their existing bodies and want them changed, no matter the pain or expense. Transvestites are not interested in changing their bodies.

If you think there is something wrong physically with your body that has caused you to question what gender you are, consult an endocrinologist or other specialist. On the other hand, there are individuals with completely normal bodies who are totally convinced they are the opposite sex. If you think this is what is going on, consult a specialist in gender identity. To find such a specialist, contact a nearby medical school, ask for the department of endocrinology, and say that you need an appointment with the staff member most familiar with problems of sex assignment and gender identity.

Changing one's physical sex is a complicated process. If you decide to pursue this, you must be prepared to spend a great deal of time and money working with specialists. Before being accepted by any reputable center for a sex change operation you will need to be evaluated by one or more psychiatrists, plus several other types of specialists. An initial evaluation will also include thorough medical tests to determine your chromosomal and hormonal status as well as your general health. Many clinics also want to interview family members and willing sexual partners and friends.

If you are accepted into a transsexual program, the first step is usually to live and work successfully as a member of the opposite sex for one year, then to continue a successful lifestyle while being on hormone therapy for another year—all before ever beginning the more irreversible surgical alterations of the reproductive organs and body. The full procedure varies, depending on the clinic, and takes several years, but has been found to produce the best overall results.

Accepting yourself for who you are when it comes to gender identity can be a painful process. If you are a true transsssexual you will more than likely discover that going through the process of making your body congruent with how you *feel* inside will be an incredibly liberating process. Instead of feeling trapped in the wrong body you will be able to love your body and feel at home inside of it.

Sexual Orientation

Our sexual orientation—whether we are heterosexual, homosexual, or bisexual—is obviously an important part of our sexual personality, but an even more important aspect of our sexual orientation is how we *feel* about it. Homosexuals and bisexuals, because they are a minority and because their behavior is outside the norms of society, often suffer from a great deal of confusion, shame, fear, and anger regarding this aspect of their sexual personality. Many heterosexuals also experience some degree of confusion regarding their sexual orientation.

Kinsey showed that about one third of all males have had at least one same-sex experience leading to orgasm. Most of these men are comfortable heterosexuals. Also according to Kinsey, about eight percent of U.S. males have had exclusively same-sex partners for at least a period of three years at some point in life. Only about four percent of men were exclusively homosexual throughout their entire lives. Among U.S. females, Kinsey found that around half of college-educated women and approximately twenty percent of non-college-educated women have at least one same-sex erotic contact past puberty; only two or three percent of these women were exclusively homosexual their entire lives.

HOMOSEXUALITY

Estimates about the percentage of the population that may be gay range between 1 and 13 percent of men and 0.5 and 8 percent of women. These numbers are based on numerous surveys, including those of Lee Ellis and colleagues and Alan Bell and his coworkers. The privacy that envelops this subject and the question about how much homoeroticism is necessary before someone is considered gay keep all these figures uncertain.

Many heterosexual and homosexual adults are biased against homoeroticism and homosexuality and believe them to be signs of psychological illness. Although some current psychological theories about persistent homoeroticism point to unfortunate childhood development, these theories do not mean that homoeroticism is an illness. Mental patterns and behavior are considered a symptom of illness only if they convincingly meet two criteria: personal distress and impaired social functioning. After thoughtful consideration by both the American Psychiatric Association and the American Psychological Association, it was decided in 1974 that the weight of scientific evidence supported the conclusion that homosexual men and women could not be considered to have a psychological or mental illness on the basis of their sexual orientation. In essence, homosexuality is not an abnormality, illness, or disorder.

Thus far, there has been no conclusive evidence as to the cause of homosexuality. While many theories have been proposed, and there have been some recent studies pointing to the possibility that it may be biological (such as the Simon Le Vay research, which found that the hypothalamus in the brains of gay men is smaller than in the brains of heterosexual men), so far most studies have not held up under careful scrutiny and none have been proven. Findings such as those of Le Vay are limited due to the fact that the test subjects were all gay men. So far, there have been no studies involving lesbian women.

While science has not yet identified what determines sexual orientation—what causes a male or a female to be heterosexual (sexually attracted to people of the opposite sex), homosexual (exhibiting a romantic attraction to, sexual desire for, or sexual behavior with a person of one's own sex), or bisexual (having a romantic or sexual attraction for both sexes), what has been established is that simple explanations (such as having a domineering mother) do not hold true for most homosexuals. It is certainly reasonable to think that biological factors do interact with social and psychological ones to influence heteroerotic and homoerotic orientations.

Based on over twenty years of working with clients with sexual concerns, I believe that there is no *one* answer when it comes to what causes homosexuality. Some people do seem to be born gay or lesbian, while others seem to become homosexual due to certain life circumstances such as childhood abandonment or neglect, childhood sexual abuse, rape, or physical abuse by a partner. I have worked with clients who seem to have been born gay based on the fact that they remember feeling different from the time they were very small children, and with clients who seemed to have been born heterosexual but who became involved in homosexual relationships much later on in life because of traumatic experiences with the opposite sex. I have also had some lesbian clients who remember being attracted to the same sex all their lives but after many years of therapy realized that they were looking for the nurturing they did not receive from their mothers.

No matter how often a homosexual is told that the behavior is not sick or perverted, many continue to suffer from terrible shame and guilt regarding their sexuality. Those who are religious and find that their religious leaders and other church members are critical of homosexual behavior usually have the most difficult time accepting themselves the way they are. If their behavior is continually labeled "sinful," "the work of the devil," or "an abomination of the Lord," then self-acceptance is almost impossible. Many gays in this kind of situation have found a great deal of solace by joining churches where homosexuality is accepted.

Another important factor influencing whether a gay man or lesbian woman can finally gain self-acceptance is whether his or her family is accepting of the gay lifestyle. Groups such as PFLAG (Parents and Friends of Lesbians and Gays) can help tremendously by educating parents and other family members about the gay lifestyle (write to Box 24565, Los Angeles, CA 90024). Families of gays need to understand that gays and lesbians do not "choose" to be gay in the way that we usually think of the word *choice*, as in choosing a career or a partner. Furthermore, they need to understand that studies indicate that homosexuals are no more neurotic than heterosexuals and that homosexuals can and do lead happy, healthy (mental and physically) lives.

BISEXUALITY

There are a growing number of people who are coming forward to state that they are bisexual. Once criticized by both the heterosexual and homosexual communities, bisexuality is finally being regarded with more respect and understanding. The following statements, made by two openly bisexual individuals, express the positive attitude of many bisexuals today:

"I have been in love with both men and women. At different times in my life I seem to gravitate more toward one sex than the other but overall I feel I am equally capable of having a gratifying sexually romantic relationship with either sex."

"I enjoy sex with both women and men. With men I tend to be more passive, while when I am with women I am more aggressive. I don't think I could ever be satisfied being with just one sex or the other because my sexual personality can be expressed far more fully with both sexes."

CONFUSION ABOUT YOUR SEXUAL ORIENTATION

Being confused about your sexual orientation is actually quite common. This is undoubtedly more true today than ever before due to the following: the amount of openness about the subject, more options available today in terms of sexual lifestyles, and the fact that more and more celebrities and public figures are becoming more open about their alternative lifestyles.

Because heterosexuals make up the majority of the population, we don't usually assume that they suffer from any problems about their sexual orientation. But even heterosexuals can suffer from the same kinds of feelings of confusion and shame that homosexuals and bisexuals do because often the lines between heterosexualism, bisexualism, and homosexualism are not rigid and firm. Many heterosexuals have thoughts, feelings, and fantasies that involve homosexual activities and attractions, which causes them to feel confused, ashamed, and afraid. They become worried that there is something wrong with them—that they are indeed homosexual. Many worry about homosexual experiences they had when they were children, adolescents, or young adults and feel they must hide their secret from even those closest to them. Many heterosexuals have gone so far as to engage in homosexual activities or even to get involved in homosexual relationships, even though they maintain an attraction to heterosexual sex or even while they maintain a heterosexual relationship.

Even homosexuals are disturbed by fantasies involving heterosexual sex since they take these fantasies as a sign that they may indeed by straight. Jules was a good example: "I feel so guilty because I keep having fantasies about having sex with a woman. If my lover ever found out he'd be terribly hurt—and confused—as I am. I'm sure this sounds weird to you, but I feel like some kind of pervert. What healthy homosexual has fantasies about having sex with a woman?"

As we learned in a prior chapter on sexual fantasies, what we fantasize about can have less to do with sexuality than with other aspects of our personality, such as whether we feel in control of our life, the amount of anger and other feelings we are holding in, and so forth.

In reality, few of us are completely heterosexual or homosexual. Many researchers believe that there are degrees to one's sexuality and that people can no longer be clearly divided into groups of homosexuals, heterosexuals, and bisexuals by simply asking about the sex of past or present sexual partners. The Kinsey scale, devised by Kinsey over forty years ago, is still widely used by sex researchers. The scale classified persons with *only* heterosexual behavior as zero, only homosexual behavior as six, and persons with mixtures of male and female sexual partners as one, two, three, four, or five. A true bisexual would be somewhere around three. More recently it has been reported that the scale can be enhanced by including separate scales for factors such as love, sexual attraction, fantasy, and self-identification. For example, if a person had sex *only* with opposite-sex partners but fantasized about having sex with same-sex partners, on the original scale that person would be a zero. On the more complex scale, the zero rating would remain on the partner scale, but the person would be somewhere between one and six on the fantasy scale, depending on what proportion of his or her fantasies included same-sex partners.

This is a difficult theory to accept because most of us are so threatened by the gray areas. We prefer to have things either black or white. "I am straight," or "I am gay." Bisexuals, as reported in books like *View From Another Closet* by Janet Bode, are not the most popular group of people, either with straights or gays. In fact, they tend to be shunned by both groups. They are accused of straddling the fence by gay groups, who see them as homosexuals who just aren't willing to come all the way out of the closet. In the heterosexual population they are often thought of as disturbed or weird, probably because they represent the unknown even more than homosexuals do.

Not only do most of us fall somewhere on the continuum between heterosexuality and homosexuality, but our rating on the scale can change over time. The Kinsey people warn that their scale should not be seen as a series of rigid, fixed descriptions that necessarily describe all behaviors or predict future behaviors because it has become clear that people do not necessarily maintain the same sexual orientation throughout their lives. Some people have a consistent homosexual orientation for a long period of time, then fall in love with a person of the opposite sex; other individuals who have had only opposite-sex partners later fall in love with a same-sex partner. And these changes are not usually a matter of "choice," just as a person can't will or force himself or herself to "fall in love" with some particular person.

There are several factors that determine your sexual orientation, including:

- How you feel inside.
- How you identify yourself.
- Who you choose to be with sexually.

ACCEPTANCE OF YOUR SEXUAL ORIENTATION

As far as your sexual personality goes, it is vital that you come to some kind of acknowledgment and final acceptance of the basic nature of your sexual orientation, whatever configuration it takes. If that means that you are basically heterosexual but have a curiosity and interest in homosexuality, that you are basically homosexual but also find the opposite sex attractive, or that you find both sexes equally attractive, try to accept this truth about yourself as part of your sexual personality—nothing more and nothing less. It requires no judgment from you, and, unless it is troubling you considerably, it requires no further analysis. Researchers have discovered that one of the most common fantasies among heterosexuals is having sex with a same-sex partner. This can be reassuring to people who worry about future behavior when the content of their fantasies doesn't match their current behavior. As with fantasies, you can have an interest in the same sex without ever acting on it. Just enjoy it.

Whatever your sexual orientation or preference it is extremely important that you remain true to your self—that whichever way you choose to express your sexuality it is a true expression of who you really are. It is also vitally important that you work on accepting yourself for who you are and not try to change yourself. Research shows that efforts to change sexual orientation through psychotherapy, abstinence, prayer, or willpower do not work. If indeed you are homosexual, the likelihood of your changing into a heterosexual is about as great as your changing your sex from male to female or vice versa.

It will probably be far more beneficial for you to surround yourself with others of your same sexual orientation as a way of building up your self-esteem and pride in your sexual orientation. Those who have a strong connection with the gay community experience a tremendous amount of pride and receive much-needed support, which in turn raises their self-esteem. Those gays and lesbians who remain isolated or closeted, on the other hand, suffer from feelings of alienation, low self-esteem, fear of being exposed, and shame.

With only heterosexual couples as role models many gay men and lesbian women lose touch with their sexuality and become confused as to what really is erotic to them. When lesbian women see women portrayed on television in roles as sex kittens to macho men how can they help but either see themselves as bimbos in their relationships or as pseudo men a la butch or dyke? Conversely, when gay men see males portrayed as macho or even sadistic, how can they help but bring that into their relationships, believing that one must be submissive while the other is dominant?

There are all kinds of people in the world with all kinds of sexual orientations. Don't try to fit into a box, no matter who is trying to put you in it.

SEXUAL INTENTION

Sexual intention—what we want to do with a partner during sex—is the most private aspect of sexual identity. Most of us have a combination of both conventional and unconventional sexual intentions that arouse us. Examples of *conventional* intentions would be:

1. To have an orgasm.
2. To sexually satisfy our partner.
3. To connect with our partner on a deeply emotional level.
4. To reduce stress.

The most common themes of *unconventional* intentions are:

1. Exhibiting or exposing one's nakedness.
2. Secretly looking at the nakedness or sexual behavior of others.
3. Hurting another person in a display of power.
4. Being subservient to a more dominant person.

However strongly we judge or reject such sexual pleasures in others or ourselves, the fact is that the potential to derive gratification from similar behavior is part of our human nature.

Lovemaking can, in fact, provide gratification of some of these pleasures. For example, during the course of normal lovemaking there is opportunity to exhibit one's body, to enjoy what are usually forbidden looks at our partner's naked body, to dominate by providing intense arousal, to carefully bite or pinch in ways that enhance the partner's arousal. These actions may be so fleeting and disguised that they are not recognized as intentions or forms of behavior that, when exaggerated, are considered forms of sexual perversion. (Again, remember that the diagnosis of sexual perversion is only made when unconventional themes recur with great intensity and are the major source of sexual arousal.)

SEXUAL DESIRE

Although sexual desire is a periodic bodily event like hunger for food, it is indeed far more. It is not just an instinct but a complex need that varies in intensity. It is a mental force, an energy that may appear before lovemaking begins and may accompany sexual arousal, a force that pushes us toward some individuals and away from others. It is a psychological energy that precedes and accompanies arousal and accounts for our tendencies to behave sexually.

Some people complain about a lack of sexual desire while others complain of too much, and still others are distressed by its unpredictable arrivals and departures. Although this energy is often baffling in its presence, absence, and intensity, we do know that health, well-being, good fortune, and inner contentment increase our tendency to be sexual and that desire is stimulated by joy, exhilaration, and personal triumph, and diminished by illness, misfortune, disappointment, depression, and a sense of failure.

In addition to the fact that repressed feelings of anger, pain, and envy can block sexual desire, as we discussed earlier, there are three other common factors that have been known to kill sexual desire: fatigue, worry over health or finances, and a lack of time for play and good companionship.

Sexual desire is not merely a biological need but the interaction of three elements—drive, wish, and motive. The mind integrates these elements and produces something we know as sexual desire. Even though these three elements blend into one another to create desire, they should not be confused with sexual desire itself.

Sexual Drive

Sexual drive is the biological element of sexual desire—the spontaneous experience of arousal. Some people notice that their sexual drive occurs regularly—daily, weekly, or twice a week—while others find their sexual drive has no predictability.

The hormone testosterone is necessary to produce sexual drive in both males and females. There is evidence that a particular small region of the brain is the sexual drive center. Many medications are known to interfere with this center.

After a vigorous beginning during late adolescence and young adulthood in both sexes, the frequency and intensity of spontaneous genital tingling, sexual fantasies, sensitivity to erotic cues in the environment, masturbation, and partner-seeking behaviors gradually decline until in old age they are minimal. Sexual excitability also diminishes, but does not disappear. The source of these changes is not understood, but may be due to the loss of cells in the sexual drive center and a decrease in the amount of testosterone in the body tissues.

When and to what extent the sex drive declines varies considerably from person to person. Despite the decline of drive, sexual behavior continues, and may even increase for some individuals throughout adulthood because the other elements—wish and motive—continue to contribute to the tendency to behave sexually.

ACCEPTING YOUR SEX DRIVE

An important aspect of accepting yourself sexually is to come to terms with your sexual drive. Unless there is a possibility that your sex drive may be affected by medication or illness, learning to accept it will go far in terms of raising your sexual self-esteem. If, for example, your sex drive has always tended to be low, it will serve no purpose whatsoever for you to be critical of yourself about it or to try to change it. Instead, accepting it and finding partners who are compatible with you (that is, who also have a low drive) will probably free you to allow yourself to be sexual when you feel like it and to enjoy your sexuality far more than ever.

The unquestioned assumption behind much of the current literature is that sex is good and that the more pleasurable sex a person has, the greater his or her self-understanding, self-esteem, and general happiness. Basic to many books, particularly the "how-to" variety, is the notion that sex is somehow a great panacea that will cure all anxieties about our worth.

The logic of today's sexologists goes something like this: Sexual activity should be emphasized in a person's life because sex leads to higher self-esteem, to self-understanding, to freedom, and to happiness; and therefore anyone who does not emphasize sex in his or her life is doomed to have low self-esteem and to be unhappy.

But I take issue with the idea that greater sexual activity and pleasure will necessarily lead to higher self-esteem. If a person has low self-esteem she or he should not go out and learn to become an orgasmic sexual gymnast as a way of guaranteeing that all feelings of worthlessness will be magically whisked away. Sex is not a substitute or a quick means to self-esteem, and the two are not one and the same.

Exercise—How Often Do You Feel Sexually Aroused?

There is a wide range of what is "normal"—everything from desiring to have sex once or twice a day to desiring sex only once a month. Begin to keep a log of how often you become sexually aroused and place a star beside those times when you would have actually desired to have had sex. This log will help you discover just how often you become aroused. It may also point out to you that: you may become aroused more often than you think; and you don't necessarily want to have sex every time you become aroused.

Sexual Wish

The sexual wish is the social aspect of sexual desire. For example, many older people whose sexual desires are infrequent and no longer strong still may have a strong *wish* to be involved in sexual activities. There are many reasons for wanting sex and these wishes are established over the many years of adulthood. Some of the reasons people wish to have sex, even when there is no physical desire, are:

- It helps them to feel more intimacy with their partner.
- It makes them feel they are pleasing their partner.
- It makes them feel loved, valued, or important.
- It makes them feel good physically.
- It makes them feel more vital or energetic.
- It makes them feel more masculine or feminine.
- It makes them feel normal.
- It makes them feel connected to another person and thus less alone.

On the other hand, adolescents and young adults with frequent, strong, unexpected arousal and high excitability may not *wish* to have sex. This wish, based on their values, ideas, thoughts, and emotions, causes them to decide *not* to express their sexual feelings—or if they do choose to, to express them with discomfort. Some of the many reasons why people decide *not* to express their sexual wish are:

- They wish to wait until they are married.
- They fear pregnancy.
- They are afraid of getting AIDS or another venereal disease.
- They have a strong conviction that it is morally wrong.
- They do not wish to disgrace or displease their parents.
- They feel emotionally unready.
- They do not know exactly how to do it.
- They are frightened of experiencing intense excitement.
- They do not like anyone enough yet.

Sexual Motive

Sexual drives are physical while sexual wishes are based on thoughts and emotions. "I want to have sex!" may be either the body or the mind speaking. But sexual desire is not simply an interaction between intellectual ideas and biological drives. The most important element, especially in adulthood, is motivation. When motive says "I want to have sex" the person is *emotionally* willing to bring his or her body to the sexual experience.

When a person's sexual life works well, drives, wishes, and motives all push in the same direction. But sexual behavior is not always the product of the three elements pushing together. Often we have drive pushing in one direction and wish and motive pushing in another. For example, if an aroused teenager considers masturbation a legitimate way of relieving sexual tensions, he or she will do so, restore calm to his or her body and psyche, and then be able to continue with other activities. But if this same teenager considers masturbation a terrible sin, masturbation may bring relief from sexual tensions but will produce terrible guilt afterward. The psyche is not calmed by the experience because now the teenager feels the tension of guilt.

The most powerful influence on sexual desire is indeed the emotional element—motive, not drive or wish. Some people with sexual drive and the intellectual wish for lovemaking still do not seem to actually want to make love. Long periods may pass with little or no sexual activity, even when they have a partner who is willing. Other people do not like to spend much time at all without having sex. These individuals do not necessarily have high sexual drives. But they do value sexual experience and have organized their private lives around it.

Sexuality is what we conceive it to be: a valued or a worthless commodity, a form of communication or a way of rebellion, a source of self-esteem or a tool of aggression (control, power, punishment, submission), a biological function or an ideal state, evil or good, a source of freedom or a duty.

WHAT DOES SEX MEAN TO YOU?

Place a check beside each item that describes what sex means to you.

___ love
___ romance
___ connectedness/intimacy
___ a means of expressing affection
___ a way to please my partner
___ pleasure
___ a release from tension
___ a defense against loneliness
___ a means of procreation
___ a duty
___ a sport
___ a skill
___ a reward
___ an escape
___ a communion with the universe
___ a mystical experience
___ other (fill in)

OBJECTS OF DESIRE

There are many different reasons for becoming sexually attracted to someone. While it is often the person's physical attributes that attract us, no one has been able to explain exactly why some people find certain attributes attractive while others do not. And while we are certainly influenced by messages about desirability from books, TV, movies, and magazines, cultural trends are only part of the answer. For the rest of the answer we most certainly must look again to our childhood. The interactions we had with parents, other family members, other significant adults, and our peers helped determine what characteristics we would eventually find desirable in a partner.

For example, a man may be attracted to women with long legs because his mother had long legs, or conversely, because his mother was short and stocky. A woman may find some men especially attractive while others may appear to be repulsive to her depending upon her early experiences with men. If her father was a loving man whom she respected and admired, she may be attracted to men who look like him. But if her father was cruel, aloof, or seductive, she might feel repelled by men who look like him.

Interestingly, if children experience abuse at the hands of a parent, stepparent, other relative, or caretaker, the physical features of that person may either attract or repel them as they grow older. As was mentioned earlier, ironically, it is often the case that abused children develop a repetition compulsion that compels them to reenact the abuse, sometimes even to the point of being involved with partners who look very much like their abusers.

By the time we reach puberty most of us become aware of our own feelings of sexual attraction and notice that we are more likely to become aroused by specific types of people and situations, while other people or situations have little or no effect on us. All of these learning experiences help us determine which people we eventually will be attracted to and also affect the content of our sexual fantasies and the pattern of our sexual behavior because we tend to imagine or seek out partners or situations that are arousing to us and ignore or avoid those that are not.

Dr. John Money, the respected sex researcher I mentioned earlier in our discussion of paraphilias, has called these internalized patterns for a person's particular sexual interests and behavior "lovemaps." He believes that these lovemaps begin to take shape early in our lives and become fixed as we go through experiences that more clearly define what contributes to sexual arousal. Most people from similar backgrounds end up with essentially similar maps in which only the details differ. For example, most men will be attracted to women within a few years of their own age whose physical characteristics, like height and weight, are more or less within average range, but each may prefer or be drawn to particular characteristics—including hair, eye, and skin color; body shape; or personality type. A few people are aroused only by individuals with very specific or rare features or attributes, as was discussed earlier.

Many men in particular believe that they should be turned on by the typical model type when in fact they are not. There are surprising numbers of men who are not attracted to the stereotypical "perfect" woman but instead have their own unique vision of beauty.

Exercise—Who Are You Attracted To?

Write a description of your ideal sexual partner, including both a physical description and a description of the person's emotional makeup.

WRITING YOUR OWN "PERSONALS" AD

While you may never actually list a personals ad in a publication, you can learn a lot about yourself by spending some time thinking about what your personal ad would say. Your descriptions will tell you a lot about your own sexual personality and that of your ideal sex partner. In addition, they will help you to determine just how important physical characteristics are to you in terms of sexual arousal.

1. Start with a self-description.

Write a paragraph about who you are sexually. Include a physical description if you wish, but more important, describe your sexual attributes.

Examples

"I am an extremely waspy looking woman who likes things that are exotic. Even though I like to be in control in the business world, I tend to be more traditional in terms of wanting the man to be more dominant than I am in bed."

"I like sex to be exciting, intense, and sometimes even a little kinky. Sometimes the most bizarre things will turn me on—like watching a movie about the people in the circus—you know, the freaks. I don't know why I find things like that exciting but I do."

2. Now describe your "ideal" sex partner.

Again, write a paragraph describing the sexual personality and sexual attributes as well as a physical description of your ideal sexual partner.

"I like a sex partner who isn't afraid to try new things and who is as adventurous as I am—someone who likes to have sex in the backseat of the car at the drive-in, on the beach at night, or in an isolated forest. I like a partner who is spontaneous and free sexually, who isn't worried about performance, orgasms, or what others think."

As you can see from the above paragraph, this person was very sure of the sexual personality he or she wanted in a partner but didn't describe any physical characteristics. As a matter of fact, we don't know what the writer's sex was or what his or her sexual preference was. One gets the idea that the sexual personality of a partner is far more important than how he or she looks or possibly even what sex the partner is.

"I like the tall, dark, and handsome type, especially if he looks somewhat exotic. It really turns me on to be with a man who is taller and bigger than me because it makes me feel small and protected. I prefer a man who doesn't have a hairy chest or a lot of body hair and who isn't too muscular—more of a runner's body than a weight-lifter's body. I like him to be very gentle and soft-spoken at first but be very strong and aggressive when intercourse begins. I like a passionate man who really gets into what he's doing and isn't afraid to show his enjoyment."

Here we see that this woman has very specific physical features that she is turned on to and that what the man looks like is extremely important to her arousal.

What Is Erotic to You?

The word *erotic* refers to anything that tends to arouse sexual love or desire—or, to put it simply, anything that stimulates a person sexually. What may be erotic to one person may be a turnoff to another.

We don't always understand why we find something erotic and

in most cases we don't need to. As long as what turns us on doesn't cause us a great deal of shame, and does not hurt others or ourselves, we can gain a great deal of pleasure by allowing ourselves to respond to the things that stimulate us.

Until recently we believed that men tended to be more *visually* stimulated, while women tended to become aroused by tactile and auditory stimulation and by connecting emotionally with their partners. Men were thought to generally become aroused by nudity, sexy lingerie, and pornography, while women tended to become more aroused by erotica (literary or artistic works having an erotic theme or quailty, such as romance novels or "art" movies with just a vague hint of nudity).

Now we know that there are women who do become aroused by pornography or by their partner's naked body and there are men who prefer erotica or subtle sexual innuendo versus full nudity. In the past several years—with the popularity of male strippers and *Playgirl* magazine, for example—women have expressed an interest in male nudity as erotically stimulating. Obviously, women are far more capable of being aroused visually than they have been given credit for. The fact is that both sexes can be aroused by a variety of stimuli, including auditory, olfactory, visual, kinesthetic, and tactile stimulation.

There are basically two sources of eroticism—that which comes from outside of us (a specific visual, auditory, or olfactory stimulant), or that which occurs as a result of the connection between two people (a touch, a look, an embrace, an understanding). Both sources of eroticism are natural and healthy, but when a person relies almost entirely on outside stimulants to the exclusion of being aroused by a human connection—that person will become more and more isolated, less able to sustain an emotional relationship, and far more limited sexually.

Sexual Triggers

WHAT AROUSES YOU?

Make a list of the kinds of stimuli that arouse you. This may take some time and you may need to do it in more than one sitting. After you have completed your list go back and prioritize it, making number one the kind of stimuli that most arouses you, and so forth.

This list was written by a workshop participant:

1. I am most aroused by visual stimuli such as seeing a beautiful woman, either in real life or in a movie or magazine.
2. I also find that I am very affected by how a woman smells. I don't know what causes it but some women smell *exotic* and that really turns me on.
3. I like women who like to touch and be touched. It really turns me on for a woman to stroke my arm or leg, or for her to rub my back. If a woman likes to be touched I almost always find that she is a good lover.

WHAT TURNS YOU OFF?

Paying attention to what turns you off sexually is as important as knowing what turns you on. Time after time while working with couples in sex therapy one partner discovers much to his or her surprise that he or she often does things during lovemaking or just prior to it that are actually turnoffs to the other partner. In fact, it is quite common for even the most intimate of partners to be unaware that a particular action on his or her part is a turnoff to the other partner.

The following are some common turnoffs:

• Someone who appears to be extremely needy about sex.
• Someone who acts like a little child while having sex.
• Bad breath.
• Body odor.
• Being the one who always has to initiate sex.
• Never being able to be the initiator.
• Talking about ex-lovers, ex-spouses, or previous lovers.

Sometimes something turns us off because it reminds us of a previous unpleasant or traumatic experience, as it did with these workshop participants:

"I get turned off to women who are like my mother. She was so passive and let my father walk all over her. Now I find that passive, quiet women are a real turnoff to me. I especially hate it if a woman whines or acts helpless."

"Ten years ago I was raped as I was getting into my car late one night after work. The man pulled me into the backseat of my car and raped me. Now, I can't stand to be kissed or even for a guy to hold my hand while driving in a car. And if a guy is wearing leather, like the rapist was, forget it—I am completely turned off."

Make a list of all the things that turn you off sexually. Include behaviors, touches, sights, sounds, smells, and tastes.

YOUR IDEAL SEXUAL RELATIONSHIP

A great sex life doesn't just happen—it takes work. Sex can easily become boring and mundane if it is not honored and nurtured, just like a relationship can become stale if it is not infused with new energy and commitment from time to time. Treating sex as the tender flower it is can help keep it not only exciting but fulfilling as well.

Exercise—What Is Your Ideal Sexual Relationship?

There is a certain quality of life that we all want to live within, a life that we all strive for. Sex is almost always a part of the ideal life we hope and fantasize about.

Write down a description of your ideal sexual relationship. Spend some time thinking and fantasizing about it before you write it down.

Here are some examples from workshop participants:

"My dream is to have a sex life that is extremely romantic. I love candlelight throughout the house, soft music, soft feathers, beautiful lingerie, satin sheets. I love sensuous foods, sensuous clothes, and long, slow sex with lots of caressing."

"My dream sex life would be to always have sex be exciting and new. I want a partner who is as creative and innovative as I am and who is willing to explore all kinds of sexual positions and act out all kinds of sex roles."

The chances are that you can have your dream, whatever it is. It may seem unreachable based on what you know right now, but with some work and dedication on your part it can indeed come true. You may have to do some work on the things in your life that have gotten in the way of your getting what you want (childhood traumas, old sexual guilt, or poor body image, for example), but once you have cleared up these obstacles, your dream sex life can indeed come true if you make a commitment to making esteem-enhancing choices and if you determine to be the one who creates your sex life instead of waiting for someone else to create it for you.

For example, I know a lovely elderly couple who recently shared with me that they have experienced a beautiful sexual life together for forty years—a sex life they swear gets better every day. When I asked them what they attributed their great sex life to, they told me this:

Husband: "Helen has always made our sex life exciting. I never know what to expect. One night I might come home and find soft music, candlelight, and a hot bath waiting for me. Another night I would come home and she had rented a French movie. She always set the stage for romance—with fresh-cut flowers, soft music, candlelight. At age fifty she signed us up for a massage class and it was one of the most wonderful things she could have done for our relationship. Ever since then we have taken turns massaging each other, depending upon who has the most energy. It has helped us connect with each other in a way we never had before. I give Helen complete credit for keeping our sex life alive."

Wife: "It's true that I have worked hard to make certain that the quality of our sex life remained high, but Arnie isn't telling you the whole story. He is a very attentive, gentle lover. And no matter how stressed he was from work, when he came through that front door he put it all aside for me. Instead of complaining about his day at work he joined with me in making our evening the most relaxed, loving experience it could be. Sometimes we were both so tired we'd just watch TV together, but we kept it to a minimum, unlike most of our friends, whose lives seemed to be centered around the TV. And even while we watched TV one of us was almost always rubbing the other's feet or neck. Arnie is the most devoted husband I have ever heard of. It's easy to love him and want to share our love together sexually."

To summarize, our sexual personality includes the following:

- Who you are attracted to sexually.
- Who you are most comfortable with sexually.
- Who you tend to get involved with sexually.
- What kind of sexual stimuli arouse you.
- What kind of sexual activities you prefer.
- How often you become sexually aroused.
- How often you like to have sex.
- Whether you prefer to be the initiator or the receiver.
- Whether you prefer to be dominant, submissive, or equal.

We each need to begin to accept ourselves for who we are, because until we can do this, we will only make matters worse. An important aspect of increasing your sexual self-esteem is learning that there is no ideal way to have sex, no ideal way to have an orgasm, and no ideal number of times you should have sex a week. The more we pressure ourselves to perform, to be what we consider "normal," the lower our sexual self-esteem will be.

While the sexual personality begins to develop in childhood, it continues to develop and evolve over a lifetime. At each stage of our lives we will focus on a different aspect of our sexuality. Some of the important stages of sexuality that each person goes through in a lifetime are:

- Discovering the sexual self.
- Becoming comfortable with the sexual self.
- Beginning partner sexual behavior.
- Forming an intense relationship bond.
- Exploring the capacity to be constant, loving, and committed.
- Managing disappointment and hostility to preserve the attachment.
- Parenting.
- Reattaching to another.

Sex consists of a whole range of experiences that are not just genital. Sex involves the whole body and is expressed in different ways at different times in a person's life.

Among older age groups, sex is heavily affected by both partners' health, the typical decrease of the male's sex drive and his ability to achieve and maintain an erection, and the quality of the couple's previous relationship during middle life. At every stage of adulthood comfort with our sexual selves enables us to love fully with our bodies or causes us to miss sexuality's richness.

Our sexuality is an integral part of our lives and as such it is both influenced by and affects every part of our lives. Nevertheless, sex should never be the focal point of our lives to the exclusion of other things. It should never become our purpose of living but rather its reward. By the same token, sex should never become the most important aspect of a loving relationship nor the glue that holds the relationship together. Rather it should be the dessert—the celebration of a loving and tender bond.

And finally, it has been discovered that what is on our minds determines our sexual abilities more than nearly anything else. Each sexual experience can be either enhanced by pleasant thoughts, fantasies, or memories, or soured by recalling painful or unpleasant memories of the past or by feelings of anger toward our partner. A positive sexual activity is any sexual activity that is viewed in a positive light by the person who experiences it.

Epilogue

TOWARD A NEW SEXUALITY

Having high sexual self-esteem won't mean that you will necessarily want to go out and have lots of sex with lots of different partners. In fact, as we have discussed earlier, this is more the behavior of someone who has low self-esteem, someone who is trying to gain approval, to bolster low self-esteem, or someone who is sexually addicted and is thus trying to fill up the emptiness inside. Persons with high sexual self-esteem value their bodies and their emotions and will thus choose their partners carefully, choosing those who are caring, accepting, and passionate.

Having high sexual self-esteem will mean that if you make a mistake (old habits die hard) and choose someone who is critical, uncaring, unaffectionate, or dispassionate you will recognize your mistake and be able to end the relationship early on and not waste valuable time.

Having high sexual self-esteem will mean that you no longer expect yourself to "perform" sexually but are able to take your time, enjoy all your bodily sensations, and appreciate the connectedness you feel with your partner. It means you no longer expect yourself to always have an orgasm or an erection or to lubricate but that you understand that sometimes you are just too tired or too preoccupied or under too much stress.

Having high sexual self-esteem means that as you get older you won't panic about a few more wrinkles, a few extra pounds, or the fact that it takes you longer to get an erection or to achieve an orgasm. You will know that anyone who truly cares about you won't care about these things and that getting older can sometimes mean getting better.

Having high sexual self-esteem means that you have discovered your sexual personality and have learned to accept yourself as you are instead of constantly trying to change yourself into something you are not. And it means that you choose partners who are compatible with your sexual personality instead of those who are not and then focus all your attention either on changing them or on feeling bad about yourself.

It means being able to be truly intimate with your partner, to trust enough to share your true self and your secrets.

It means you will no longer be plagued by self-doubt, shame, or a fear of being who you really are, but that you will feel free to express your sexuality, your feelings, and your passion.

Having high sexual self-esteem will mean that instead of worrying about what other people are doing you will be able to focus on enjoying every minute of intimate and sexual contact.

The work you have done on yourself concerning your sexual self-esteem will continue to pay off—not just in the short term but in the long term as well. You will continue reaping the benefits for a long time to come.

Your sexual self-esteem will be more constant instead of soaring up and down depending upon how your partner views you, or whether you have gained a few pounds. This is not to say that you won't need to remind yourself now and then of what you have learned. We are all vulnerable from time to time to the opinions of others, the whims of fashion, or the ghosts of the past. At these times give yourself a "refresher course" by rereading key sections of this book, reviewing your sexual history, or discussing your concerns with a supportive friend or therapist.

Some of you may have discovered in the process of reading this book that you were either emotionally, physically, or sexually abused as a child or that you were severely deprived of parental affection and care. As I have recommended throughout the book, this kind of childhood history normally requires individual psychotherapy, group therapy, or a twelve-step program in order to more fully recover from such trauma.

Others of you may have discovered that you have a sexual dysfunction or other sexual problem that requires professional help. When you feel your problem probably does not involve medical or physical factors, you should locate a sex therapist or marriage counselor. The following suggestions will help you find a professional who has been specifically trained to make discussing sensitive personal problems easier and more comfortable for you.

HOW TO LOCATE A SEX THERAPIST OR MARRIAGE COUNSELOR

• If you are comfortable doing so, ask friends, family members, or coworkers who have gone to a counselor whether they can recommend someone.

• Ask your family physician or clergyman for a recommendation.

• Write to one of the following groups and ask for a list of certified counselors and therapists in your area (there may be a nominal fee):

American Association of Sex Educators, Counselors and Therapists (AASECT)
11 Dupont Circle N.W., Suite 220
Washington, D.C. 20036

American Association for Marriage and Family Therapy (AAMFT)
1717 K Street N.W., Suite 407
Washington, D.C. 20006

• Call your local community health center and ask for recommendations, or call the nearest medical school or large hospital and ask if it has a sex dysfunction clinic.

• Look in the yellow pages of your telephone book under: "Marriage, Family, Child Counselors"; "Psychologists"; "Psychiatrists" (may be listed under "Physicians & Surgeons—Medical, M.D." or separately under "Psychiatrists"); or "Mental Health Services."

If you suspect your sexual or relationship problems may include medical or physical factors, locate a sex therapist who works closely with medical professionals or a physician with special training in sexual medicine.

Call the nearest medical school, university, or large hospital and ask if it has a special clinic for diagnosing and treating sexual problems (dysfunctions). If your town does not have such a facility, most libraries have telephone directories of nearby large cities where such facilities may be found.

RECOMMENDED READING

The following list contains books that may be of further help to you in raising your sexual self-esteem. These resources present information on sexuality in general, sexual dysfunction, sexual abuse, and other relevant topics. Because sexual self-esteem is a new topic, few references address it directly or in much detail. Therefore you will need to pick and choose relevant material from what you read.

SEX EDUCATION AND ENRICHMENT

Barbach, Lonnie. *For Yourself: The Fulfillment of Female Sexuality.* Garden City, N.Y.: Anchor Books, 1976.
———. *For Each Other: Sharing Sexual Intimacy.* New York: New American Library, 1984.
Henderson, Julie. *The Lover Within: Opening to Sexual Energy.* Barrytown, N.Y.: Station Hill Press, 1987.
Kennedy, Adele, and Dean, Susan. *Touching for Pleasure: A 12-Step Program for Sexual Enrichment.* Chatsworth, Calif.: Chatsworth Press, 1988.
Kitzinger, Sheila. *Woman's Experience of Sex: The Facts and Feelings of Female Sexuality at Every Stage of Life.* New York: Penguin Books, 1993.

Montague, Ashley. *Touching: The Human Significance of the Skin.* New York: Harper and Row, 1986.

Zilbergeld, Bernie. *Male Sexuality: A Guide to Sexual Fulfillment.* Boston: Little, Brown, 1978.

INTIMACY AND RELATIONSHIP ENHANCEMENT

Beaver, Daniel. *More Than Just Sex: A Committed Couples Guide to Keeping Relationships Lively, Intimate, and Gratifying.* Lower Lake, Calif.: Aslan Publishing, 1992.

Covington, Stephanie. *Leaving the Enchanted Forest: The Path from Relationship Addiction to Intimacy.* New York: Harper and Row, 1988.

Lerner, Harriet. *The Dance of Intimacy: A Woman's Guide to Courageous Acts of Change in Key Relationships.* New York: Harper and Row, 1989.

Love, Patricia, and Robinson, Jo. *Hot Monogamy: Essential Steps to More Passionate, Intimate Lovemaking.* New York: Dutton, 1994.

Marlin, Emily. *Relationships in Recovery: Healing Strategies for Couples and Families.* New York: Harper and Row, 1990.

Pearsall, P. *Super Marital Sex: Loving for Life.* New York: Doubleday, 1987. (Based on a study of 1,000 couples; addresses sexual satisfaction in committed relationships.)

Scarf, Maggie. *Intimate Partners: Patterns in Love and Marriage.* New York: Random House, 1978.

Woititz, Janet. *Struggle for Intimacy.* Pompano Beach, Fla.: Health Communications, Inc., 1985.

SEXUAL DYSFUNCTION

Heiman, Julia, LoPiccolo, Leslie, and LoPiccolo, Joseph. *Becoming Orgasmic: A Sexual and Personal Growth Program for Women.* New York: Prentice Hall, 1988.

Kaplan, Helen Singer. *The New Sex Therapy: Active Treatment of Sexual Dysfunctions.* New York: Brunner/Mazel, 1974.

———. *How to Overcome Premature Ejaculation.* New York: Brunner/Mazel, 1989.

Knoph, Jennifer, and Sieler, Michael. *I.S.D.: Inhibited Sexual Desire*. New York: William Morrow, 1990.

Masters, William, and Johnson, Virginia. *Human Sexual Inadequacy*. Boston: Little, Brown and Company, 1970.

YOUR BODY AND BODY IMAGE

The Boston Women's Health Book Collective. *The New Our Bodies, Ourselves*. New York: Simon and Schuster, 1984. (A complete sourcebook on women's health care issues from birthing to aging.)

Chernin, Kim. *The Obsession: Reflections on the Tyranny of Slenderness*. New York: Harper and Row, 1981.

Hutchinson, Marcia Germaine. *Transforming Body Image*. New York: Crossing Press (Box 640, Trumansburg, N.Y. 14886), 1985. (Step-by-step exercises to help integrate your body, mind, and self-image, and to begin to love and accept yourself just the way you are.)

McFarland, Barbara, and Baker-Baumann, Tyeis. *Shame and Body Image: Culture and the Compulsive Eater*. Deerfield Beach, Fla.: Health Communications, 1990.

SEX AND AGING

Burnett, R. G. *Menopause: All Your Questions Answered*. Chicago, Ill.: Contemporary Books, Inc., 1987.

Butler, R. N., and Lewis, M. I. *Love and Sex After 60*. Rev. ed. New York: Harper and Row, 1988.

Cutler, W. B.; Garcia, C. R.; and Edwards, D. A. *Menopause: A Guide for Women and the Men Who Love Them*. New York: W. W. Norton and Co., 1983.

Doress, P. B., et al. *Ourselves, Growing Older: Women Aging with Knowledge and Power*. New York: Simon and Schuster, 1987.

Schover, L. R. *Prime Time: Sexual Health for Men Over Fifty*. New York: Holt, Rinehart and Winston, 1984.

ILLNESS, SURGERY, DISABILITIES, AND SEX

Cutler, W. B. *Hysterectomy: Before and After.* New York: Harper and Row, 1988.

Schover, R., and Jensen, S. B. *Sexuality and Chronic Illness: A Comprehensive Approach.* New York: The Guilford Press, 1988.

Weiner, Florence. *No Apologies: A Guide to Living with a Disability.* New York: St. Martin's Press, 1986.

SEXUALLY TRANSMITTED DISEASE (STDs)

Cass, V. *There's More to Sex Than AIDS: The A to Z Guide to Safe Sex.* Richmond Victoria, Australia: Greenhouse Publications, 1980. (An encyclopedic guide to various sexual behaviors and how to make them "safer" in the age of AIDS.)

HOMOSEXUALITY AND BISEXUALITY

Berzon, Betty. *Positively Gay.* Los Angeles: Mediamix Associates, 1979.

Bode, Janet. *View From Another Closet: Exploring Bisexuality in Women.* New York: Pocket Books, 1977.

Klein, E., and Wolf, T. J., eds. *Two Lives to Lead: Bisexuality in Men and Women.* New York: Harrington Park Press, 1985. (Scientific articles on bisexuality.)

Loulan, J. *Lesbian Sex.* San Francisco: Spinster's Ink, 1984. (Written by a lesbian counselor in a nontechnical style. Sections on sex and disability, sobriety, sexual abuse, and aging.)

———. *Lesbian Passion: Loving Ourselves and Each Other.* San Francisco: Spinsters/Aunt Lute Book Co., 1987. (Addresses self-esteem, intimacy, and relationship issues.)

McWhirter, D. P., and Mattison, A. M. *The Male Couple: How Relationships Develop.* Englewood Cliffs, N.J.: Prentice-Hall, Inc., 1984.

SEXUAL COMPULSIONS AND ADDICTIONS

Carnes, Patrick. *Out of the Shadows: Understanding Sexual Addiction*. Minneapolis: CompCare Publications, 1985.

————. *Contrary to Love: Helping the Sexual Addict*. Minneapolis: CompCare Publications, 1988.

————. *Don't Call It Love: Recovering From Sexual Addiction*. New York: Bantam, 1991.

Earle, Ralph, and Crow, Gregory. *Lonely All the Time: Recognizing, Understanding, and Overcoming Sexual Addiction, for Addicts and Co-dependents*. New York: Simon and Schuster, 1989.

Money, J. *Vandalized Lovemaps*. Buffalo, N.Y.: Prometheus Books, 1990. (A book about how paraphilias develop.)

Mura, David. *A Male Grief: Notes on Pornography and Addiction*. Minneapolis: Milkweed Editions, 1987. (Convincing thesis on the negative effects of using pornography. The address for Milkweed Editions is P.O. Box 3226, Minneapolis, MN 55403.)

SPOUSAL ABUSE

Engel, Beverly. *The Emotionally Abused Woman*. New York: Fawcett Columbine, 1990.

Forward, Susan. *Men Who Hate Women and the Women Who Love Them*. New York: Bantam Books, 1986.

Martin, Del. *Battered Wives*. Rev. ed. San Francisco: Volcano Press, 1981.

Sonkin, Daniel, and Durphy, Michael. *Learning to Live Without Violence: A Handbook for Men*. San Francisco, Calif.: Volcano Press, 1985.

Walker, Lenore. *The Battered Woman*. New York: Harper and Row, 1979.

RAPE AND SEXUAL HARASSMENT

Levy, Barrie. *Dating Violence: Young Women in Danger*. Seattle, Wash.: Seal Press, 1991.

Parrot, Andrea. *Coping with Date Rape and Acquaintance Rape*. New York: Rosen Publishing Group, 1988. (For adolescents and teens in recovery.)

Powell, Elizabeth. *Talking Back to Sexual Pressure*. Minneapolis, Minn.: CompCare Publishers, 1991.

CHILDHOOD SEXUAL ABUSE
Recovery

Bass, Ellen, and Davis, Laura. *The Courage to Heal: A Guide for Women Survivors of Child Sexual Abuse*. New York: Harper and Row, 1988. (Section on intimacy and sexuality.)

Engel, Beverly. *The Right to Innocence: Healing the Trauma of Childhood Sexual Abuse*. New York: Ballantine, 1990.

Lew, Mike. *Victims No Longer: Men Recovering from Incest and Other Sexual Child Abuse*. New York: HarperCollins, 1990. (General information about sexual effects; helpful section on sexual orientation confusion.)

Love, Patricia. *The Emotional Incest Syndrome: What to Do When a Parent's Love Rules Your Life*. New York: Bantam Books, 1990.

Sexual Recovery

Maltz, Wendy, and Holman, Beverly. *Incest and Sexuality: A Guide to Understanding and Healing*. Lexington, Mass.: Lexington Books, 1987.

———. *The Sexual Healing Journey: A Guide for Survivors of Sexual Abuse*. New York: HarperCollins Publishers, Inc., 1992.

General Information

Butler, Sandra. *Conspiracy of Silence: The Trauma of Incest*. San Francisco: Volcano Press, 1985. (Updated.)

Crewdson, John. *By Silence Betrayed: Sexual Abuse of Children in America*. Boston: Little, Brown, 1988.

Finkelhor, David. *Child Sexual Abuse: New Theory and Research*. New York: The Free Press, 1984.

Forward, Susan, and Craig, Buck. *Betrayal of Innocence: Incest and Its Devastation*. Los Angeles: Jeremy P. Tarcher, Inc., 1978.

Herman, Judith. *Father-Daughter Incest*. Cambridge, Mass.: Harvard University Press, 1981.

Masson, Jeffrey Moussaieff. *The Assault on Truth: Freud's Suppression of the Seduction Theory*. New York: Farrar, Straus and Giroux, 1984.

Rush, Florence. *The Best-Kept Secret: Sexual Abuse of Children*. Englewood Cliffs, N.J.: Prentice-Hall, 1980.

Russell, Diana. *The Secret Trauma: Incest in the Lives of Girls and Women*. New York: Basic Books, 1986.

SURVIVORS SPEAK OUT

Armstrong, I. *Kiss Daddy Goodnight*. New York: Hawthorn, 1978.

Angelou, Maya. *I Know Why the Caged Bird Sings*. New York: Bantam, 1980.

Bass, Ellen, and Thornton, Louise, eds. *Writings by Women Survivors of Childhood Sexual Abuse*. New York: Harper and Row, 1983.

Brady, Katherine. *Father's Days: A True Story of Incest*. New York: Dell, 1979.

McNaran, Toni, and Morgan, Yarrow, eds. *Voices in the Night: Women Speaking About Incest*. Minneapolis: Cleis Press, 1982.

Morris, Michelle. *If I Should Die Before I Wake*. New York: Dell, 1982.

CHILD ABUSE

Farmer, Steven. *Adult Children of Abusive Parents: A Healing Program for Those Who Have Been Physically, Sexually, or Emotionally Abused*. Los Angeles: Lowell House, 1989.

Gil, Eliana. *Outgrowing the Pain: A Book for and About Adults Abused as Children*. San Francisco: Launch Press, 1983.

Miller, Alice. *Thou Shalt Not Be Aware: Society's Betrayal of the Child*. New York: New American Library, 1986.

―――. *The Drama of the Gifted Child: The Search for the True Self*. New York: Basic Books, 1981.

―――. *For Your Own Good: Hidden Cruelty in Child-rearing and the Roots of Violence*. New York: Farrar, Straus and Giroux, 1984.

HELP FOR PARTNERS (of Survivors, Abusers, Sex Addicts)

Beattie, Melody. *Codependent No More*. San Francisco: Harper/ Hazeldon, 1987.

———. *Beyond Codependency*. San Francisco: Harper/Hazeldon, 1989.

Engel, Beverly. *Partners in Recovery: How Mates, Lovers & Other Prosurvivors Can Learn to Cope with Adult Survivors of Childhood Sexual Abuse*. New York: Fawcett Columbine, 1991.

McEnvoy, Alan, and Brookings, Jeff. *If She Is Raped: A Book for Husbands, Fathers, and Male Friends*. Holmes Beach, Fla.: Learning Publications (P.O. Box 1326, Holmes Beach, FL 33509), 1984.

Norwood, Robin. *Women Who Love Too Much: When You Keep Wishing and Hoping He'll Change*. Los Angeles: Jeremy P. Tarcher, Inc., 1985.

Schneider, Jennifer. *Back from Betrayal: Surviving His Affairs*. New York: Harper and Row, 1988.

Wegscheider-Cruse, Sharon. *Choice-Making: For Co-Dependents, Adult Children, and Spirituality Seekers*. Pompano Beach, Fla.: Health Communications, 1985.

Resources

VOICES (Victims of Incest Can Emerge Survivors) in Action, Inc.
P.O. Box 148309
Chicago, IL 60614
312-327-1500

A national network of female and male survivors and prosurvivors which has local groups and contacts throughout the country. Offers a free referral service that provides listings of therapists, agencies, and self-help groups.

Incest Survivors Anonymous (ISA)
P.O. Box 5613
Long Beach, CA 90805
310-428-5599

Survivors of Incest Anonymous
World Service Office
P.O. Box 21817
Baltimore, MD 21222
410-282-3400

Co-Dependents Anonymous (CODA)
P.O. Box 33577
Phoenix, AZ 85067
602-277-7991

Adult Children of Alcoholics (ACA)
P.O. Box 3216
Torrance, CA 90505
310-534-1815

Sexaholics Anonymous
P.O. Box 300
Simi Valley, CA 93062
615-331-6230

Alcoholics Anonymous World Services, Inc.
P.O. Box 459
Grand Central Station
New York, NY 10163
212-870-3400

Sex and Love Addicts Anonymous (SLAA), Alcoholics Anonymous (AA), Adult Children of Alcoholics (ACA), and Incest Survivors Anonymous (ISA) are national organizations whose local chapters should be listed in your telephone directory. If you have trouble locating a group, call your local hospital, outpatient treatment center, community service agency, college counseling center, library, or any mental health agency.

INDEX